WHERE AM I WEARING?

WHERE AM I WEARING?

A Global Tour to the Countries, Factories, and People That Make Our Clothes

Revised and Updated

KELSEY TIMMERMAN

WILEY

John Wiley & Sons, Inc.

Published by John Wiley & Sons, Inc., Hoboken, New Jersey.
Published simultaneously in Canada.

For general information on our other products and services or for technical support,
please contact our Customer Care Department within the United States at (800) 762-2974,
outside the United States at (317) 572-3993 or fax (317) 572-4002.

Wiley publishes in a variety of print and electronic formats and by print-on-demand. Some
material included with standard print versions of this book may not be included in e-books
or in print-on-demand. If this book refers to media such as a CD or DVD that is not
included in the version you purchased, you may download this material at http://
booksupport.wiley.com. For more information about Wiley products, visit www.wiley.com.

Library of Congress Cataloging-in-Publication Data:

Timmerman, Kelsey, 1979–
    Where Am I Wearing?: A Global Tour to the Countries, Factories, and People That
Make Our Clothes / Kelsey Timmerman. — Rev. and updated.
        p. cm.
    ISBN: 978-1-118-27755-3 (pbk)
    ISBN: 978-1-118-35608-1 (ebk)
    ISBN: 978-1-118-35609-8 (ebk)
    ISBN: 978-1-118-35610-4 (ebk)
        1. Clothing trade. 2. Clothing workers. 3. Wages—Clothing workers.
    4. Consumers—Attitudes. I. Title.
    HD9940.A2T56 2012
    338.4′7687—dc23

                                                                    2012003583

Printed in the United States of America

10 9 8 7 6 5 4 3 2 1

To all the people who make the clothes I wear.
And to Annie,
who makes sure all the clothes I wear match.

We are all caught in an inescapable network of mutuality, tied into a single garment of destiny. Whatever affects one directly, affects all indirectly.

—*Martin Luther King Jr.*

Contents

Preface

Below me is the Caribbean. Behind me is a global adventure that changed my life and the way I live it. Ahead of me is Honduras, where all of this began six years ago.

The world has changed since I last visited Honduras and stood in front of the factory where my T-shirt was made.

The first edition of this book came out in November of 2008. You likely remember this as a time where any investments you held suddenly halved. Jobs were lost. Home values continued to plummet. In other words, it was a *great* time to have a book come out.

"The world is coming to an end," a crazed-hair friend may have warned. "Better stock up on guns and gold! Oh, by the way, have you heard about this book called *Where Am I Wearing?* This fella named Kelsey went to Bangladesh because his underwear were made there! It's only $25, which is about how much your stock portfolio lost in the last five minutes."

Bullet sales in the United States went up 49 percent while book sales dropped 9 percent, but the down economy had a much wider impact than the publishing industry and the lives of first-time authors. The global financial crisis impacted every single person I met on my global quest to meet the people who made my clothes. Food prices skyrocketed. Arifa, the single mother of three in Bangladesh, was now forced to spend over half of her income on rice for her family. Sixty-four million people fell into extreme poverty—living on less than $1.25 per day. Eighty-two million more people were going hungry.

Orders for just about everything declined, and global unemployment increased by 34 million. The blue jean factory at which Nari and Ai—two of the workers I met in Cambodia—worked closed. There were reports of workers—primarily women in their late teens and early 20s—turning to prostitution. Were Nari and Ai and the others I met in Cambodia among them?

My wardrobe has changed, but not as much as I have.

Since I last sat on a plane nosing toward San Pedro Sula, Honduras, I got married and had two kids. I see the world through a dad's eyes now. Eyes that water when I watch *Toy Story 3* with my daughter, Harper. Eyes that look toward a future beyond my own. Eyes that better see where I fit in as a local citizen in my hometown of Muncie, Indiana, and where I fit in as a global citizen. This second edition of *Where Am I Wearing?* is essentially about the sacrifices parents and children make for one another in the hopes of a better life. Until I looked upon my own children, I only saw the world through the invincible eyes of a son. Having kids changed me, but so did the mothers and fathers, sisters and brothers I met tracking down who made my clothes and where.

The other day I was on a stage at one of the universities that selected this book for their freshman common reader program. All incoming freshmen read and discussed the book—an amazing experience to have as an author. This particular university dressed me in regalia—Harry Potter robes with shoulder pads sans magic wand. I tried to convince the university that if they make an author wear regalia they should give him an honorary degree, but they wouldn't bite. (I would have questioned their integrity if they had.) I felt silly. Then I clicked to the first slide of my presentation—a 20-foot-tall picture of Arifa in Bangladesh—and completely forgot about the pomp and circumstance.

When I met Arifa in Bangladesh, I had no idea I would be able to share her story in the way that I have. There was no promise of a book. But there I stood before 1,500 students and faculty, and they all knew her name. They all knew her story. I've stood on other stages at universities and high schools across the country, and it never gets old. It is an absolute honor to share her story and all of the others.

When my editor, Richard, called me about updating this book, I was in the middle of brushing my daughter's teeth. He asked me if I had any ideas for new material. Boy, did I.

I've always felt that this book was missing something. The whole experience began in Honduras where I followed my favorite T-shirt's tag. At first it was an excuse to travel. I went jungle hiking, SCUBA diving, and taught an entire island village to play baseball. But when

I showed up at the factory and met a worker named Amilcar, I completely chickened out. I didn't ask the questions I wanted to know about him: Does this job provide a better life for you and your family? What do you get paid? What are the working conditions like? And so on. I think deep down I really didn't want to know about the realities of Amilcar's life, so I didn't ask.

Not knowing what life was like for Amilcar or any of the other garment workers around the world really began to eat at me. So I pulled out a pile of clothes and went to Bangladesh, Cambodia, and China—this time to ask the questions I wanted to know.

But what about Amilcar? All of this started with him. While I have a somewhat better idea of what his life might be like, I still don't really know.

But now I'm going to find out.

I'm armed with two out-of-focus 5 × 7's of Amilcar. He's wearing the shirt that was made in his factory and a grin that says, "Some gringo came all the way here to give me this shirt, and now he's standing next to me with no shirt?" I've got the photos, I know his name, and I know where he was employed six years ago. That's about it.

In addition to my search for Amilcar, I've included updates at the end of each section about what life is like for the workers who I've been able to keep in touch with—as well as what life *might* be like for those whom I haven't. I've also added more about my adventures to be an engaged consumer, which have taken me as far as a shoe factory in Ethiopia, and as near as the Goodwill a few blocks from my house. I've highlighted some additional companies that are changing the world one job at a time, included a few new tips to help you on your journey to become an engaged consumer, and compiled a chapter-by-chapter discussion guide to help guide your book club or class discussions.

In a way, this adventure is an explanation of what I did with my college education. My degree—a bachelor of arts in anthropology from Miami University—hangs on the wall of my office. The degree is worth less than the frame that holds it—because I never got a job due to my degree in anthropology. But the curiosity for the world that my studies inspired and the empathy that anthropology taught me have been priceless. They helped me find my way. Still, I look back on my college experience with some regret, so I've written a "Letter to Freshman Me" at the end of the book. It's the kick in the pants I wish I had had as a freshman. Since so many freshmen across the country start their college careers reading this book, I hope they will find it useful.

My *Where Am I Wearing?* adventure changed the way I see the world, the way I give and volunteer, and the way I shop. The people I met have inspired me to be a better neighbor, consumer, donor, volunteer, and a better glocal (global and local) citizen. I've learned that we can't always control the impact that invisible forces like globalization have on our life, but we can control the impact our life has on the world. And all of this started with Amilcar in Honduras.

Most of me hopes I find him, but part of me doesn't. I'm worried what the past six years have meant for him. Wherever he is, he's 31 now. Maybe he has a family. Maybe he still works at the garment factory. Maybe. Maybe. "Maybe" has haunted me since that fateful day in 2005 when I met Amilcar.

I scan the notes that 26-year-old me scrawled, and I stare out at the blue beyond. I turn back to the 5 × 7's of Amilcar.

Maybe it's time to find out.

—**Kelsey Timmerman**

Prologue

We Have It Made

I was made in America. My *Jingle These* Christmas boxers were made in Bangladesh.

I had an all-American childhood in rural Ohio. My all-American blue jeans were made in Cambodia.

I wore flip-flops every day for a year when I worked as a SCUBA diving instructor in Key West. They were made in China.

One day while staring at a pile of clothes on the floor, I noticed the tag of my favorite T-shirt read: MADE IN HONDURAS.

I read the tag. My mind wandered. A quest was born.

Where am I wearing? It seems like a simple question with a simple answer. It's not.

This question inspired the quest that took me around the globe. It cost me a lot of things, not the least of which was my consumer innocence. Before the quest, I could put on a piece of clothing without reading its tag and thinking about Arifa in Bangladesh or Dewan in China, about their children, their hopes and dreams, and the challenges they face.

Where am I wearing isn't so much a question related to geography and clothes, but about the people who make our clothes and the texture of their lives. This quest is about the way *we* live and the way *they* live; because when it comes to clothing, others make it, and we have it made. And there's a big, big difference.

PART

The Mission

A Consumer Goes Global

The Mississinawa Valley High School class of 1997 voted me *Best Dressed Guy*. This isn't something I usually share with people. You should feel privileged I told you. Don't be too impressed; there were 51 members of the class of 1997, only 29 were guys, and rural Ohio isn't exactly the fashion capital of anywhere.

I would like to think that I won the award for my stellar collection of Scooby-Doo and Eric Clapton T-shirts, but I know what clinched it— junior high, when my mom still dressed me. Basically, I was *the* Bugle Boy. You might not remember the brand of clothing known as Bugle Boy, but you probably remember their commercials where the sexy model in the sports car stops to ask the guy stranded in the desert: "Excuse me, are those Bugle Boy jeans you are wearing?" I had entire Bugle Boy outfits.

As far as most consumers are concerned, clothes come from the store. Consumers don't see the chain of transportation and manufacturing that comes before they take the pants off the rack. Clothes came even later in the chain for me during this time—from gift boxes on holidays or birthdays or just magically appearing on my bed with Post-it notes hanging from the tags:

"Kels, try these on and let me know if they fit—Mom."

I really didn't care much about clothes until they were comfortable—jeans with holes, black T-shirts faded to gray—and then it was about time to stop wearing them anyhow. If clothing made it to this extremely comfortable stage, I normally established some kind of emotional attachment to it and stashed it away.

My closet and drawers were museums of me.

In high school, I remember Kathie Lee Gifford, the beloved daytime talk show host, crying on television as she addressed allegations that her clothing line was being made by children in Honduras. I remember Disney coming under similar fire, but I didn't wear clothes from either of these lines. I had bigger problems in those days, such as, finding time to wash my dirty car or how I was going to ask Annie, the hustling sophomore shooting guard with the big brown eyes, to the homecoming dance.

Globalization was a foreign problem of which I was blissfully unaware. I did know that it existed, and that I was against it. Everybody was. My friends' fathers had lost their jobs and their pensions when local factories closed or were bought out. Huffy bicycles that were made in the *county* to the north were now made in the *country* to the south. Buying American was *in*. To do so, we shopped at Walmart—an all-American red, white, and blue store with all-American products.

It wasn't until college that I learned about the other aspects of globalization. Not only were Americans losing jobs to unpatriotic companies moving overseas, but the poor people who now had the jobs were also being exploited. Slouching at our desks in Sociology 201, we talked about sweatshops—dark, sweaty, abusive, dehumanizing, evil sweatshops. Nike was bad, and at some point, Walmart became un-American. I felt morally superior because I was wearing Asics. Thankfully, the fact that my apartment was furnished with a cheap, laminated entertainment center from Walmart wasn't something I had to share with the class.

A degree in anthropology and a minor in geology left me eager to meet people of different cultural persuasions who lived far from the squared-off, flat fields of Ohio. While my classmates arranged job interviews, I booked plane tickets. I had seen the world in the pages of textbooks and been lectured about it long enough. It was time to see it for myself. The first trip was six months long, and the second and third trip each lasted two months. I worked as a SCUBA instructor in Key West, Florida, in between trips.

A love for travel came and never went. It wasn't so much an itch as a crutch. I didn't need much of an excuse to go anywhere.

And then one day while staring at a pile of clothes on the floor, I thought, "What if I traveled to all of the places where my clothes were made and met the people who made them?" The question wasn't some great revelation I had while thinking about my fortunate position in the global marketplace; it was just another reason to leave, to put off committing to my relationship with Annie, the sophomore shooting guard turned growing-impatient girlfriend of 10 years. I traveled, quite simply, because I didn't want to grow up.

I was stocking up on travel supplies—duct tape, tiny rolls of toilet paper, water purification tablets, and waders to protect against snake-bites in the jungle—when I bumped into a classmate from high school working in the camping department of Walmart.

"So, I hear you're a beach bum now," he said, his years of service marked beneath a Walmart smiley face.

What can you say to that?

"Where you heading next?" he asked.

"Honduras," I said.

"What's in Honduras?" he asked. "More beaches?" I had fallen from the *Best Dressed Guy* to *Beach Bum*.

"No," I said, "that's where my T-shirt was made. I'm going to visit the factory where it was made and meet the people who made it." Then I told him the entire list of my clothes and the other places I intended to visit.

"Oh, you're going to visit sweatshops," he said.

This was the response I received time and time again. When you tell a normal person with an everyday job, rent or a mortgage, and a car payment that you are spending thousands of dollars to go to a country because you want to go where your T-shirt was made, first they'll think you're crazy—and then they'll probably say something about sweatshops.

I understood that the people who made my clothes were prob-ably not living a life of luxury, but I didn't automatically assume they worked in a sweatshop. In fact, I found this automatic assumption to be rather disturbing. The majority of people I talked to, and even members of a nationally syndicated program that reports on the world's poor, assumed all of my clothes were made in sweatshops. It seemed to be a given: The people who make our clothes are paid and treated badly. Since few of us make our own clothes, buy secondhand, or are nudists, it appears that there is nothing we can do about it, we really don't give a darn. Besides, we saved a few bucks.

In beach bum terms, my trip to Honduras was wildly successful, but in terms of my excuse for going to Honduras, it wasn't. I went to the factory and met a worker, but I wasn't comfortable learning about his life and chose to abandon the quest. I returned home, every bit the beach bum I was before the trip. I tried to forget about Honduras, the worker I met, and my pile of clothes and their MADE IN labels, but I couldn't. A seed had been planted.

Events changed me. I got engaged to Annie, the growing-impatient girlfriend of 10 years turned fiancée. I bought a home. I started to become a normal American—a consumer with a mortgage, a refrigerator, and a flat-screen television. I began to settle into my American Dream, and comfortably so. However, the pile of clothes appeared once more, and I became obsessed once again with where my stuff was made.

I started to read books about globalization and the history of the garment industry, but I felt that they all missed something. I didn't just want to know about the forces, processes, economics, and politics of globalization; I had to know about the producers who anchored the opposite end of the chain. The lives, personalities, hopes, and dreams of the people who make our clothes were lost among the statistics.

I decided to resume my quest to meet these people. To finance it, I did perhaps the most American thing I've ever done—I took out a second mortgage.

It's probably obvious to you by now that I'm not Thomas Friedman, the *New York Times* columnist and author of best-selling globalization books such as *The World Is Flat*. I don't have an intricate understanding of the world's economy. No one met me at the airport when I arrived in the countries where my clothes were made. No company CEO was expecting me. I didn't have an expense account. I had no contacts, no entourage, and no room reservations. However, I had plenty of mental ones.

I was simply a consumer on a quest. If you asked me what I was doing, I would have told you something about bridging the gap between producer and consumer. You probably would have thought I was a bit off, recklessly throwing time and money to the wind when I should have been at home paying off my mortgage and putting my college degree to work. And I don't blame you.

But I did have priceless experiences that changed me and my view of the world. I went undercover as an underwear buyer in Bangladesh, was courted by Levi's in Cambodia, and was demonized by an American brand's VP in China.

I did my best to find the factories that made my clothes. If I wasn't allowed in to see the factory, I waited outside for the workers. I took off my shoes and entered their tiny apartments. I ate bowls of rice cooked over gas stoves during power outages. I taught their children to play Frisbee, and rode a roller coaster with some of them in Bangladesh. I was challenged to a drinking game by a drunken uncle in China. I took a group of garment workers bowling in Cambodia. They didn't like the game—which was just one of many things I discovered we had in common.

Along the way, I learned the garment industry is much more labor intensive than I ever thought. It is at the forefront of globalization in constant search of cheap, reliable labor to meet the industry's tight margins. Activists tend to damn the industry, but it isn't that simple. Some economists refer to it as a ladder helping people out of poverty, empowering women, but it isn't that simple.

The reality of the workers' lives is harsh.

It's true the workers are glad to have jobs, even if they only receive $50 a month. And they don't *want* you to boycott their products to protest their working conditions. (I asked.) But they would like to work less and get paid more.

Family is everything, but feeding that family is more important than actually being with them. And I saw things that made me think the unthinkable: that maybe, given certain circumstances and a lack of options, child labor isn't always bad.

There is a long chain of players from producer to consumer. It is made up of workers, labor sharks, factories, subcontractors, unions, governments, buying houses, middle men, middle men for the middle men, nongovernmental organizations (NGOs), importers, exporters, brands, department stores, and you and me. Each takes a cut. Some play by the rules; some don't. Exploitation can occur on any level, except one—the workers aren't in a position to exploit anyone.

*   *   *

James Bond fought communism. So did my grandpa's underwear.

Following World War II, the US War and State Departments decided to rebuild the textile industry in Japan—because when you drop a pair of atomic bombs on a country, it's a good idea to avoid helping them rebuild industries that could easily be converted to the production of weapons, since the people of that country are probably still a bit peeved.

It was important that the United States establish strong relations with Japan; if we didn't, it was likely that the commies would. So we shipped them our cotton, and they shipped us our underwear. And that meant that Grandpa was able to buy his cheap.

Trade liberalization in Europe and Asia was seen as a way to win people over to democracy and prevent the spread of communism from China, Korea, and the Soviet Union. This was not an economic decision, but a political one.

In the aforementioned *The World Is Flat* (New York: Farrar, Straus and Giroux 2005), Thomas Friedman describes this thinking in present-day terms with his Golden Arches Theory of Conflict Prevention:

> *I noticed that no two countries that both had McDonald's had ever fought a war against each other since each got its McDonald's . . . when a country reached the level of economic development where it has a middle class big enough to support a network of McDonald's, it became a McDonald's country. And the people of McDonald's countries didn't like to fight wars anymore. They preferred to wait in line for burgers . . . as countries got woven into the fabric of global trade and rising living standards, which having a network of McDonald's franchises had come to symbolize, the cost of war for victor and vanquished became prohibitively high.*

In other words, capitalism and garments spread peace and cheeseburgers around the world.

Eventually, though, economics took over. Developing nations wanted our business, and we wanted their cheap products. The garment industry within our own country was apt to go where labor was the cheapest and regulations the least, as evidenced by the flow from the North to the economically depressed South in the 1960s. So it is no surprise that as international trade became freer, and our own standards of living higher, the industry hopped our borders and sought out cheaper conditions abroad.

Despite protectionists' efforts of fighting to keep the industry in the United States, a race to the bottom began. *Sweatshop* became a buzzword that fired up activists, caused consumers to hesitate, and made brands cringe.

*   *   *

Globalization affects us all. It forces change into our lives whether we are ready for it or not. Globalization is both good and bad. It's a debate taking place in books, politics, boardrooms, at universities, and in shoppers' minds. And it isn't going away.

The Decent Working Conditions and Fair Competition Act was introduced in the Senate in 2007, backed by senators on both sides of the political aisle, including my home state senator, Sherrod Brown (D-OH). The bill, also known as the antisweatshop bill, proposed banning the import, export, and sale of sweatshop goods. Just as the bill's predecessor introduced in the previous congressional session, it died in committee.

The debate rages on in Congress.

Most companies have developed codes of conduct for sourcing their products abroad. Some align themselves with monitoring agencies and labor rights groups. They struggle with what is right and what is profitable. But hardly any company wants its customers to think about where its products are made—because brand images are built on good times, sunny beaches, dancing, cold beer, and freedom, not factories, poverty, and separated families. Other companies don't shy away from the realities of their production. Levi's welcomed me as a concerned consumer. Patagonia has videos posted on its website of the factories from which they source and interviews with the workers who make their products.

The debate rages on in boardrooms.

Labor rights activists make companies accountable to their codes of conduct. If a brand isn't meeting basic worker's rights, they pressure the company to change. If they pressure too much, the company might cut and run, taking with them the jobs of the workers for which the activists were fighting. So how much do they ask for? How much do they push?

What are we as consumers to do? If we buy garments made in some developing country, we are contributing to an industry built on laborers whose wages and quality of life would be unacceptable to us. But if we don't, the laborers might lose their jobs.

My conclusion, after visiting the people who made my favorite clothes, is that we should try to be *engaged* consumers, not mindless pocketbooks throwing dollars at the cheapest possible fashionable clothes we can find. Companies should give us some credit for being twenty-first–century humans. We can handle knowing where our clothes were made. We will buy from companies that make a real effort to be concerned about the lives of the workers who make their products. We need activists and labor organizations to work with the companies and to tell us which ones aren't.

Walk into Target or Kohl's or JCPenney or Macy's, and you'll find that some of the clothing was made by hardworking individuals who, in terms of the context of their country, were paid and treated fairly. They are supporting their families, trying to save up money to attend beauty school or to pay off a debt. Other products are made by workers who aren't treated and paid fairly. After my quest, I want to know which is which (but preferably without having to dig through websites and lengthy reports). Money moves faster than ethics in the current global marketplace, and will probably continue to do so until companies, activists, and consumers advance the discussion by asking the money to slow down and explain where it's been.

The people who make our clothes are poor. We are rich. It's natural to feel guilty, but guilt or apathy or rejection of the system does nothing to help the workers.

Workers don't need pity. They need rights, and they need to be educated about those rights. They need independent monitors checking the factories, ensuring the environment is safe and that they are treated properly. They need opportunities and choices. They need consumers concerned about all of the above. They need to be valued.

This book follows me from country to country, from factory to factory, from a life as a clueless buyer to that of an engaged consumer. Although it's mind-boggling to compare the luxuries of our lives to the realities that the people who make our clothes face every day, on

Figure 1.1   The author in front of the abandoned factory in Phnom Penh, Cambodia, where his blue jeans were made.

occasion I reflect on my own life—so that neither you nor I lose sight of how good we've got it.

In the past, I didn't care about where my clothes were made or who made them. And then I met Amilcar, Arifa, Nari, Ai, Dewan, and Zhu Chun. Now I can't help but care. And I'm certain that the more you know them, the more you'll care too.

Please, allow me (Figure 1.1) to introduce you.

CHAPTER

2

Tattoo's Tropical Paradise

July 2005

T-shirts are windows to our souls. They say who we are and what we believe, whom we support and whom we despise. A good one will make us laugh or think just a little. A bad one will draw our ridicule. More than any other item of clothing we own, our T-shirts deliver our message to the world.

The character Tattoo from the 1970s TV show *Fantasy Island* is on my favorite T-shirt. His eyes sparkle with mischief. His smile is too wide, his comb-over perfect. COME WITH ME TO MY hangs over his head, and TROPICAL PARADISE sits just beneath his dimpled chin.

My cousin Brice bought it for me when I lived in the tropical paradise of Key West. People who remember *Fantasy Island* and Tattoo's catchphrase "De plane . . . De plane!" get a big kick out of my shirt. A bit of nostalgia, a dash of lighthearted humor; it's a perfect T-shirt. Its tag reads, MADE IN HONDURAS.

Workers flood the narrow alley beside the Delta Apparel Factory in San Pedro Sula, Honduras, and rush to catch one of the many waiting buses at the highway. Merchants hoping to part them from a portion of their daily earnings—$4 to $5—fight for their attention. Vehicles push through the crowd. A minivan knocks over a girl in her mid-twenties and then runs over her foot. She curses, is helped to her feet, and limps onto a waiting bus.

The buildings behind the fence are shaded in Bahamian pastels and are very well kept. The shrubs have been recently shaped, and the grass has been trimmed. In the bright Honduran sun, they seem as pleasant as factories can be.

The lady at Georgia-based Delta Apparel giggled at me on the phone when I told her my plans. She was happy to tell me that their Honduran factory was located in the city of Villanueva just south of San Pedro Sula. She even wished me good luck.

Now that I'm in Honduras, the company doesn't think it's very funny.

I stand overwhelmed among the chaos. A thousand sets of eyes stare at me; perhaps they recognize my T-shirt. The irony that this is Tattoo's tropical paradise wore off long ago—somewhere between the confrontation with the big-bellied guards at the factory gate who had guns shoved down their pants and the conversation with the tight-lipped company representative who refused to reveal much of anything about my T-shirt or the people who assembled it. I realized almost immediately that there was no way I was getting onto the factory floor. All I learned was that eight humans of indiscriminate age and sex stitched my shirt together in less than five minutes—not exactly information that required traveling all the way to Honduras to obtain.

Since arriving in Honduras, I've been SCUBA diving and jungle exploring, and have obtained enough writing fodder to support a couple months of travel columns and articles for the few newspapers and magazines to which I contribute, which would pay me a pittance of the expense I've incurred. I often write in my column, which covers years of traveling on a shoestring, about being a *touron*—one part eager tourist and one part well-meaning moron. I first heard this term when I was working as a SCUBA instructor in Key West. The locals used it to refer to the tourists who ride around on scooters honking their little scooter horns and asking jaded tour guides questions like: "Does the water go all the way 'round the island?" In Honduras, I've been nothing else—while ignoring the main reason I was here. I'm here to meet the people who made my shirt; but now that I'm surrounded by them, I'm feeling less "tourist" and more "moron."

The workers break around me like salmon swimming around a rock with a bear on it. They steer clear from of me when I approach them. It's almost as if they have been warned to stay away from the likes of me.

Finally, one hesitantly steps aside.

I find out that his name is Amilcar and that he lives in a nearby village with his parents. He attended school until seventh grade and likes to play soccer. His cheeks are skinny and his brow prominent. He has worked at the factory for less than a year.

"Ask him his age," I tell my translator.

I know enough Spanish to make out that he's 25 before my translator tells me.

Twenty-five. When I was 25, I was working part-time as a retail clerk in an outdoor store and part-time as a SCUBA instructor. Now, I'm 26, and I don't have a job, unless you count the meager amount I make writing. My mom recently received a survey from my alma mater, Miami (of Ohio) University, that asked about my professional status. Because I was in Baja, Mexico, SCUBA diving at the time, she filled it out for me. When I received the results several months later, I found that I was the only person in my graduating class of thousands who was "unemployed by choice."

As a college-educated, white male living in the United States, I have too many choices—and I can't decide on any of them. I suppose this is how the quest started—a search for something, anything that would keep me from choosing a path just a little while longer.

The difference between Amilcar and me is that I *have* a choice. I can work for eight months and take off four months. I can settle down into a real job, but I choose not to. When I do opt to work, I do something fun. I'm mobile with no intention of planting roots.

One in four people are unemployed in Honduras. Jobs aren't easy to come by. For his day of work, Amilcar probably made four to five times less than my cousin paid for my Tattoo T-shirt.

My translator asks if I have any more questions for Amilcar. I want to ask him how much money he actually makes. I want to see where he lives and what he eats, hear about what he hopes to become, and discover what he thinks about my life.

Part of me wants to know about Amilcar, but the other part is content *not* knowing—and maybe even a little scared about what I would learn. Do I really want to find out if the factory is a sweatshop?

This is my chance to prove myself, to show that the quest isn't silly.

So I do something stupid. I give Amilcar the Tattoo T-shirt off my back. We pose for a few pictures before Amilcar rejoins the stream of workers flowing from the factory gates.

I'm a crazy shirtless gringo, a spoiled American. I'm a consumer, and my job is to buy stuff. Amilcar is a producer, and his job is to make stuff. Perhaps we are both better off not thinking too hard about the other's life.

CHAPTER 3

Fake Blood, Sweat, and Tears

Anti-Sweatshop Protestors, April 2006

"Diet, Cherry, or Vanilla, Coca-Cola is a killa!" "Diet, Cherry, or Vanilla, Coca-Cola is a killa!"

I pretend to participate in the chant, but I find it ridiculous. Plus, Coca-Cola is my soft drink of choice.

I'm attending the first International SweatFree Communities conference in Minneapolis, Minnesota, with lots of angry young people who blame Coca-Cola for the deaths of union leaders in Colombia. According to one of the speakers, "If a company is big enough that we know their name, they probably have human rights violations."

This is not the kind of place where you would want to walk in munching on a Big Mac and carrying a Walmart shopping bag. Most of the weekend-long conference is focused on the wrongdoings of the apparel industry. No major corporation is left unblemished.

In the middle of a session on labor abuses in Haiti, the participants break into a solidarity clap. It gradually increases in tempo and, at its height, a woman from Haiti yells, "We need to connect workers worldwide!"

The workshop session participants don't take notes; they write manifestos in fancy leather-bound notebooks that tie or latch shut. Bright, young, organized people dedicated to changing their world are overrepresented, but so are people with green hair, Mohawks, and body piercings. One of them appears to have blood all over his shirt.

"What's on your shirt?" I ask.

"Fake blood. I just came from a die-in."

"What's a die-in?"

"It's where you pour fake blood all over yourself and lie on the ground and pretend to be dead."

"Wasn't it cold?" To me, April in Minnesota doesn't seem like a good time to pour fake blood on yourself and lie on the ground.

"Not too bad," he says. "We had tombstones blocking the wind."

I don't even ask what they were protesting.

It's easy to dismiss SweatFree's message as antiestablishment; after all, they probably disapprove of the truck I drive, the clothes I wear, and the food I eat. Plus, I'm not big on clapping and chanting in public; it seems a bit on the fringe. But for the past decade, this group has become our consumer conscience. With limited funds and a whole lot of passion, they've chased companies around the globe and made abominable working conditions public. If it weren't for them, I would have never learned about labor rights in developing countries in Sociology 201. I wouldn't have considered where my shirt was made or who made it.

Other than the die-ins in April in Minnesota, SweatFree's strategies seem quite reasonable. First, they targeted large companies like Nike and GAP, which incited public awareness. Now they are concentrating on municipalities, public schools, and states, by arguing that taxpayers' money is being used to purchase uniforms made under unacceptable conditions. The market in their crosshairs is big—billions of dollars—and unlike the retail market where consumers vote with their pocketbooks, citizens have actual votes. If a bunch of voters complain that mistreated Mexican workers are making your uniforms, you listen—or risk not being reelected.

By this point, 9 states, 40 cities, 15 counties, and 118 school districts have adapted SweatFree procurement policies, and more than 180 colleges and universities have adopted similar rules. Students might not care about how big of a mess they leave for the janitor in their dorm's corridors, but they care about where and under what conditions that janitor's uniform was made. Concerned tax and tuition payers are being heard.

Since I left Honduras, Amilcar's face haunts me each time I pull on a T-shirt. I've become obsessed with tags. If an item of clothing was made somewhere I don't recognize, I pull out the atlas and find it. I know that each tag must have a story behind it—of faces, places, hands, families, struggles, and dreams. I want to know more workers like Amilcar around the world. That's why I'm attending this conference.

Most of the attendees have never met the workers to whom they dedicate so much of their fake blood, sweat, and tears. So naturally, they are eager to ask me questions when I tell them that I've been to a factory in Honduras.

The problem is that I don't have any answers. My quest to Honduras was a failure.

The conference leaves me with more questions, which I realize won't get answered unless I find them on my own.

If I knew what these people knew, would I be angry like them? Do Honduran or Haitian workers even *want* a 20-year-old philosophy major in Minnesota participating in die-ins in their name? Maybe they're glad to have a job—despite one that pays a shockingly low wage by US standards—because it's enough for them and their families to get by.

The conference and my engagement give new urgency to my quest. I have questions that need to be answered before I can settle down into an all-American life. While Annie begins planning our wedding and settling into the home we buy in Muncie, Indiana, I pack my bags. As Annie begins her quest to find the perfect wedding dress, I set out to find the people who made my underwear.

My Underwear:
Made in Bangladesh

CHAPTER 4

Jingle These

April 2007

"So, I hear you are interested in women's panties." Salehin, a middleman in the Bangladeshi garment industry, magically whips out a pair of sea-foam green granny panties and splashes them down across the desk between us. They're see-through.

I've just taken a swig from a skinny can of Coca-Cola and fight hard not to spit it all over Salehin and his granny panties. Composure is required when you're undercover as an underwear buyer.

"No . . . I'm interested in *boxers*," I pull my boxers out of my Domke camera bag, "like these."

I bullshit my way through a discussion about my underwear: how they were printed, what their thread count is. The sad thing is that I don't know squat about any of this—and Salehin still salivates at the thought of doing business with an American buyer.

I experience a mix of emotions: nervousness (that I'll be caught in my fib); exhilaration (because he's actually buying the fib); and guilt (again, because he's actually buying the fib.)

I describe to Salehin how I want my boxers designed.

"We can make those," Salehin says. "We can make anything."

He smiles at me—a glowing sack of American greenbacks.

"Now," Salehin says, "tell me more about your business."

I never intended to pass myself off as a garment buyer. It just kind of happened. Really, Dalton is to blame. But first, here is all you need to know about my favorite underwear.

*   *   *

My underwear aren't sexy. They're an inside joke with myself.

I didn't get my first pair of new underwear until I was five. I was a younger brother, and younger brothers wear hand-me-downs—even underwear. I never had a pair I could call my own until Mom decided that I deserved a pair of Scooby-Doo Underoos for being good while she shopped in The Boston Store, a small family clothing store where the store clerks knew how to measure and make adjustments. The Boston Store has since gone out of business along with the other department stores in Union City, Ohio—including Kirshbaum's, Kaufman's, and McClurg's Five and Dime. They went under in the mid-1980s when all of the local factories started to close or leave the country. Westinghouse moved to Mexico; Sheller Globe downsized their production of plastic moldings for vehicles under the pressure of foreign competition; and the Body Company, which made chasses for step vans, was bought and lost the majority of their work to cheaper labor in the South.

Globalization came to Union City, a small town that straddles the Ohio and Indiana border. It took jobs. It took stores. Today, I'm not sure if it's even possible to purchase a pair of underwear anywhere in town. You might be able to at Rite Aid, but they likely wouldn't be comfortable or funny.

Unfortunately, I can't show my favorite pair of boxers in public. Not only would it be in poor taste; it would be illegal. So I wear them to meetings, classes, funerals, weddings—places where no one ever gets to enjoy them. And I'm pretty sure that most people would like them. They have multicolored Christmas ornaments printed on them and the phrase *Jingle These* running around the waistband.

I got them as a gift years ago and, ever since, they've maintained a regular place in my underwear rotation regardless of the time of year or holiday season.

If you look closely, you can still read the faded tag. It reads, MADE IN BANGLADESH. And though a country whose population is 83 percent Muslim couldn't give a hoot about Christmas, I'm about to learn that they get pretty excited about my underwear.

*   *   *

Bangladesh is surrounded by India to the west, north, and east, with the Bay of Bengal to the south. The country, slightly smaller than Iowa, is bursting at the seams with people. However, while Iowa's population is 3 million, Bangladesh counts 135 million, making it the most densely populated country in the world. And getting around the capital Dhaka isn't easy.

Dhaka's streets are drab and dusty, with rickshaws and colorful artwork providing a relief to the eye. Their tinkling bells, which cut through the motorized chaos, are a treat to the ear and, if you're viewing Dhaka from one of its taller buildings, are the most prominent sound drifting to the rooftops. The Dhaka police estimate that there are 600,000 rickshaws operating in the city (Figure 4.1).

The rickshaw is an old technology, and cell phones are a new one. Today, 29 million Bangladeshis have cell phones. There are many stores and service centers in Dhaka, but there's only one Motorola store, which I had a heck of a time finding.

I had been trying to find someone who would know how to unlock my phone, and having visited several stores with no luck while braving multiple street crossings and taxis, I got the advice that shaped my stay in Bangladesh, "Go see Mr. Dalton with Motorola in Banani."

So I took a rickshaw to see Mr. Dalton. It was my first, and I was somewhat concerned about the attention I might draw—because it turned out that I was basically a rock star in Bangladesh.

I've never worn leather pants or trashed a hotel room. My rock stardom is purely a function of the rareness of being a blond-haired,

Figure 4.1   A traffic jam of rickshaws in Dhaka.

blue-eyed foreigner. Heads turn when I walk down the street, and crowds form when I stop. A riot nearly broke out when I attended a Bangladeshi rock concert (featuring the legendary guitar licks of Ayub Bachchu) and was sucked into a Bangladeshi mosh pit. If you haven't seen one, there's a lot of hand-holding, gyrating, hugging, basically everything that you would do at a rock concert in the United States—if you wanted to get your ass kicked real fast. People get sucked into these things and are never heard from again.

Luckily, the ride to the Motorola store was devoid of mosh pits.

*   *   *

Dalton, the general manager of the Motorola store, has a look in his eyes as if he's always up to something or knows something you don't. It's kind of a squint out the side. His blue-black hair is combed over to the right, and he regularly flips his head back and smoothes it into place with his hand.

"Where is your country?" Dalton asked. "Why you come to Bangladesh?"

I told him. His eyes sparkled with excitement.

"I'm a journalist, too," he said.

When it was all said and done, Dalton had my phone repro-grammed and gave me a SIM card to use for free. But we hardly talked about phones that first afternoon. Instead, Dalton showed me his portfolio of published stories, his book of poetry, and photographs.

"This is life in Bangladesh." Dalton held up a photo of two street boys sleeping on the sidewalk with their heads resting on a scrawny dog. The picture surprised me. It wasn't the sight of the boys on the street that was unexpected. A short walk anywhere in Dhaka will yield such a sight. What surprised me about Dalton's photo is that Dalton actually sees this. Most people in Bangladesh don't bat an eye at street children sleeping in the midafternoon sun. Dalton sees and captures such sights.

Dalton is different—which made us instant friends.

After Dalton showed me nearly every picture he had ever taken, we returned to the topic of my quest in Bangladesh and how I should go about meeting the people who made my underwear and locating the factory where they were produced.

"You no need to think," Dalton said. "I take care of everything."

I came to Bangladesh alone on my quest. Now I had a partner.

*   *   *

Dalton has a tendency to introduce me as someone much more important than I am. In his boyhood village of Ludhua, I was the *honored journalist*.

The village elders assembled at a tea stand alongside the main thoroughfare, not much wider than a golf-cart path. They wanted to talk politics with the *honored journalist*. What did I think of George W. Bush? They didn't like him.

They told me that Bush was manipulating the Bangladeshi government to do his bidding because oil had recently been discovered. He was responsible for something bad in their country. I never learned what. Was it the regular flooding, getting worse by the year thanks to rising sea levels that wipe out crops and leave a wake of hunger? Was it the fact that Bangladesh has no government at this particular time? The incumbent party had fixed the last election, but the military took control of the government to try to end the corruption before the election could take place. There were so many problems it was impossible to fathom which ones they were pinning on Bush.

I doubt that Bush or anyone in his administration rolled out of bed in the morning and thought much about Bangladesh. Maybe this is part of the problem. But the village elders—men who have likely never seen a computer, who live a day's trip from Dhaka via boat trips on which before you board you are repeatedly asked if you can swim, or bus rides that seem even sketchier than the boats—blame the president of the United States for their situation.

The village chairman met with the *honored journalist* in his office. He sent one of his boys for soda pop and cookies. He apologized for not having more time to talk, but he was very busy. Bags of rice were stacked in the corner, which had been donated from a foreign organization, and he had the difficult job of deciding who in his village needed them most.

I was meeting with the chairman to learn about his village's role in the textile industry, since many of the garment workers in Dhaka come from villages like his. Dalton wanted to introduce me to village life and thought there was no better way than to have me play a game of Kabaddi. When he told the chairman about his plans, the chairman laughed. Kabaddi was the perfect way to break the ice with the villagers. I just hoped I wouldn't be breaking anything else.

A good portion of the village assembled to see the *honored journalist* play Kabaddi. It was rare to see a foreigner, but a foreigner playing Kabaddi . . . that was unheard of.

Kabaddi is a sort of full-contact tag meets ultraviolent Red Rover in which whoever is *IT* must chant repeatedly "Kabaddi . . . Kabaddi . . . Kabaddi. . . ." in one breath while trying to tag someone on the opposite side and make it back across half-court. Once tagged, the opposing team tries to tackle him.

I stood on one baseline with five of my teammates. Twenty feet in front of us was half-court and another 20 feet was the other baseline with our opponents. The court is carved into the dirt, the field worn with use. It was the largest open space in the village that wasn't a rice paddy.

Dalton gave out instructions that I gathered included: Don't hurt the *honored journalist*. I was the biggest and oldest of the bunch. The other players were knots of stringy muscle and showing ribs. I recognized one as the rickshaw driver who had pedaled us around the village earlier in the day.

On the first play, my teammates wrapped the opposing player low, and I tackled him high. The village watched, cheering loudly. Then it was my turn to be *IT*. The five opposing players immediately stopped my progress, and I forgot to keep repeating "Kabaddi" because I was laughing too hard.

The score was six to five, my team on the low end. The sun was excruciatingly hot, and I could feel my face flushed with blood, pumping at the temples. Dalton called for the last point of the game, and I told him I wanted to play to ten. The villagers loved it. My turn again. Dalton addressed the players. I crossed half-court and began chanting. I tried to move faster than my first attempt and stay as light on my feet as possible. I knew I could overpower one of the smaller, lighter players but not all five. I tagged a scrawny teenager and dashed toward the line. They all grabbed me, and I started pumping my legs and squirming through grips. I moved the pile, and the line was within reach. Since all of the players had touched me, I'd score five points and my team would win if I crossed—and I would be written about in the Ludhua Kabaddi history books.

Their grips gave way and I tumbled across (Figure 4.2). My teammates and the rest of the village swarmed me. It just might have been my proudest moment in sports.

But then I started to think about it. What was it that Dalton told them? Did they throw the game? It *had* felt like they were trying hard to bring me down; so maybe not.

That's how polite the Bangladeshi people are. They'll let you win, but they'll play just hard enough to make you doubt it, so you'll still feel good about yourself.

Figure 4.2 The *honored journalist* reaching to score the game-winner.

* * *

The floor of Dalton's childhood home is dirt, but it is the cleanest dirt floor one could possibly imagine. Dalton's aunt swept the dirt floor with a broom while we sat and talked about his growing up in Ludhua and his adult life in Dhaka.

The village was peaceful. Locusts hummed. Heat waves rose. A fisherman pulled a net through his pond. Ponds lined the main road, and narrow elevated paths between them provided access to the homes. Some homes were brick, some were tin, but even the fanciest ones were still simple. Behind the homes and patches of fruit trees and brush, the rice fields began—Crayola green stretched to the horizon. If you looked closely, you could see workers standing up straight like prairie dogs stretching their backs, then bending and disappearing once again to their work.

Although Dalton works for a multinational company, he is lower middle class. He owns next to nothing and is responsible for his entire family—his two brothers, his mom, and his dad who left his mom a few years ago. Someday he hopes to take down the tin walls around his mother's home and replace them with brick.

He is highly respected in his village, as he is one of the few who has achieved a measure of success. He is educated, has a good job, and is able to support his family. But life for Dalton is still a struggle. He scraps for every ounce of respect.

"I have social status but not land," he told me. "My mind is middle class, but my bank account is not."

Before he began working for Motorola at the age of 19, he was put in charge of the construction of one of Dhaka's fanciest hotels, the Lake Shore Hotel. You may not believe that someone would put a 19-year-old in charge of a multimillion-dollar project, but you haven't met Dalton. You haven't been with him in the hotel where everyone still treats him with the utmost respect years later. You haven't stood by his side as he talked with executives of hotels and multinational corporations, or heard people approach him, "You're Dalton from the Lake Shore, right?"

You also weren't there with Dalton when he introduced me as the *honored journalist*, or when he told a businessman over a cup of tea that I was a Motorola executive, or when he introduced me to a factory owner, without advance warning, as a big-time American garment buyer in the market for shipments of underwear.

CHAPTER 5

Undercover in the Underwear Biz

Before I left home, I knew very little about my underwear. I knew they were made in Bangladesh for the brand Briefly Stated. A few minutes searching online told me that Briefly Stated sold in 2005 to Li & Fung, a buying house that claims on its website to manage the supply chain of brands and department stores in over "40 economies." I'm not sure if an economy is the same as a country, but Li & Fung is big—and you probably have worn something they've handled. Their client list reads like a Who's Who of American retail—Walmart, Target, Kohl's, and Levi's, to name a few. I called Li & Fung's New York office to locate the factory in Bangladesh where my underwear were made and to attempt to arrange a tour.

It didn't go well.

The receptionist sent me to the underwear department, who sent me to a voicemail. When I called back, the receptionist sent me back to the underwear department, who sent me to the president's assistant, who sent me to the production manager, Mr. Cohen, who said, "Describe your underwear"—which my inner juvenile found hilarious. He said that they no longer sourced my underwear in Bangladesh, and he couldn't give me the location of the factory where they were made or any contact information of anyone who might be able to help me in Bangladesh. Eventually, with no help from a living, breathing representative of Li & Fung, I found their Bangladesh address online.

Fortunately for me, Dalton knew right where the address associated with my *Jingle These* underwear was. He led me into a tall office building located on Dhaka's Gulshan-II Circle, a kind of mini–Times Square.

"All right, Dalton," I said in the elevator on the way up to the twelfth floor, "tell them exactly why I'm here. That I'm a writer from the USA, and I followed my underwear all the way here to learn about them and see how they were made. Got it?"

Dalton smacked his lips open and was about to say something when one of his cell phones rang. Yes—*one of* his cell phones. He has four of them—two for work, one for friends, and one mystery phone whose number he doesn't give to anyone. He had to discuss some issue back at the Motorola store, which he did in minutes before turning his attention back to me.

"You no need to think. I take care of everything."

The office was modern, bright, and comfortable. A fella sat on the maroon couch next to a pile of garment samples. This definitely wasn't the factory. Dalton approached the receptionist, a man in his early thirties with a large head and a face chubbier than that of most Bangladeshis.

Dalton coolly chatted with him, occasionally nodding in my direction. The first time the receptionist followed his nod and gave me a half wave. I nervously tried to read his reaction, comparing it with my Honduras experience and worrying that I had fooled myself into a strange, expensive vacation under the delusion it was some kind of worthwhile quest.

Dalton's phone rang, and he stepped away from the counter to answer it. I stood, pulled out my underwear, and approached the counter.

There's something you need to know.

I don't lie. Not for moral reasons, but more because I'm lazy. I don't want to take the time and effort to spin a story and then try to remember what I told this person or what I did there. I know that I would get caught up in my own web. I'm not clever enough.

"I'm not sure what he told you," I motion toward Dalton, "but I'm a writer from the USA." I set my *Jingle These* underwear on the counter. "And I would like to talk to someone about my underwear."

It wasn't until I said it that I realized how stupid that sounded. Tracking down a T-shirt in Honduras was one thing. They are used to their gringo neighbors from the north visiting to preach them some religion, save them, hike through jungles, pay to throw themselves down raging rivers in rafts, and a variety of other strange things. A gringo on a mission was nothing new in Honduras. But the few westerners that visit Bangladesh are all business. Underwear is a commodity, not a grail after which to be quested.

He responded in broken English.

"I make factories list," he said. "Tomorrow you go."

I started to go into the finer details of my quest and tell him that I needed to know the exact factory that made this particular pair of underwear. Thankfully, Dalton hung up, took the card from the receptionist, and led me out the door.

Dalton had told the receptionist I was in the underwear business.

"Kelsey, if you say you're on business, people will be happier to you and show you more. Tomorrow he calling me to set up a visit. Remember, you no think."

* * *

I could only "no-think" when Dalton was around. But sooner or later, I would have to do it on my own.

Buying houses act as middlemen between garment factories and buyers. The factories don't have sales and marketing departments. Some don't even have computers, so they rely on the buying houses to communicate and handle potential and present buyers. Li & Fung isn't interested in working with one-man shows like the imaginary company Dalton said I owned. The receptionist had understood this and decided that I was an opportunity for his own small buying-house business on the side. Instead of arranging a visit to a factory through Li & Fung, he and Dalton scheduled me to meet with his business partner Salehin who thought I was in the market for granny panties.

"Now," Salehin says, "tell me more about your business."

Unfortunately, Dalton couldn't make the meeting today. There's lying to be done, and I'm on my own.

"It kinda happened by accident," I say, trying to remain as close to the truth as possible. "I'm a travel writer who coined the term *touron*—a combination of the words *tourist* and *moron*. My readers loved the term. Eventually, I started working with a cartoonist. Together we created a comic strip known as *The Touron*. I opened an online store, thinking that some of my bigger fans would enjoy owning a *Touron* T-shirt, a mug, or underwear. I called the store *Touron Attire*."

The truth is, I didn't quite coin the word *touron*, but I had written a travel column titled "The Land of Tourons" for a newspaper in Key

West. I did work with a cartoonist, and I do have an online store. But I don't have any customers, never intended to. I'm the store's owner and lone customer, designing and purchasing gifts for family and friends. I custom-make shirts, mugs, and coasters for holidays and birthdays.

I pull out a few printouts from *Touron Attire*'s online catalog and lay them on top of my underwear, and Salehin flips through the pages. He has a rounded nose that's too large for his face and a belly that's too large for his small frame. He wears the worst toupee I've ever seen. It hovers above his scalp leaving an endless black hole of space beneath. It is also too short, and he is constantly pulling it down so it doesn't ride up and reveal the gap on the sides of his head between his real and fake hair.

It's not so easy to lie to Salehin because I like him.

"It was never my intention to get into the business," I say, "but last year I sold 3,000 T-shirts. I paid $9 per shirt and sold them for $16, for a profit of $21,000. That's $21,000 into my pocket. I don't have any staff to pay. I'm hoping to more than double my profit by sourcing in Bangladesh."

"Good . . . Good," Salehin says, handing back the papers. "We don't have such [online] businesses yet in Bangladesh. Your partner, Mr. Dalton, said that you wanted to see a few factories?"

"Yes. I'm new to all of this, and I want to learn the process from start to finish. I don't have to do anything with the online store—just make the design and cash the checks."

"Please, wait." Salehin grabs his mobile phone and leaves the room. The concrete walls are bare and so are the desks. There isn't a computer in sight. The floor is tile covered in dirt that scrapes under each step. The electricity is out, and the room is lighted by a single glassless window. It's not so much a buying house, but a buying apartment. Stacks of garment samples are scattered about. Salehin had apologized for the mess earlier, just as he had apologized for not picking me up in his personal car that was "in the shop," resulting in our having to take a rickshaw to his office.

"Okay, we go to visit factory," Salehin says, poking his head around the corner.

We are on a bus leaving Dhaka.

*   *   *

"I have one son," Salehin shows me the wallpaper on his phone of a half-smiling little boy wearing nothing but a T-shirt. "He's 10 months.

My wife was visiting family in India and for one-and-a-half months, it was just me and him." He smiles, proud of his solo parenting.

Garment middlemanning isn't Salehin's only business. He also runs an NGO that he says is "for mother and child" that funds 31 medical clinics across Bangladesh and another business that places Bangladeshi students at universities abroad.

I know that he's just trying to make it in the world like everybody else, with one major priority: providing a good life for his family. And I'm completely wasting his time.

I think about this and how his breath smells like he mistook mothballs for Certs. I think about the lie, what I'm going to say at the factory, and how not to blow my cover. I feel guilty about all of it.

We pass flooded rice paddies. Six people lean out the sides of a small wood boat doing something. I don't know if rice has tassels that need detasseling, but that's what I imagine they're doing. Others wade through the mud and water. The sun is smoking hot. If it weren't for the breeze coming through the window courtesy of our great speed, I would be a sweaty mess. You can feel the breeze in Bangladesh, not just through your hair, but sticking to your skin and in your eyes. Another rice farmer guides a team of oxen from a wagon with a whip. When he wants to turn right, he hits the one on the left. The wagon is heaped with straw, and the oxen pull their feet in and out of the mud.

I think about how it would suck to be a beast of burden.

"Where exactly are we going?" I ask.

"The city of Saver," Salehin says. "It's not far. Have you been there before?"

CHAPTER 6

Bangladesh Amusement Park

I have been to Saver before; it's probably the place in Bangladesh where I left my biggest impression on the locals. If I were going to be recognized anywhere in Bangladesh, it would be here.

I stare out at the rice fields and think back to my first visit to this place, and the day I spent at its otherworldly amusement park with 19 children and one old man who weren't going to forget me anytime soon. I just hope they don't blow my cover.

* * *

Sixty-seven dollars admits one child for one day at Disney World in Orlando, Florida.

Sixty-seven dollars admits 20 people for one day at Saver's Fantasy Kingdom.

All we had to do was find them.

"One girl and one boy would be best," said Ruma, a 20-something Bangladeshi sportswriter who took the day off to help me with my crazy idea: take as many Bangladeshi kids as we can into the amusement park. Riding a roller coaster is a luxury they'd probably never know and, as a lifetime roller-coaster enthusiast, that was something I hoped to change. At the time, I didn't think this plan had much to do with my quest to find the people who made my *Jingle These* boxers. However, that was before I knew that the park was surrounded by garment factories that employ many of the locals and their kids.

"I want 20," I said. "Ask those kids."

Ruma approached three boys. While she talked, they stared at me.

"Tell them to go and bring back more kids."

We waited while they did.

Behind us were the gates of Fantasy Kingdom, the brightest, cleanest, and most out-of-place sight in all of Bangladesh. The walls are plastic but look like sandstone. Standing atop them are two very happy cartoon kids looking out onto the crowded streets and nearby garment factories. The boy holds a scepter and the girl a long-handled mirror. They give thumbs-up signs with their free hands.

Kids and adults came from every direction, and soon we had a crowd. Once we bought the tickets, the hard work began: Who got one?

We lined up the kids shortest to tallest and started handing out tickets. I noticed a group of middle-aged men in the back pointing to an old farmer. I pushed my way through the crowd and handed him a ticket.

There were no lines inside the park. *We* were the line, in fact; our personal ride-operator followed us wherever we went. We chose one that I know as the Spider from the rural county fairs of my childhood for our first ride. The kids hooted and hollered as it spun.

Our group had been somewhat reserved and unsure of what was happening before the ride. There was a sort of nervous energy that I couldn't put my finger on. They were kids (except for the old farmer) at an amusement park who *weren't* going bonkers. They stayed together and listened to whatever Ruma had to say. There wasn't even much chatter.

But the Spider changed everything. They started acting like kids, all of them, even the old farmer. They talked wide-eyed to each other with open mouths and waving arms. I knew what they were saying: "Did you see me? I wasn't holding on." Or, "I had my eyes closed." Or, "Did you try spittin'? I did and. . . ."

You don't ride rides when you are a kid; you conquer them. And those who go along with you are your brothers-in-arms. When I was a kid, I remember giving high-fives to my buddies as we strutted away from the Scrambler, the Vortex, and the Hurricane. We would look back at the nervous kids waiting in line and revel in the superiority of our shared experience.

We talked over a lunch of pizza and soft drinks. I told them that I was a journalist and I was trying to locate the factory that made my underwear. They thought this was funny. And then they told me about themselves.

Russell spoke a little English because he had gone to school for six years. He was a garment worker, as were Habir and Zumon. Habir was only 18, but was a five-year factory veteran who supported his family on $115 per month.

Five of the children were street scavengers. They picked through trash for plastic bottles, pieces of paper, cardboard, anything that they might be able to sell. None of them had attended a day of school.

A nine-year-old girl, the youngest of our group, wasn't wearing shoes or a shirt, but she was wearing earrings. Her hair was parted to the side and held with a clip. Her ten-year-old cousin had burn scars running from her fingers to her elbow. She had put her arm in a stove when she was very young and did not know better.

Life is work in Bangladesh for adults and for children. These kids were professionals.

Two of the boys sold jalmoni, a sort of spicy rice, on the street. Also in our number were two shopkeepers, a 14-year-old herbal doctor, two vegetable salesmen, two barbers, and the old farmer—Mr. Azhar, A father of seven with a white beard and whiter teeth, his distinguished face was lined with years of smiles, pain, and hard work.

"Who has been here before?" I asked.

Ruma relayed the question and only Russell raised his hand.

"Who has eaten pizza before?" I asked.

Again, only Russell raised his hand. I didn't need to ask if they liked pizza. They didn't. Half-eaten slices sat on their paper plates. I had assumed they would be hungry and expected them to wolf down whatever was put in front of them.

After lunch, we passed a wealthy couple that Ruma referred to as lovers. They sat on a ride, just the two of them. They were rich. Any Bangladeshi that could afford the $3 admission is. Some can't afford shirts for their daughters. I bought a baby-blue one that had FANTASY KINGDOM written on it for the shirtless girl with the earrings. It cost $1. I checked—it was made in Bangladesh.

There were strange metal seesaws at the playground. I got on one with one of the older boys. It hurt my knees to land and push off. I rubbed them, and the old farmer laughed. The girls played on the slide. One of the boys motioned for me to take his picture on a spring-loaded rocking kangaroo. The old farmer posed for a photo on the kangaroo, too.

People stared at us trying to figure out exactly what was going on. They couldn't make sense of our group: an upper-class Bangladeshi girl, a western man, a bunch of poor kids, and one old farmer.

There are two roller coasters in Fantasy Kingdom: a big one that would be a weenie one at any other amusement park, and a weenie one that would be a child's ride at any other amusement park. When I pointed to the big one, the kids cheered.

On the way, we passed a group of adults on the weenie coaster. We pointed and laughed. Weenies.

As we walked, some of the kids started hopping. The sun-baked stone was torture to bare feet, but they didn't complain. They just skipped.

The first coaster filled with kids and there was no room for me or the old farmer. The kids buckled in and off they went. They climbed up the hill and dropped. Fear delayed the screams, but they came all the same. The ride lasted less than 30 seconds. As the coaster pulled into the station, one of the jalmoni vendors, terrified, wiggled out from beneath the leg bar and dove for the platform before the ride came to a complete stop.

I boarded the second train and took the front car with the old farmer. He eyed the seat belt, bewildered. I buckled it for him and then pulled down the lap bar. We passed the first group of kids on the ground, and they cheered as we started to climb the hill. I motioned for everyone to hold up their hands. The old farmer did, but dropped them at the top of the hill, his veins bulging as he death-gripped the lap bar. The old man's head fell to my shoulder as we rounded a sharp

Figure 6.1   Kings and queens for a day at Fantasy Kingdom.

curve. By the ride's end, we were both laughing so hard we had tears in our eyes.

We walked through the park victorious.

The old farmer told Ruma that every day he walked by this place but had never visited. "This place was my dream place. I never thought that I would be able to come here. I'm a farmer, and it was not possible. Now, I'm quite happy."

For some in Bangladesh, $67 is more than a month's wage. Maybe I should have done something more practical for the kids with my money. After all, every kid deserves to have shoes and a shirt. But if while walking by on their way to work or while picking through trash, they look up at the park's high-arched gate and remember the roller coaster and how their stomach was in their throat and the wind in their hair, and escape just for a bit—well, then it was money well spent.

We live in a turbulent, imbalanced world. It can be depressing to think about. But we all have the right to a little fun. For a few hours, we were the kings and queens of Fantasy Kingdom. And we had a blast. (Figure 6.1.)

CHAPTER 7

Inside My First Sweatshop

Back in the city of Saver for my second time, the bus drops Salehin and me directly in front of Fantasy Kingdom. Salehin leads me from the bus stop toward the factory. I half expect one of the Fantasy Kingdom kids to run up to me at any time and blow my cover.

I know we're getting close because I can hear the drone of the machines pulling at a generator. The electricity must be out. With the factory in sight, I'm relieved to have gone unrecognized.

Through the factory's windows I see rows and rows of sewing machines and heads. Each floor of the building is leased by a separate garment business. On the way up, Salehin and I pass guards on each landing that stand from their metal folding chairs and salute us as we pass. It is weird, as if they have been told, "Make sure you salute if you see any foreigners, okay?" We aren't generals, and they sure aren't soldiers. They have permanent slouches and wear ill-fitting uniforms. Their salutes are limp. The guard on the sixth floor shows us into an office and, after some brief chitchat, we get down to business.

Three men wearing pink frocks are examining my *Jingle These* underwear. I mean *really* examining them. They pull them, stretch them, rub the fabric between their fingers, look closely at the seams, hold them up to the light. They do pretty much everything but smell them.

I packed light for this trip, and the boxers still hold a place in my underwear rotation. As I watch the examination take place, I try to think of when I wore them last and if I have washed them since. I never expected them to come under such scrutiny.

The pink men take my underwear and leave the room. Apparently, there are some types of underwear examination tools that are housed elsewhere in the factory.

The factory owner, Asad, sits across from me behind a wide desk. He's holding his three-year-old son, who plays quietly with a small length of thread on his lap. We talk about the power outage, and he tells me they cost him $700 per month in diesel to power his generators.

For the most part, I can't understand what Asad says. He speaks fast, and my attempts to read his lips are thwarted by his lazy eye that drifts to the right. I can't stop staring at it.

I think he asks me if I want to see the factory. When he stands and walks toward the door, I follow. Salehin holds the door open, and I step onto the factory floor.

*   *   *

The garment industry accounts for 76 percent of the country's annual exports, or about $8 billion. Yet the Bangladeshi industry thought they were doomed in 2005, after the Multi Fibre Agreement (MFA)—a policy that set limits on how much apparel developing countries could export—was lifted. As one of the poorest countries in the world, Bangladesh had been allowed to export with limited restrictions and duties under the MFA. This meant that they could compete on the global stage with a country like China, whose exporting was much more heavily restricted by the agreement. But without the MFA, China was free to export as much as they wanted to the developed world—causing the industry in Bangladesh to hold its breath. How could they compete with China? China has infrastructure. China doesn't have to import raw materials. They have nearly everything in that big old country of theirs, including enough poor people to work cheaply.

However, Bangladesh underestimated the value and savings they could provide. They have some of the cheapest labor in the world, even cheaper than China. The garment industry in Bangladesh not only survived; it is expected to double in size over the next eight years.

The industry's newest concern is the Decent Working Conditions and Fair Competition Act (2007), also known as the anti-sweatshop bill, introduced in the US Senate. Though the bill may mark the first time the US Congress has introduced such legislation, it's certainly not the first time United States citizens took action against working conditions in Bangladesh.

In 1992, the television show *Dateline NBC* aired footage from inside a garment factory in Bangladesh that featured a Walmart production line where kids as young as seven were operating machines and trimming garments. Walmart argued that the individuals who appeared to be seven-year-old kids were actually malnourished adults whose growth has been stunted.

The American consumers weren't buying it. MADE IN BANGLADESH became synonymous with MADE BY CHILDREN. Out of concern for the child laborers of Bangladesh, we took action the only way we knew how—by boycotting clothing made in Bangladesh. But the children didn't want our help. In fact, *they* protested the American boycott— along with Bangladeshi children's rights NGOs and other garment workers. The children didn't want to lose their jobs. They had to help support their families.

In 1994, the Bangladesh Garment Manufacturers and Exporters Association (BGMEA), under pressure of the boycott and the damaged image of the MADE IN BANGLADESH label, required the factories under their power to fire all children under the age of 14 without compensation. The local NGOs and labor unions protested this decision as out-of-work children flooded the streets of Dhaka.

In response to the crisis, the United States and Bangladeshi governments, along with international organizations such as the International Labor Organization (ILO) and United Nations Children's Fund (UNICEF), funded schools for the displaced child workers to attend until they were of working age.

And that's how the widespread use of child labor in the Bangladeshi apparel industry ended. Now you can buy clothes made in Bangladesh and know that they may have been stitched together by uneducated 15-year-old kids, but at least they (probably) weren't stitched together by uneducated 14-year-old kids. However, this is of little consolation— because heart-wrenching levels of child labor continue. According to the 2002/2003 National Child Labor Survey conducted by the Bangladesh Bureau of Statistics, 93 percent of working children work in the informal sector. And while there are a small number of kids making our clothes in Bangladesh, there are 4.9 million children between the ages of 5 and 14 holding down other jobs (Figure 7.1).

*   *   *

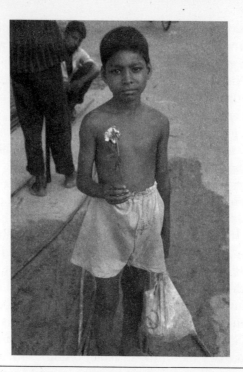

Figure 7.1 A boy selling a flower on the streets of Dhaka.

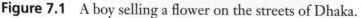

Asad leads us past a high table with neat stacks of cloth. A few of the workers are holding what appear to be giant electric bread cutters with blades two feet long. One woman marks the cloth using a pattern and then sets to slicing. She cuts the outline of a T-shirt. Plumes of cotton dust fill the air. Another woman is armed with a pair of oversized scissors—somewhere between the size of regular scissors and those used for ribbon-cutting ceremonies. She trims a piece of cloth and adds the scrap to a large pile beside her.

The factory is clean, exits are marked, and fans maintain a nice breeze. The conditions seem fine. In fact, I'm relieved to see that they're much better than I had expected.

Today, they are making T-shirts; but, I'm assured, they can produce almost anything, including underwear.

There are eight production lines, each consisting of 40 people—none of whom seem to be children or "malnourished Bangladeshis whose growth has been stunted"—and 15 sewing machines. We walk down one of the lines, and I notice cotton cobwebs frosting the dark hair of the workers. There is no chatter, just thumping needles and quick hands. I wonder if their hands move that fast when their boss and some foreigner aren't looking over their shoulders.

As with Asad's lazy eye, I try to pretend the workers aren't there. I'm a garment buyer. I'm not interested in workers. I'm interested in the products they produce.

"With this type of shirt," Asad says, picking up a completed shirt at the end of the line, "in one day we can produce 12,000 pieces."

I nod my approval and take the shirt from him. Keeping the pink men in mind, I pretend to examine the seams around the neck and sleeves and whatever else I think should be examined on a T-shirt. I stretch it, hold it to the light, and then add it to the pile.

We go back to Asad's office. I tell him about my company, and we start crunching numbers.

"I guess my order would be around 5,000 T-shirts and 3,000 boxers. How large is a typical order?"

"Normally, 20,000 pieces," Asad says. "But we are willing to make exceptions for first-time customers."

The pink men return with my boxers. They hand them to me and give Asad a sheet of paper. He punches numbers into a calculator.

"Three thousand pieces will cost $2.60 per piece," he says, and then punches in a few more numbers. "Add $0.50 per piece for shipping. That comes to $3.10 per piece."

For $9,300, I could be in the underwear business. If I sold them for $15 per pair, my profit would be $35,700—minus whatever the shipping costs would be to get them from the port in the United States to my warehouse, which I suppose would be my parents' garage. Add that to my imaginary T-shirt profits, and I could easily make over $70,000 per year. All I had to do was get an export license and have my people send their people the cash.

I thank Asad for his time. Salehin talks to him in Bengali. I'm guessing it has something to do with the $3.10 price tag per pair of underwear, which is probably more than a little high. I'm the sucker, and together they are working to reel me in.

I've concluded it would be impossible to locate the actual garment factory that made my underwear. There are over 3,000 factories in Bangladesh, and twice that many middlemen. The factories are privately owned and work with multiple brands. Today, they may be making underwear, but tomorrow maybe they'll switch to jeans, and the day after, T-shirts. To top it off—as I'm sure the pink men will attest—my underwear are old. The factory in which they were made has likely been sold, closed, burnt, or perhaps converted solely to the production of sea-foam green granny panties.

We exit back through the factory floor. I don't look at the workers, but I can feel them looking at me.

I wonder what they eat, where they sleep, what they laugh about. I wonder what they think about me.

Child Labor in Action

I was a child laborer at 11.

The factory I worked in was hot. Plumes of sawdust rose into the air off screaming saw blades and settled onto my skin. I got splinters, cuts, and scars. Once I had to get stitches. I cut wood. I swept floors. I worked around machinery that could crush and dismember. I earned $4 an hour.

My contract with the company was written in blood.

In the United States, there is no minimum age limit if your parents own the business for which you work. Lucky me. While my friends spent their summers sleeping in and going to the pool, I worked for my parents' wood truss manufacturing company, cutting boards to be made into trusses for chicken, hog, and turkey barns. Some of my friends suffered similar plights. Adam probably had it the worst. Pity the son of a dairy farmer.

I would rise at 5:42 AM and sleepwalk my way across the gravel drive to the long white barn. Some of the boards were too heavy for me to lift. I could handle all lengths of 2 × 4's, and most of the 2 × 6's, but anything bigger than that and it was time to sweep the floor. When I wasn't carrying wood or sweeping, I daydreamed or caused trouble. If you packed certain tubes on the large component saw with sawdust and waited for just the right moment to blow it with the air hose, you could really get somebody. I also enjoyed playing with grease. If you left your hammer or tape around me very long, you could bet that I was going to apply a nice layer of grease onto it so that when you picked it up your hand was a mess.

Unfortunately, I got more than I gave. Everybody liked messing with the boss's son. If you've never had sawdust down your pants, I wouldn't recommend it.

I wasn't the best truss builder, but I would have been an even worse garment worker. A good garment worker is docile and out of options. Like many kids my age, I had big aspirations and was raised on a steady diet of "you can do anything you put your mind to." I spent half my time figuring how many hours I had to work before I could afford that Trans Am I wanted. Sixteen was only five years away. The rest of the time, I tried to decide which NBA team I preferred to draft me in the 2001 draft, following my hugely successful collegiate career in the Big Ten.

I had confidence (too much), dreams (big ones), and was outgoing. I also had six years of education. These are all things that make for one crummy garment worker. Since the Industrial Revolution, our clothes have always been made by those who are less privileged— primarily, young, uneducated women who are desperate for work.

In nineteenth-century England, the industry favored women and children for their abundance, the cheap wages paid to them, and their obedient temperament. Since child labor was frowned upon when the industry jumped the pond to New England, it relied primarily on young, single women from rural areas. When it moved to the South, guess who worked at the garment factories? Young, docile, women from rural areas—just as when it moved to Japan, Honduras, China, and Bangladesh.

In fact, the more docile, the better.

*   *   *

Dalton took me to a few sweatshops in the city of Narsingdi, northeast of Dhaka. And by sweatshop, I don't mean the socially loaded term that refers to employees being paid below the federally mandated minimum or treated poorly—although they may have been that, too. I mean the factories were friggin' hot.

Of course, the garment factories aren't the first step in my underwear's production. Cotton is grown, picked, made into giant spools of thread that are turned into long sheets of cloth, then colored, and only then shipped to the garment factories—which are the last step of the process, and the textile factories are just one step before that.

Dalton's uncle has a small textile factory on his property. A broken-down pickup truck sat outside the tin shack in a bed of weeds. Inside the building, two shirtless men wearing loose skirts wrapped up tight like a pair of shorts worked away. The process was completely manual. One of them turned a big wooden wheel fed by a hundred or so spools of thread. The other sat beneath the rainbow of thread and guided them into the wood contraption. The men worked in the silence of monotony, ignoring us. I imagined cloth had been produced like this for centuries.

The next factory was more modern, and the neatly dressed boss man gave us free rein. We could walk where we wanted, talk to whomever we wanted, and take pictures of what we saw. Dalton told the truth this time: that I was a writer from the United States. Still, the owner had no problems. He was happy to show a foreigner around.

We walked in the door and saw two teenage boys working on a small machine. The best I could tell, their job was to prep the rolls of thread for the bigger machines by unrolling them and rolling them back again.

The one boy picked through the thread with a tool that appeared to be a small version of a hot dog holder (Figure 8.1). His upper lip looked as though a pathetic woolly worm had crawled up on it and died. He couldn't have been more than 15. Dalton asked him to slow down so I could see what he was doing, but his hands still moved too fast.

Electric looms pounded out a rhythm that could be heard anywhere in town. Shirtless men tended machines once again, but these were unlike the first wheel crank we saw. Flywheels spun belts. The looms pumped up and down. One of the men motioned me closer, but I chose to keep my distance from all the moving parts. A safe uniform is no uniform, and

Figure 8.1   Boys working in a textile factory.

I was wearing a baggy shirt. The room had row after row of similar stations attended by similar skinny half-naked guys. I'm not sure if I could stand it. So hot. So loud. In the United States, there would be guards and stickers all over the place, and hearing protection. Here there's nothing.

We were shown into the boss man's office and given grapes, oranges, and soft drinks. We learned about how his father started the business in 1965, and he was proud to have taken it to the next level with this new factory. He sells the fabric to garment industries in Bangladesh and internationally, mostly to Japan and some to the Carolinas.

Employees shuffled in with poster boards of photos of the boss man receiving awards for his work in the community. They, including Dalton, kept referring to him as a "social worker." He donated a lot of money to the hospital down the road. He was a nice man, broad through the shoulders with a slightly receding hairline and a strong face. I was most welcome in his factory, even if my purpose was to take photos of his underage workers. He owned five other factories.

"They work around the clock," said one of the locals that accompanied us on our tour. "One man—12 hours at a time. The machines never stop."

I asked him if there are many injuries.

"Not too bad, but . . ." he motioned a slice across his finger and then his forearm to show me that fingers and arms were lost.

The coloring factory was the sweatiest of all the shops. Huge, worm-like furnaces with glowing red mouths sucked in long sheets of cloth. The heat helps affix the dye to the cloth. It was stifling. We watched the teenage boys work through a mist of rising steam, using wood sticks to help feed the cloth into the furnaces.

"Ask them their age," I told Dalton.

"No need to ask," Dalton said, firmly denying my request to translate a question that might get us into trouble.

The stores lining the streets of Narsingdi were closing for the night, but the rolls and mounds of cloth were still being shuffled this way and that by any means of locomotion possible. An overfilled truck coming from a narrow alley toward the main road stopped before the power lines. It was heaped full with bags of cloth and too tall to pass beneath. On top, two men reached forward with a bamboo pole and lifted up the lines—death no farther away than the width of the pole. The truck lurched back and forth as the driver tried to make it up the rough incline. The workers on top balanced the line on the pole. A rickshaw hauling a load of long skinny rolls of fabric rang its bell, signaling me to step aside as it passed. No one else seemed to think anything of the workers cheating death on the truck. The textile industry stops for nothing here in Narsingdi.

I was feeling pretty crummy by the time we left for Dhaka. I had come all the way to Bangladesh to see workers working, and I didn't like what I had seen. Kids who should have been in school were instead working. Dalton assured me that if these kids didn't work there, they would beg in the middle of the road, or work at a welding shop in Old Dhaka, or at a brick factory where they would crush bricks into stone. Or, they might do hundreds of worse things on the streets, some harder, more dangerous, and for less pay than working at a textile or garment factory.

It's really easy to be against child labor. In the United States, there are few things we value more than a child's innocence. Children should be skipping through sprinklers, chasing lightning bugs, drinking Kool-Aid or Tang, believing in Santa Claus and the Easter Bunny, making forts out of blankets and furniture, watching cartoons, and, in general, not worrying about anything other than going to school and having fun. If they work, it's not for income to pay for food or shelter; it's to learn responsibility, build character, or to save for what promises to be a bright future. American children are protected from the realities of the world.

The children of Bangladesh are not. I've never known anyone in the United States who died from diarrhea or malaria. I've never met a leper. It would be great if all the kids in Bangladesh who spend their days trying to earn money for their family's next meal could go to school instead of work. But it's not reality. Not yet.

One can make the argument that factories that employ children are doing good, and the westerners who call for an end to child labor are actually doing harm. I read about one factory owner who would offer underage children jobs when they were down and out and needed money. He thinks he's actually helping the children. Maybe he is.

Not having children make our clothes does not eliminate the reality that many children in Bangladesh must work, but it eliminates our guilt in the matter. It clears our conscience and helps us forget that we live in such a world.

Does a mother who sends her eight-year-old daughter off for a day of picking up plastic bottles, or begging, or working in a factory love her daughter any less than a mother in the United States who sends her daughter to school? Is she being immoral? My own conclusion, after visiting Bangladesh, is that we should not be ashamed that our clothes are made by children so much as ashamed that we live in a world where child labor is often necessary for survival.

Child labor or not, the working conditions in Bangladesh's garment and textile industries are the living conditions of the country.

This is the culture of poverty.

CHAPTER 9

Arifa, the Garment Worker

Two million people live and work as garment workers in Bangladesh. I've seen them walking on the streets in the early morning with their lunches; I've seen them working beneath fluorescent lights at their machines, and I read about their struggles and the industry's triumphs in the local papers each morning. A single morning's headlines from Dhaka's English language paper, the *New Age*: "25 Hurt as Garment Workers Clash," "Knitwear Factory Workers Stage Demo for Arrears," "Garment Worker Commits Suicide," "Exports Grow by 21 Percent to $8 Billion in 8 Months."

Economist Jeffrey Sachs, Director of The Earth Institute and Special Advisor to the United Nations Secretary-General Ban Ki Moon, believes that the garment industry in Bangladesh and other developing countries is an opportunity to get a foothold on the first rung of the global economic ladder. In his book, *The End of Poverty* (New York: Penguin, 2005), he writes:

> Not only is the garment sector fueling Bangladesh's economic growth of more than five percent per year in recent years, but it is also raising the consciousness and power of women in a society . . . this change and others give Bangladesh the opportunity in the next few years to put itself on a secure path of long-term economic growth.

Women who have jobs are likely to have fewer children. Missing work while pregnant, having a baby, or caring for a newborn is, in a sense, expensive. Therefore, working women have fewer children to feed, clothe, and keep healthy, and more money to do so. Sachs writes that the total fertility rate—the average number of children a woman has over her lifetime—in 1975 in Bangladesh was 6.6. Today, it's 3.1. Educating and employing women is one of the best ways to lift a society from poverty.

*   *   *

Mr. Moon of the National Garment Worker's Federation is a squat, serious-looking man. His bare office, furnished with a single table and two unoccupied chairs, is dark—so dark that it takes me a moment to notice that the walls are papered with newspaper pages picturing dead and beaten garment workers. He has a lot of reasons to be serious.

He agrees to introduce me to some garment workers and takes me to an apartment building full of them. We talk with young and old workers about their lives, families, and futures. I meet a 45-year-old man who has worked in the garment factories for 20 years and makes $45 per month. I talk with a pretty 18-year-old girl with a nice smile and a name that translates to "Singer" who makes $24 per month. She tells me she wants to be a doctor, which is like me saying I want to fly the Space Shuttle.

But it is a woman by the name of Arifa who impresses me the most. I get the sense that she might be the type of woman Sachs is talking about in his book. When she talks, everyone listens. I arrange to spend a day with her from sunup to sundown to see whether Arifa is socially empowered—or dehumanized by her work making clothes for people like me.

I came to Bangladesh to meet the people who made my clothes just as I had when I went to Honduras. But I let myself down in Honduras. I didn't ask what I wanted to during the few minutes I had spent with Amilcar—questions I wasn't prepared to have answered. It was as if I had walked up to the edge of a cliff, looked over, said "No thanks," and walked away. Now, I have every intention of taking the plunge— learning about Arifa's work as a garment worker, her struggles living on less than $1 a day, and her hopes as a single mother for her children.

*   *   *

It's 5 AM. The streets of Dhaka are empty. It's creepy being the only moving thing in the most crowded city of the most crowded country in the world.

The hotel clerk warned me not to go.

"This [idea] is very dangerous. Maybe you can go after 10 AM, but at *that* time of day there are many hijackers," the clerk said.

"What if I go with nothing? No money. No camera. No passport."

"At a minimum," he said, "you'll get stabbed because they'll be angry that you don't have anything."

Yikes.

"Could your driver take me there and walk me up to the apartment? Kind of act as my security man?"

The driver is five inches shorter than I am, but he struts with his shoulders thrown back. His biggest muscle is his gut, and it hangs over his belt. All in all, he looks a bit like the bouncer of a bar that has nightly specials of 50¢ beer. Of course, he wouldn't be a bouncer at a bar here; Bangladesh is for the most part a dry country.

The driver is still blinking the sleep out of his eyes as he guides the hotel's car down the street. I almost hugged him when he agreed to accompany me the previous night. But we were too manly for such shenanigans. After all, we were going to brave the empty streets of Dhaka.

I'm on the lookout for hijackers, highwaymen, robbers, crooks, thugs, gangs, bandits—you name it. I spot some talking on the corner, and, to my horror, the driver pulls over to ask them directions. He lowers my window and leans across the armrest to talk with them. Two of the potential hijackers step back, and their leader rests one hand on our car's roof and his other on the door. His fingers dangle inside the car. The nails are long and yellow, especially the pinky's that appears sharp enough to slit throats of soft-skinned foreigners who dare to face the small, dark hours of the day. He consults his gang and then points around the corner.

We do this again and again—pull over and ask nearly every person we see on the street for directions. If there are any evildoers about, we give them ample opportunity to do their evil.

"This is it," I say, motioning the driver to stop.

The driver finds a place to pull the car out of the way in the narrow alley. We walk down a narrower alley. I recognize the smell—a mix of rotten cabbage and shit—and the way it burns in my nose and my chest. I lead the driver into the concrete building on the left to which Mr. Moon first brought me.

No attempt at all has been made to have this building appear aesthetically pleasing. From the outside, and especially the inside, it looks as if a fire has scarred the concrete and done away with any paint.

The steps are rounded from wear and crumbling, and look like they could go at any time. There used to be a railing, as evidenced by the occasional green support sticking out from the wall. We reach the sixth and top floor of the building. The driver is huffing and puffing, and I'm a bit winded myself.

"Arifa?" I whisper. The hallway is lit by the flame of a gas stove hugging the edges of a pot of rice.

The cook at the stove gives me a half smile and disappears into a room down the hall. I hand the driver a fist of Bangladeshi taka and thank him for his help. He looks at me, puzzled. His English isn't good enough for me to explain to him what I'm doing. To him, it must look like I'm up to no good: meeting a prostitute or buying drugs.

Even in the dim light, I recognize her face. She has a strong jaw, big eyes, and a sloping forehead. She's wearing a baggy purple shirt and blue pants, and a scarf with a rainbow of color tied around her neck. Both her face and outfit are still wrinkled from sleep.

She waves me into the room and has me sit on a bed crowded with her kids. Little Sadia, who's four, sleeps in the corner by the wall, flopping silently this way and that. Each time I look at her, she is in a different position. Abir, 11, sleeps much more soundly.

Arifa motions for me to lift up my legs. I do, and she pulls a bucket of rice out from under the bed and starts to scoop out cupfuls. I count them to myself . . . four . . . five . . . six. In the early morning silence, I can hear each grain tink against the pot.

The room is constructed out of anything and everything. Cardboard insulates the roof and the walls. The studs are bamboo, the floor concrete. Wood boards make up the interior ceiling and walls. The exterior wall is sheet metal dimpled with holes that are lit with the slightest hint of dawn. There are two cabinets, one directly in front that's long with sliding glass doors and upper and lower compartments. The upper has clothes, bed sheets, and towels, and the lower, dishes, silverware, and two stuffed animals.

The majority of space in the room is taken up by the two large beds, which slept four people last night. The fourth person, Didder Khan, is Arifa's sister's husband. He works for Gillette and speaks a little English. He brushes his teeth for a half hour. The first time he spits, he does so on the wall of the steps, adding to the white stains that look like runny bird poop. The next time is through a hole in the wall near his bed.

Arifa returns. The rice is on, and it's time to prepare the rest of breakfast. She pulls out a bowl of vegetables from beneath the other bed and sits on the floor. She places a curved blade face up on the floor and begins to expertly chop onions, potatoes, and other veggies by running them across the blade's edge. She's quick and doesn't have to be watching to do this. Sometimes she looks at me, and we try to communicate; sometimes she looks up at her children and smiles. The cut veggies pile up on the floor before she scoops them up and takes them into the kitchen.

I walk down the hallway, the gas from the stove burning my eyes, and step onto the roof. Dhaka is just waking; the first rickshaw bells cut the silence of the morning. Below, the beggars are getting an early start, and the market's first deals of the day are under way. Merchants transport their goods to their stores in large wicker baskets balanced on their heads. A man on a nearby roof stretches, and on another roof, a small boy is doing his morning chores, but stops long enough to wave at me.

I go back in and sit on the bed. Arifa offers me breakfast. I don't want to take the food. They have so little. After refusing three times, I finally take the tortillas, and the green goop made from the vegetables she mixed and mashed. It's a little spicy for my taste, but I eat it.

Across the hall in a small room, three guys watch me from their bed—a bamboo frame with slivers of board on top. All three are garment workers.

Arifa subleases the room to the workers. They pay her $14.60 per month for room and board. Arifa cooks for no less than seven people at a time. The men scoop rice from large bowls with their hands, mix it with the green goop, and shovel it in. Light through the window behind me lights the edge of their bed. I can make out the bowl, but barely their faces. I just see hands shrinking the pile of rice.

Sadia wakes and the first thing she sees is me. She starts to cry. After I tickle her feet with my pen, she starts to giggle. It's not hard to win the friendship of a four-year-old. The giggling only lasts as long as the tickling, and then she cries again and doesn't show signs of stopping.

"What's wrong with Sadia?" I ask Didder.

He stumbles around with the sentence before finding the words, "Sadia is very hungry."

Arifa sits down on the bed and reaches underneath the mattress and pulls out a wad of taka, mainly red 10s and hands them to Abir. Abir returns with some tortillas and gives them to Sadia. After a few bites, she has more interest in playing with her food than eating it.

At first, it's hard to tell if Sadia is a girl or boy. She has short hair, and her clothing provides no clues. Her smile is mischievous and exposes her complete set of top teeth. Her skin is bumpy. I think she must have some problem with rickets, ringworm, or some other thing I've never had to worry about in my life. I ask Arifa about it.

"The water is no good," she says. "It comes from the roof."

Abir sits down on the bed and pulls out a plastic briefcase.

"I bought that for him when I was in Thailand with the Garment Federation," she says.

Abir works on math problems with long division and parentheses using Arifa's cell phone for its calculator function. He's lanky and wears a ball cap pulled down over his eyebrows. When he carries Sadia, he does so just like his mom—jutting out a hip. Sometimes he squats down so Sadia can ride on his back piggyback-style, which she clearly loves.

Arifa has another son, Arman. He is 18 and living and working in Saudi Arabia, which is common practice for young men in Bangladesh. He makes $146 per month and sends half of it home to his mom.

"He has been gone for five months," she says, "and will be gone for at least another five years." I see the sadness in her eyes as they drift to Abir. If given the opportunity, he would have to go, too. "Their father was a crook, and the government doesn't take care of my children. It's not like the USA or the U.K. They don't have a choice. I would like them to go to school longer, but this isn't possible."

After breakfast, Abir heads for school and Didder for Gillete. Arifa, Sadia, and I go to the market.

Arifa works at the Standard Garment factory, but injured her leg somehow and is taking a month off to recover. When she is working she makes 10¢ an hour and works 60 hours a week, earning a total of $6 per week.

Merchants have their foods laid out on plastic tarps. Flies buzz fish. A meat stand—think child's lemonade stand in size and structure—has slabs of unidentifiable meat hanging from hooks. People selling produce dip their hands in water and spritz their veggies.

Regardless of the crowd, Arifa walks up and takes care of business. I can tell she always gets the price she wants. The sellers know better than to try to negotiate with her. People stare at me, and Arifa smiles and laughs as she nods to me while continuing her conversation. It's typical staring, but there are more little kids than usual grabbing my arms and hands. With a word from Arifa, they scatter. I'm always looking for Sadia among the crowd, and Arifa looks at me and says, "No problem."

If it takes a village to raise a child, that's definitely the case here. Sadia is always with someone she is calling auntie or uncle.

Arifa begins preparing lunch for the workers. I sit on the corner of a bed and scribble down some notes. It begins to rain, and the rhythmic pitter-patter on the tin roof puts me to sleep. I wake and find a pillow beneath my head and a fan directed on me.

Sadia returns with one of her aunts. I draw a smiley face on the palm of my hand and show her. She laughs. I add a tongue, close my hand, and then reveal it. She laughs. I add ears . . . a body . . . an arrow through the head . . . . We keep up the game until lunch.

I'm served rice. Not just any kind of rice, but some kind of smaller-grained, imported rice reserved for guests of honor. The honor is lost on me until someone points it out. To me, rice is rice.

The heat of the day is beating down on the tin roof. It's inescapable. To make matters worse, the electricity is out, and the fan sits motionless with its on-button pushed in. We sit on the beds and chat.

Sadia plops a dollop of Brylcreem onto her hair. She rubs it in with her tiny hands and giggles. She's a kid and likes to show off. Arifa ruffles her hair and gives her a hug. She's a mom.

Sadia's aunt tells me to sit by the window so I can take advantage of what little breeze there is outside. The thin, shredded curtains barely move. They are see-through and a pathetic, almost heartbreaking attempt to spruce up the place.

I look down on more tin roofs, rusted and holey, like the wall I lean against. It's a harsh, hard-to-imagine concept that on the sixth floor of a smelly, crumbling building, where 16 people share a single shower, I'm witnessing economic progress and the future of Bangladesh.

*   *   *

I've got $20 in my pocket, and, economic progress or not, Arifa could use it more than me.

Arifa is leading me to her factory, Standard Garment, to meet some of the workers being let out for the day. The sun is low in the sky and turns the dust from the rush-hour hustle and bustle pink. Some guy, maybe her boyfriend, met us at her apartment and is walking with us. He's creepy in a Lurch sort of way. In her room, I tried to communicate with him using my repertoire of hand gestures and facial expressions, but he met them all with the same blank, unwavering, serial-killer stare. I would just hand her the money if it weren't for him. He might question what she has done to earn it, and we don't need that.

We pass a steady stream of people all of whom Arifa identifies as garment workers. She stops and talks with them to explain who I am. She snags a peanut from a vendor and pays him with a little attention. People are glad to see her. She's confident and popular.

The streets become more crowded as we get closer to the factory. Trucks jerk from forward to reverse and back again as they maneuver around tight corners. Their headlights throw the shadows of the workers across the muddy street.

Arifa stops 300 feet short of the factory gate. If we go any further, my presence might cause a problem. It's unnatural for producer and consumer to meet. And while it's okay for me to inspect their work in the factory as a potential buyer, it's not okay for me to stand beside them on a muddy street as anything other than that.

The scene is similar to the one I witnessed at the factory in Honduras—an endless stream of workers, haggling vendors, people, and vehicles jockeying for position. To me, it's controlled chaos; to them, it's six o'clock. In Honduras, I knew nothing about any of workers' lives. Here, I know a little about Arifa's and enough to know that many of the hundreds of workers passing by have harder lives than I could ever imagine.

The sun has set on my day with Arifa. She flags a taxi. The first is too expensive, and she sends it packing. The next, she bargains down. Whether a pillow under the head, a fan directed on me, the honor of short-grained rice, or saving me a few cents to get back to my hotel, Arifa looked after me the entire day. I wish there was more I could do for her.

I finger the $20 in my pocket. It's nearly an entire month's worth of Arifa's wages or, to me, about one pair of *Jingle These* boxers. Lurch is standing beside her. I pull my hand out empty and wave goodbye.

Arifa knows how much my underwear cost. Workers at her factory add the price tags onto the garments before they are shipped out. She knows the world that I come from is one of luxury. I know hers is one of hardship. We know, but we can't imagine.

She waves and then disappears—just another garment worker.

CHAPTER 10

Hope

"Now is a good time," Bibi said. "The electricity is out." I have never interviewed a supermodel before or even talked to one, for that matter. I never expected that she would be there—up three flights of stairs off the chaotic streets of Dhaka sitting in the dark.

When she stood I almost said, "Boy, you sure are tall and skinny," but I didn't. I would say dumber things later.

"Do you smoke?" she asked in her elegant, full-bodied smoker's voice.

"No. . . ."

"Good," she said.

"But go ahead." As if she needed my permission to smoke in her own office.

Bibi Russell graduated from the London School of Fashion in 1975. At her teacher's suggestion, she modeled in her own fashion show. She was discovered and soon became a famous international model who appeared in *Vogue, Cosmo,* and *Harper's Bazaar.* And then she did a strange thing. In 1994, she moved back to her home country of Bangladesh (Figure 10.1).

"How could I forget all of this," Bibi said. "This is where I grew up."

She loves the people of Bangladesh; as she tells me, "Everything I do is for them. They made me Bibi. Everything I have, I owe them."

And Bibi is paying them back big time. Through her business, Bibi Productions, she directs the work of local weavers in villages across Bangladesh and India. The weavers don't know what sells and

Figure 10.1   Model and fashion designer Bibi Russell.

what is in style. Bibi does. They also don't have access to the global market. Bibi gives it to them.

"Everything comes from the grassroots people—everything."

In a way, she is like the major clothing brands—directing factories through buying houses as to what they want, how they want it made, and ultimately buying the finished product.

However, there's one way in which she's not so much like the brands: "We help people come out of poverty through dignity."

You can argue that the mainstream garment business provides Bangladesh 2.5 million jobs that they wouldn't have otherwise and therefore is a blessing in an impoverished country. But the pay is so very poor that most garment workers, at best, are barely able to tread water. If a family member becomes sick, or the workers themselves are unable to work, they all sink. Bangladesh is a country of obscene realities.

Dalton and I once saw a one-legged rickshaw driver. He didn't hassle us for a ride. He just sat there and watched as we walked by. He had lost his leg to an infection, but still had to support his family.

It takes a full-body effort to get his rickshaw rolling, but once it is, you can barely tell that he's missing a leg. But you'll never forget.

And Bibi chose to come back to deal with such things, to make a difference, to leave the glossy, touched-up world of fashion for this.

I joined her for tea one evening in her apartment for which her mother pays the rent. Bibi has given all of herself and all that she was worth financially. Her brothers, sisters, and children help pay her daily expenses. Her mom thinks she's a bit too selfless. A few years back, she had broken her wrist while in Indonesia aiding the victims of the 2004 tsunami. Her mother gave her money to have the necessary surgery, but Bibi gave the money away. There was a man in one of the villages that she worked with who had had a heart attack and needed a double bypass. For her selflessness, she was appointed an UNESCO Special Envoy: Designer for Development.

I sat in her living room and drank watermelon juice and ate cookies. Her place was decorated with indigenous instruments of wood and metal. The decorated carriage of a rickshaw stood in one corner. She pointed out a picture of Gandhi, and I asked if she had met him.

"He died in the 1940s," she politely informed me.

"Well, if he would have been alive, you probably would have met him." I'm an idiot, and nothing I can do or say can change that. (Although in my defense, Ben Kingsley—who played Gandhi in the movie—is still alive.)

"Probably," she said politely.

She's the closest thing to a saint I've ever met. She loves her country. She believes in it.

* * *

Nobel Peace Prize winner Mohammad Yunnus believes in Bangladesh, too. He formed the Grameen Bank, which gives microcredit loans to people who couldn't get loans from a traditional bank. I went with a representative of the bank to see the program in action.

Thirty women sat shoulder-to-shoulder on wood benches in the bare building framed with bamboo and covered in corrugated metal sheeting. The bank's regional manager called out names from his ledger. One-by-one, the women approached his table at the front of the room and made their group's loan payment.

To get a loan from the bank, a woman must find other women to form a small group. Failing to pay it back hurts the other women's chances of obtaining future loans; as such, the group provides support and a sort of peer pressure to repay the loans. A borrower who cannot pay reflects poorly on her group. However, this is the only penalty. The bank doesn't take their home or their livestock. There is no collateral.

Amazingly, 98 percent of the loans are paid back, and the bank has lent to over 7 million borrowers.

Lovli is only 55, but she looks 75. That's what life as a beggar will do to you. She used her loan to buy bags of gummy candy to sell, making twice as much money as she did begging.

Shokinan bought a cow with her first loan. After she paid the loan back, she bought a home. After she paid that one back, she built rooms near her home to rent out. Now, she owns more than 60 rooms. Her first loan was for $57 and her last for $4,200. She has come a long way from owning one cow.

Shilpi works at a garment factory earning $25 per month, but she has started her own business on the side making pants and shirts. She used her loans from the Grameen Bank to buy her sewing machine and materials. She's 26, has two sons (9 and 11), and only attended three years of school. When I asked her where she saw herself in 10 years, she got really excited. She smiled, pointing this way and that. I didn't have a clue as to what she was saying, but I could tell she had big plans.

A first-time loan might be only $5. But that's all it takes to empower these women to see beyond today's needs, to imagine a better life for their children—to give them hope (Figure 10.2).

Figure 10.2   A borrower of the Grameen Bank with her child.

Like money, hope is in short supply in impoverished nations. Ask kids what they want to do when they grow up and they'll look at you funny. They know what they are going to do. They are going to do what their moms and dads do—just try to get by.

But as long as Bangladesh has people who believe in it like Bibi and the dedicated workers of the Grameen Bank, hope has the potential to grow.

CHAPTER

11

No Black and White, Only Green

"We predict the garment sector will grow $8 billion in the next three years." Habib works at the Bangladesh Garment Manufacturers and Exporters Association. He's about my age and eager to chat. It's apparent that not too many potential garment buyers stop in at their headquarters.

"For quality and price you can't beat Bangladesh," says Iqbal, one of Habib's coworkers, as he wipes sweat from his forehead with a napkin. "Our service is best, too. It's in our culture. Sometimes factory owners will take a job and just break even or lose money to establish good relations with a new customer."

I've already given them my *Touron Attire* spiel, and now I'm telling them that I'm also visiting Cambodia and China to see where I want to source from.

"You go to China, they don't speak English," says Iqbal, "and their quality is not as good. All my shirts are made in Bangladesh. I could buy ones made in China for $6, but I buy ones made in Bangladesh for $20." He pulls at his sweaty shirt.

The electricity is out once again, and the office workers who were napping in front of their blank computer screens have gathered around to listen in on our conversation. I'm not sure if they speak English or not, but they laugh when we laugh; when we get serious, they get serious.

"What do you think about the US-proposed anti-sweatshop bill?" I say, curious to know if they had heard of the bill that's currently in Congress. "Whatever a sweatshop is." I roll my eyes.

Iqbal, along with everyone else in the garment sector, is worried that the bill might lead to more boycotting of the MADE IN BANGLADESH label, like the one in the 1990s did.

"Child labor is not a problem here. If we find out that one of our members is breaking this rule, we fine them $10,000 on the spot. If this happens three times, we take away their license to export."

Before I came to Bangladesh, met Arifa, and visited the factories, I would have completely supported any bill against sweatshops and child labor. But I've come to realize that the world isn't black or white, good or bad. The bill's intentions seem good; if carried out, they could lead to the improvement of working conditions worldwide. However, it could also bring job loss in Bangladesh. If it passes, I hope that lawmakers will consider the results it could have on the Bangladeshi worker and plan to assist those who lose their jobs.

I let a new fella who's taken a seat on the corner of the desk know my story: how I'm hoping to source in Bangladesh and turn my private little *Touron Attire* business from a $21,000 profit to over a $70,000 profit.

"Mister Kelsey," Iqbal interrupts me, "your thinking is wrong. Don't think thousands. Think millions."

Everybody smiles and nods. It's *that* easy for foreigners to make money in Bangladesh.

The electricity comes back on. I'm sweating from the walk to their headquarters, the tea they gave me, and maybe a little bit from the lying. They point the fan at me and hand me some napkins.

One of them brings me a T-shirt, "This is a gift for you. We hope it's the first of many shirts you'll have from Bangladesh."

I thank them and tell them that I'm still considering whether or not I want to take the next step. A few of them give me their cards and ask whether I'd be interested in the small garment businesses they have on the side. They all encourage my progress.

"Who wouldn't want to be in this business?" Iqbal says. He leans back in his chair and looks at me over his glasses.

*   *   *

One person who certainly does is Dalton's cousin, Sapon. I'm standing with Sapon and his two partners inside Tatting Fashion Ltd., a company that is nothing more than a name—right now, at least. Our voices echo off the concrete walls of the empty factory floor.

"The garment industry in Bangladesh is growing fast," Sapon says. "We hope to benefit from it. Large factories get big orders and will send us work."

"Your company will be a subcontractor?" I ask.

"Yes."

If you are looking for labor or human rights violations in the garment industry, the best place to look is the subcontractor, if you can find one. Buyers and brands place orders with large factories, which they might even visit to make sure that the working conditions meet whatever standards they have outlined. But subcontractors are dark holes in the wall that are often overlooked by any sort of monitoring. They are too small and abundant. It took the bad press of the 1990s to compel major clothing brands to take responsibility for the working conditions in the factories from which they sourced; however, subcontractors are contracted to the factory, not the brand, thereby adding another layer of separation. The sweatshops I pictured in Sociology 201 in college look an awful lot like the subcontractors' factories. But the evil lords that ruled over the sweatshops I pictured look nothing like Sapon.

Sapon is Mr. Rogers—soft-spoken, polite, and eager to teach me about all things Bangladeshi. I first met him in Dalton's village of Ludhua. He accompanied us during our walks, often putting a hand on my shoulder as he explained something about the village. Whereas, Dalton has the squinty-eyed shiftiness thing going on, Sapon is genuinely open.

His father worked hard to support Sapon's family and paid for a few years of schooling. However, once he was unable to work, the onus fell on Sapon. He quit school and, with his uncle's help, got a job managing a hotel. It was Sapon's sole responsibility to support his mother, father, sister, and two brothers. He paid for both of his brothers to go through school and eventually for them to leave Bangladesh and work abroad—one in Singapore and the other in Dubai. Now they send money back to Sapon to invest in his business venture.

"We ordered 60 machines from China for knitting and 24 for linking," Sapon says, laying out rows of machines with his hands. The room is about the size of a cozy family restaurant.

We walk up a set of stairs and leave his partners behind. "This is the washing room, and this the prayer room."

Sapon's eyes tend to bug out of his head when he really concentrates; that's what they are doing right now as he scans the room. "We can put a few more machines up here and maybe an office." The room currently has a table and two chairs where we sit.

"What do you see for the future of your business?" I ask.

"In two months, the machines should be here, and then we start working for factories."

"What do you think the business will be like if I come back in five years?" I ask.

He takes a deep breath. After all the planning and hoping and remittances from his brothers abroad, the opening of the factory is so near I can tell that it's hard for him to see beyond it. "If our business continues to grow up, we get license to export after five years."

"How will it change your life if your business succeeds?" I ask.

Again, he gathers his thoughts before answering, "When I get more money and the business grows, maybe then I can stop working at the hotel and work here with my partners. Maybe I buy some land, build a house, and bring my parents to live with me."

"How about a wife?"

"Actually, I have been of age to marry for 10 years, but because of my family's economic crisis, I could not. But at the moment, I have no good relations with a girl to make my wife." He gives a bashful smile. At the age of 35, a wife is a luxury he has been unable to afford. "I try to find a sweet girl to marry."

"How many employees will you have?" I ask.

"About 200."

"I've spent a lot of time with garment workers here in Bangladesh," I say. "What is their life like?"

"The Bangladeshi worker is very cheap. That's why Bangladeshi garment sector is in a good position. Eighty percent of people live in the village and most don't go to school. Their family is not educated. That's why maybe one couple has five, six, seven, eight children. And their children when they are teenagers come to Dhaka City and work in garments. Ten years back my family was very poor, and then I came to Dhaka City to get a job and help my family and my village. I think garment workers can do the same."

Sapon is a man with a dream, one that is tied to the success of the garment industry. An evil lord of the sweatshop, he is not (Figure 11.1).

*   *   *

Figure 11.1 Sapon in front of his factory.

"This is where our worlds meet," Dalton says.

We're sitting in the lobby of the North Shore Hotel. For the two years it took to build, Dalton worked as the project manager. His role included but was not limited to being accountant, architect, and security guard. He bought supplies. He hired and fired people. He lived at the hotel day and night. And he was let go once it was completed. The hotel owner told him that he didn't have enough experience to work customer service, management, or in any other position at the hotel. Despite being somewhat bitter about this, Dalton brought me here to witness the nightly ritual.

We watch as an American man rides down to the lobby in the glass elevator. He's wearing flip-flops, cutoff shorts, and a T-shirt. I imagine that he's from Southern California, but honestly, who can say? Many people think that my blond curly hair means that I'm from California, so I guess he could be from Ohio. A Bangladeshi woman draped in a colorful sari stands to meet him. In a country where some women will not look at or touch a foreigner, she shakes his hand. They sit in high-backed, wraparound chairs. The man hands her a T-shirt. She examines it while nodding her head.

I know what she's saying. "Yes, we can make this. We can make anything cheaper than almost anywhere."

The bright lights reflect off the polished marble floor. They always do—the hotel has a generator. A fountain trickles. Stone goldfish hold up tables of glass. Everything looks excessively expensive and, in a feng shui sort of way, ultramodern.

There are several such meetings going on with buyers from Europe and India. The Bangladeshis in attendance carry duffel bags of their factories' handiwork.

"Every night it is like this," Dalton tells me. "Business bridging the world."

Once the meeting ends, the American takes the elevator up to his room. The Bangladeshi woman has her orders, which workers—maybe Arifa—will carry out. The doorman holds the door for her as she exits with her duffle bag. With a step across the threshold, she leaves the hotel, a western oasis, and enters the all too real world of Bangladesh.

Life in the hotel is much more like the life I live than the life outside the hotel. As I sit in a cushiony chair and listen to soft music from hidden speakers, I think about something Bibi Russell told me: "Beauty lies in poverty."

The world we come from seems to be less real in comparison to Bangladesh (Figure 11.2). A child's laugh when surrounded by our modern luxuries isn't as beautiful as Arifa's daughter's on a sultry day where hunger wakes her before the heat. A mother's smile while chopping veggies on the floor seems more genuine than an American mother's while dishing out mac 'n cheese onto an Elmo plate. Nothing—a smile, a laugh, not even a single pair of underwear—is taken for granted.

If beauty lies in poverty, then Bangladesh is very beautiful.

Figure 11.2   Overlooking Dhaka, Arifa holds her daughter, Sadia.

Hungry for Choices

*The man helped a young woman step onto the windowsill, then held
her away from the building—like a dancer, perhaps. . . . He let go.*

*The fourth [woman] was apparently his sweetheart. Amazed, the
bystanders saw them embrace and kiss. Then he held her out into space
and dropped her.*

—Scenes from the Triangle Shirtwaist Factory fire in 1911,
passage from *Triangle: The Fire That Changed America* by
David Von Drehle (New York: Grove Press, 2003)

They stood at the windows of the building, 100 feet above the ground,
skin boiling, with fire behind and nothing ahead.

There was no choice.

Was it more courageous to stay and burn or to jump? It takes about
two-and-a-half seconds for a person to fall 100 feet. That's two-and-
a-half seconds of air cooling enflamed skin, two-and-a-half-seconds of
relief before the end.

One of the advantages—and there are few—of jumping was that
your family could identify your body. Eight workers jumped. Workers
on the ground thought they were bails of clothing being thrown out
the windows—as if that made sense, as if clothes need saving.

This isn't 1911, but it is. This isn't the Triangle Shirtwaist factory fire that killed 146 trapped workers in New York City, outraged the
public, and helped propel labor rights forward. This isn't then. This is
now. This is 100 years—a year for every foot the jumpers fell—after that
fire. These aren't Americans. These are Bangladeshis.

Twenty-nine Bangladeshi garment workers burned alive, were asphyxiated by smoke, or jumped to their deaths during the garment factory fire near Fantasy Kingdom on December 14, 2010.

Charles Kerneghan, director of the Institute for Global Labour and Human Rights, talked with Democracy Now! about the fire:

> *It was lunchtime. There were workers in the cafeteria on the 11th floor, and they started to smell smoke. They didn't panic. They did just what the workers did at Triangle: they started to go towards the exit. The workers tried to get out the exit, and the flames were so great and the smoke was so dense that they had to retreat. They ran through the cafeteria to the other side of the building, the west side, and they tried to go out the fire exits, and the exit doors were locked. They were trapped. . . . And do you know what the workers told us? They said that, often, management locks the exit gates during a fire so that the garments can't be stolen.*

Over 100 were injured. And 400,000 children's dungarees destined for a GAP store near you fueled the flames.

The families of those who died were paid $2,080 for their loss. GAP has helped lead the way making sure that those affected by the fire were compensated and that factory fire safety standards were improved.

This is nothing new. Between 2006 and 2009, 414 garment workers lost their lives in 213 factory fires. Growth in the Bangladeshi garment industry is manic. Buildings are slapped together, and renovations are accelerated. Because of this haste, one factory collapsed like a stack of pancakes, killing 64 workers in 2005.

The industry has nearly doubled since my visit in 2007. It now accounts for $15 billion in exports and employs 3.5 million people.

Arifa is no longer among them. She left her job at the factory in 2009 to stay home with her daughter, Sadia, who is now eight years old.

"It is risky to leave a girl alone anywhere in our country," Arifa told Ruma, the reporter who accompanied me to Fantasy Kingdom in January of 2012. "Until a certain stage, I won't leave my daughter alone. And, if for that I am to remain unemployed, I will."

They live in the same room in the same crumbling building, which Arifa manages and lives rent-free.

Garment workers are paid more now, but it wasn't an easy fight. The workers took to the streets and blocked highways. Labor leaders were arrested. Factories were vandalized. The industry came to a screeching halt. Eventually, the minimum wage for a worker was increased from $24 to $43 per month—still the lowest wage on the planet. And while this might seem like a life-altering wage increase, it hasn't changed much—since the cost of living in Bangladesh has doubled in the past five years.

I checked in with Arifa in 2009 when she was still working at the factory. She was earning $24 per month and paying $15 per month for rice.

Workers who took to the streets weren't hungry for more rights or increased wages; they were just plain hungry. The increase in wages didn't even bring their standard of living to what it was when I was there in 2007; however, it was just enough to get them back into the factories.

"It is true that the overall garments sector of Bangladesh has been developed in regard to salary," Arifa told Ruma. "But simultaneously, [the] living standard has also been so expensive. The increased salary hasn't added anything to our life. The salary is increasing, but the price of every household material, food, and beverage is also increasing day by day. So it is really tough to live a minimum standard life for people like us."

Arifa's eldest son, Arman, returned from Saudi Arabia and now works at a garage in Dhaka where he earns $49 per month. His income, along with Didder's—Arifa's brother-in-law who still lives with them—supports the family.

Her 16-year-old son, Abir, who she feared would have to be sent away to get a job, just completed his eighth year of school. Arifa would like for him to continue on in school, but their financial crisis has forced her to help him look for a job.

Arifa doesn't want Abir to be a garment worker. She attributes the pains she suffers in her neck and her arms to her years working in the garment factory. She doesn't want Abir to suffer like her; but like so many in Bangladesh, he might not have a choice.

III

My Pants:
Made in Cambodia

CHAPTER 12

Labor Day

May 2007

It's Labor Day in Phnom Penh, Cambodia, and the beggars are working hard.

A little girl with three unevenly spaced ponytails is wearing a soiled denim dress. It's too big for her and falls off her shoulder. She scoops at the inside of a coconut with a piece of its outer shell. She's a messy eater; bits of white flesh are stuck to her face and in her hair. A pocket on her chest is overflowing with money. When she's done with the coconut, she passes it on to her older sister who is wearing nothing but shorts and a pair of oversized flip-flops. The girl gets back to work looking sad, holding out her tiny little hands for tourists or worshippers to fill (Figure 12.1).

The girl and her sisters have a lot of competition. There are old women and men and amputees on crutches and in wheelchairs or sitting on wood planks with wheels pushing themselves around with their arms. They jockey for positions in the shade near the line of worshippers doing their best to appear more down on their luck than the person next to them. Their faces seem even more pathetic set against the happy music radiating from a stage in front of the shrine, played by a six-piece band that consists of drums and xylophone-like instruments.

Cages of birds for sale sit in a row to the left of the shrine. Their owners lean back on plastic chairs beneath umbrellas. A Cambodian woman in a white bucket hat hands over a few riel (Cambodian currency)

Figure 12.1   Girls begging worshippers and tourists for money.

and reaches into the chicken-wire cage to extract a chirping bird. She prays with her hands together and head bowed. A little head peeks out the top of her hands and a pathetic wing sticks out between her fingers. She kisses the bird's head, extends her arms, and opens her hands. Wings in a flourish, the bird flutters off over the Tonle Sap River. The bird seems lost in its new freedom, almost as if it doesn't remember how to fly.

The Cambodian people are primarily Buddhist. For them, releasing caged birds is an act meant to let go of one's sorrow, pain, sickness, hunger, and, likely in Cambodia, memories of war.

I watch the bird flutter wildly, flying upriver and descending ever closer to the water. I wonder what the woman prayed for.

The bird is now dangerously close to the water, and I wonder if the woman cares that the life she just released is falling from the sky.

Splash.

The speck in the water struggles among the offerings of trinkets, trash, and pollution deposited by other worshippers. I turn to find the man who sold her the bird. He sees the bird in the water, and he sees that I see. Another one of his customers has just released a bird that immediately flies into a nearby tree, and the birdman stalks it. He creeps up to the tree and holds out a stick. He pulls the stick from the tree, and the bird is stuck to it. This is his racket. He doesn't sell birds. He sells hope. And today his karma recycling business is good.

I walk down the bank and upriver toward the still-struggling bird. I feel a little silly. There are humans near the shrine pushing their legless selves on makeshift skateboards, and I'm walking briskly to a bird's rescue.

I get the attention of a group of kids playing at the water's edge and motion out toward the bird. From here I can hear it chirp—sounding panicked, if that's possible. The situation is urgent. I grab a dollar bill from my pocket and offer it to the kids if they save the bird.

No takers.

I know I could get it myself. I start to set down my bag, which holds my passport and digital camera, and realize what a bad idea this is. *Farangs*, what locals call western tourists, aren't rare. However, one stripping to his *Jingle These* boxers, leaving his valuables behind and swimming to a bird's rescue would attract some attention and likely result in said valuables disappearing.

I turn to find the birdman standing behind me, his clothes in a pile at his feet. He has the outline of a bird with its wings spread tattooed on his right shoulder. He steps gingerly into the shallows and starts to swim while looking back at me. I point to the bird like a lifeguard. He reaches it, grabs it like a floating plastic bag, and lops it on top of his head where it sits motionless. He returns to the bank winded from effort and holds out the bird. It has a long beak, red eyes that don't show a hint of panic, and matted black feathers streaked with yellow.

I've just arrived in Cambodia, and I don't know how to say "thank you" in Khmer; so I just smile and turn to walk away, relieved the bird is okay. The birdman grabs my arm and holds out his hand. I shake it. I turn to walk away, and again he grabs my arm and holds out his hand.

He wants the money I was offering the kids. It's his damn bird. He's going to turn around and sell it to someone else in his game of catch-and-release karma, and he has the nerve to ask me for money.

I give him the dollar.

Today is May 1, Labor Day around the world for everyone except a few countries, including the United States. On this day in 1886, some

(when does start)

40,000 workers marched down Chicago's Michigan Avenue in efforts to bring about an eight-hour workday. A few days later, a riot broke out at a labor rally in Haymarket Square—complete with a bomb and police firing into a crowd. Seven police officers and two protestors were killed, and many more were wounded. Four of the "anarchists" were rounded up and later hung. Since President Grover Cleveland didn't want to celebrate the "socialist" movement, US Labor Day moved to the first Monday in September.

So, today is the day that Cambodians commemorate events that the United States is officially trying to forget, events that eventually led to factories in the United States paying their workers more for working less. These were events that, extrapolated over time, priced American laborers out of work and led to their jobs being relocated to places like Cambodia, where workers' rights and pay are less, where sorrows are released and recycled, but never forgotten. They are places where capitalism is chaotic, where there are more labor unions than factories, and where union leaders are killed.

It's also where my blue jeans were made.

*   *   *

Picture a cowboy, a worker building the Hoover Dam, a miner panning for gold, an American doing American things. What are they wearing?

Why, the most American of all things you can wear: a pair of blue jeans.

Entire books have been written about them. James Sullivan wrote one simply titled *Jeans* (New York: Gotham Books, 2006), which is peppered with quotes deifying the garment: "First they built the country's infrastructure, then they populated it with a collective identity."

What other garment could actually get credit for building a country and a national identity? Certainly not *Jingle These* boxers.

Jeans were first worn by the Italian Navy, but riveted jeans were first produced in San Francisco by Levi Strauss, a German immigrant. So, maybe blue jeans aren't as all-American as we would like to think, but I've got two words for you: James Dean.

Here's one more: Fonzie.

We didn't invent blue jeans in the United States; we just made 'em cool.

Sullivan goes on to write:

All blue jeans, whether they are rough as sidewalk or burnished to a hand as fine as cashmere, share an "Americana" feel. They may be cut and sewn in Japan, Vietnam, or Hong Kong, using denim from mills in Mexico, India, Italy, or Turkey and synthetic indigo dye from Germany or Brazil. Yet wherever its origins, a pair of blue jeans embodies two centuries' worth of the myths and ideals of American culture. Jeans are the surviving relic of the western frontier. They epitomize our present-day preoccupations—celebrity and consumer culture—and we'll likely be wearing them long after the business suit, say, has been relegated to the dustbin of fashion.

I don't remember any other article of clothing that my mom would patch, but some of my jeans had patches on patches. Each hole was a battle scar of sloppy slides into second base, wrestling matches in the house, bicycle wrecks, and afternoons of play during which good always prevailed over evil. I've ripped, grass-stained, and bled through jeans. In the wintertime, I've played in the snow until my jeans were frozen. When I remember my childhood, I'm wearing jeans and having a blast.

Like baseball, like apple pie, and like my childhood, jeans are as American as you can wear. Yet the label inside my favorite pair reads, MADE IN CAMBODIA.

CHAPTER

13

Year Zero

"Two days ago, a cow exploded over there," says Tim Rem—who along with his wife, Suay, doesn't live near but *in* an actual minefield. Red-and-white-striped bamboo poles hold up signs with stenciled skulls and crossbones. Khmer script hovers above the skull, and below is its English translation: DANGER! MINES! Tim Rem and Suay are in the shade beneath their wood plank house on stilts. Tim Rem sits on a wood chest, and Suay sways in a hammock.

"Yesterday," Tim Rem says, "someone stepped on a mine and was taken to the city for treatment."

Tim Rem and Suay are old and skinny, with heads that look too large for their weak bodies. They have one tooth between the two of them. It sits on Tim Rem's lower gum like a crooked, faded white tombstone. Even their wrinkles have wrinkles. From their frailty to their gray-stubbly shaved heads, they've aged to look like one another. Tim Rem has suffered a stroke that shows when he walks and in the way he holds his right arm. Suay isn't doing too well herself.

I'm west of Cambodia's second largest city, Battambang; my Cambodian buddy Kim has agreed to accompany me into the countryside. Kim works for the Mines Advisory Group (MAG), a nongovernmental organization (NGO) that works to clear Cambodia of mines and unexploded ordinance (UXOs). The group has been hard at work since 1992, and theirs is a job that is seemingly never done.

In an article entitled "Bombs over Cambodia" that appeared in the October 2006 issue of Canada's *The Walrus* magazine, Taylor Owen and Ben Kiernan claim that Cambodia may be the most bombed country

in history. They point out that although World War II saw Allied
forces drop 2 million tons of bombs—including those on Hiroshima
and Nagasaki—the United States dropped 2.7 million tons of bombs
on Cambodia, a country slightly smaller than Oklahoma, from 1965
to 1973. The bombings started in secret in 1965 under the Johnson
administration, and were likely done to support the movements of
CIA and US Special Forces on the ground. In 1969, under Nixon,
bombing was elevated in order to destroy the mobile headquarters of
the Viet Cong and the North Vietnamese Army and to provide an
exit strategy from the Vietnam War. Henry Kissinger passed Nixon's
orders on to General Alexander Haig, "He wants a massive bombing
campaign in Cambodia. He doesn't want to hear anything. It's an
order; it's to be done. Anything that flies on anything that moves.
You got that?"

Owen and Kiernan argue that the Khmer Rouge, Cambodia's
communist insurgency, used the bombings to recruit villagers and
grow their number from a few thousand to over 200,000. Eventually,
the Khmer Rouge rose to power in Cambodia, enforcing an extreme
form of agrarian communism. They simply executed anyone they saw
as an enemy, carrying out a genocide that killed 1.7 million people.
Although the Khmer Rouge fell from power in 1979, they maintained
a stronghold in nearby Pailin into the late 1990s. And according to
MAG, they planted millions of landmines to protect their region.

"I know where the mines are," Tim Rem tells us. "I planted
them." Tim Rem is a former Khmer Rouge soldier. I heard that a lot
of leaders and soldiers still lived in these parts, but I never expected to
meet one.

"I built this place in 1990," Tim Rem continues. "My brother and
I moved some of the mines, but I'm not sure we got them all. Because
there still might be some around, we put down a bunch of dirt first.
We cleared some of the land," he smiles, "and the cows cleared some
of the land."

The mines that Tim Rem planted blew up his neighbors' cows
and his neighbors.

US bombs killed tens if not hundreds of thousands of Cambodians
from 1965 to 1973. And, coupled with the landmines planted by the
Khmer Rouge, they have killed and injured Cambodians at the rate of
about two people per day ever since.

"He's 72, he can't be removing mines anymore," Suay says,
content to sit and listen until now. "He can't remember where they
all are."

As Kim and I say good-bye to Tim Rem and Suay, their two dogs start barking at something in the distance. Husband and wife simultaneously turn and tell them to shut up.

*   *   *

I'm following Sokpisith (Sok) step-for-step into his family's field.

If the last thing you want to hear in a minefield is "Boom," the next to last thing is. . . .

"Kelsey! Kelsey! Take care where you step," which is what Kim says as he points at the ground beneath me. I freeze, my right foot hovering above what I believe to be some sort of nasty explosive.

Kim bursts into laughter, joined by Sok and the chief of the nearby village. Laughter *is* what you want to hear in a minefield.

"No problems." Kim points to a red-and-white marker in the middle of the field. "MAG has cleared this land." Kim translates the marker, "MAG started clearing this land in August of 2006 and completed it February 23rd. They removed 174 antipersonnel mines and 22 UXOs."

"We will move to this land as soon as possible," Sok says. "But I'm a farmer, and right now is a busy time."

Sok, his three boys, and wife currently live with his parents in the village at a house similar to Tim Rem and Suay's, but slightly bigger and somewhat general-storeish—odds and ends for sale and more people just hanging out than could possibly live in the house.

The land he outlines with a finger toward the distance is six or seven acres. He starts to describe his plans. He sees a pond that needs digging near a rock and pile of brush. In a stand of bamboo, he sees a field that needs clearing and a small grove of mango and banana trees that need planting.

"Before, I had a bad feeling; I would not use this land." Sok says. "Now that it's cleared, I am very happy."

Sok adjusts his torn baseball cap and picks his teeth with a grotesquely long fingernail. He tells us that he actually started to clear this land of bamboo before MAG cleared it of land mines.

"Isn't that a bit dangerous?" I ask.

Sok doesn't wait for Kim's translation, but just pulls up the leg of his pants revealing hamburger scarring on his lower leg. Well, there's my answer. Then he nods to the village chief, who is wearing a T-shirt with cartoon kids and cows being thrown through the air by a blast in a field. Cartoons like that are featured on billboards lining roads throughout Cambodia. The chief rolls up the right leg of his pants and reveals a faded and chipped prosthesis with a light blue flip-flop glued to the plastic foot.

We had spent the last hour together, and I hadn't noticed.

"This land is my life now," Sok says, staring down at the chief's leg. "This is the future of my children. I hope they will farm this land someday."

This is a common sentiment, of course. Home is where we want our parents to become grandparents, our grandparents to become great-grandparents, and our siblings to become aunts and uncles. It's where we want to raise a family.

It is where it is, even if it's in a minefield.

*   *   *

We are three grown men on a scooter heading back toward Pailin—nothing new in Cambodia. We pass entire families on scooters, kids sleeping with their heads resting on a parent's back. One scooter crawling along extra slowly has a huge wicker basket lashed on it. A pig's head pokes out the top.

The shocks of our scooter crunch with each bump we cross in the dirt road. I'm in the middle behind our driver, and Kim is on the back. We descend into a valley with a small pond in the middle. Pink lotus flowers carpet the surface of the pond and sway in the light breeze. Three Cambodian flags, red and blue with a silhouette of Cambodia's iconic temple, Angkor Wat, stick out of the pond on skinny bamboo poles.

The sky is perfect-day blue, and the hills are jungle green. It's the kind of day that kids should spend skipping or rolling down hills, but as the landmine warning signs dictate, much of the land in these parts has been stolen.

Kim and I continue our conversation about the effect of land-mines on the local people and how organizations like MAG try to educate kids about mines and bombs.

"We try to teach them that if they see bones on the ground they should leave," Kim says. "It's probably a mine field."

"There are bones just lying around all over the place?" I ask.

"Yes."

Cambodia has the highest number of amputees in the world. One out of 350 people is missing some kind of body part.

Unsuspecting children are attracted to the shiny bombs they find in the forest while collecting wood. Farmers collect bombs and sell them for scrap metal. Bombs are so common that locals use them for fishing. Mines maim and kill with complete indifference. The war is long over, but they lie in wait. It may be safe to step here today during the wet season, but tomorrow—thanks to erosion transporting or uncovering a mine or UXO—it's not.

On the other side of the valley, we pass a home much different from all of the others. It's made of concrete, stone, and tiles.

"That is the home of a Khmer Rouge leader." Kim peeks around my shoulder while holding onto his military style hat. "Now he's an old man, but he lives good."

For 30 years, the leaders of the Khmer Rouge have gone unpunished. In August of 2006, a formal inquiry headed by the United Nations began with hopes to prosecute former leaders of the Khmer Rouge. Many of them have died or are ailing, including Pol Pot, the leader of the movement who died in 1998. It's not until the summer of 2007 that charges were brought to a commandant of one of the many killing fields—execution grounds of the Khmer Rouge.

As we bounce down the dirt road, covering our faces when we pass an oncoming vehicle or scooter, Kim tells me his experience with the Khmer Rouge.

"I was herding the cows in the woods when I heard some voices," Kim says. "I went to look and saw a family shot just like this," he mimics a gun to the back of my head, "and then shoved in a hole. I ran fast. My mother told me that no one could know about what I saw. Soon after that, she and my father sent me to Thailand to find one of their friends. I was a refugee of the war. I was eight."

Tim Rem was a former Khmer Rouge soldier, and Kim talked to him the way he would talk with anyone else. He pointed out the house of a former leader and didn't sound bitter. How is it possible?

Anthropologist Alexander Laban Hinton has studied the Cambodian genocide and spoken with people about their feelings toward neighbors who were involved in the killing of their friends and family. In his book *Why Did They Kill? Cambodia in the Shadow of Genocide* (Berkeley: University of California Press, 2005), he writes about a woman named Chlat who told him:

> I continue to think of revenge. But this thought of revenge, it doesn't know how to stop. And we should not have this thought or the matter will grow and keep going on and on for a long time. We should be a person

who thinks and acts in accordance with dharma. [A person who seeks
revenge] only creates misery for our society. It is a germ in society. . . .
The people who killed my brother . . . are all alive, living in my village.
To this day, I still want revenge . . . but I don't know what to do . . . the
government forbids it.

Whether it is due to religion or legalities, the people of Cambodia
don't have a choice but to carry on with the memories of their past. But
how could they forget?

I would like to ask Kim about his feelings toward the former
Khmer Rouge. Does he want the justice that his government and the
international community have failed to bring? Does he want revenge
against the people who separated him from his family? But I don't.
Kim has worked for CARE where he helped combat the sex trade, and
now he works for MAG where he educates locals about mine awareness. I suppose that the good he is doing for people who have experienced
so much evil is, in a way, his revenge.

The Khmer Rouge referred to 1975, the year they rose to
power, as Year Zero. *Year Zero* represented the idea that all culture,
tradition, and history before 1975 was irrelevant and washed away, that
Cambodia was a blank canvas that they would paint in the tradition of
Mao. Essentially, the Khmer Rouge hit the reset button.

They emptied cities and filled farms. Their number-one priority
was to produce rice—three times more than previously produced. The
Khmer Rouge said a surplus of rice was needed to "raise the standard
of living." Cambodia was a blank slate. Government institutions were
gone. Religion went unpracticed. Doctors, lawyers, and others who
had been educated were killed; in fact, 20 percent of the population
was eliminated. The economy was crushed.

When the Khmer Rouge were removed from power, it was time to
rebuild. The international community came to help. They brought money.
They brought workers. They brought tourism. They brought jobs. They
brought exploitation. They brought good people. They brought bad
people. They brought hope.

They brought blue jeans.

CHAPTER 14

Those Who Wear Levi's

I'm at the re-grand opening of Steve's Barbecue in Phnom Penh, and there isn't a Cambodian in sight.

Tonight is Steve's 55th birthday, and the all-you-can-eat buffet costs $5.55 and the draft beer 55¢. That's US dollars, by the way. Dollars are accepted and actually preferred in many locations in Cambodia.

The tables are full of western men and women eating heaping piles of food. I grab a plate, load it up at the buffet, and sit at one of the few remaining stools at the bar next to a man with gray hair and pasty skin. He stares at the TV behind the bar turned to ESPN's *SportsCenter*.

"Is it against some eating etiquette to eat both fries and mashed potatoes?" I ask, during a commercial break while dipping another steak fry into the potatoes and then into the ketchup.

"Where you from?" the man asks.

"Ohio."

"You?" I ask.

"Connecticut," he says, sounding a little down on his luck. "We used to run a travel business that led trips to Asia—Nepal, India, Cambodia, et cetera. September 11 pretty much put an end to that three years ago. So, I moved here."

We used to run? *I* moved? In the past three years, this poor fella lost his business and went from a *We* to an *I*.

"Now I teach English for Steve." He tips his beer toward the boisterous American behind the bar trying to fix the broken tap of

Tiger Beer. Steve's barbecue? Steve's English school? It seems that Steve has quite the Steve empire running here in Phnom Penh.

On my second plate of steak fries dipped in mashed potatoes dipped in ketchup, an extra chubby American joins us. His triple-X black T-shirt says something, and I'm trying to read it in the mirror behind the bar. I can't, so I ask him.

"Oh, I don't even know." He seems a little embarrassed about it and looks down at the words: "Caution 1990 Tool Style." The shirt makes absolutely no sense, but I guess if you need an XXXL shirt in Asia, you buy one whenever you find one—regardless of how stupid the words are.

He's also one of Steve's English teachers and talks with a superiority of all things Cambodian to let me know he's been here awhile. When he learns that the Tiger Beer tap isn't working, he rolls his eyes and settles for a Beerlao.

More of Steve's teachers arrive, and we move to a table.

A man in his late thirties joins us. He looks like Data, the pale android from *Star Trek: The Next Generation*, and talks with a monotone voice that hints at sarcasm. Data and Mr. Tool Style are close friends. Soon they start bitching about the lack of food on the all-you-can-eat buffet.

"I'm not paying five dollars," Tool Style says. "It's not worth it."

"It's ridiculous," Data says. "Steve says he has 10 people in the kitchen working. If he had three that were competent, the buffet would be fully stocked." He turns to me and continues his rant. "I lived in Thailand for a year. The people are great, but if you had to get something done it was impossible. But the Khmers make the Thais look like fucking rocket scientists."

More English teachers join us, including a Brit who marvels at the brilliance of his own words and a short Kiwi fella who is hunched over from some kind of industrial accident. The group starts to talk about a friend trying to get a visa for Vietnam.

"He's been getting *Khmered-up* a lot lately," says Tool Style, replacing "fucked-up" with "Khmered-up."

The group continues to blast the incompetence and laziness of the locals until the buffet is restocked. They decide after seconds and thirds of heaping plates of hamburgers and fries that it is worth $5.55.

The sky falls, literally. The corner of the porch roof caves in on the pool table, sending clay tiles flying. Steve runs over to survey the damage. First the beer tap, now this. He places his hands on his head, which he shakes in disbelief. This wasn't the way the re-grand opening/birthday party was supposed to go.

Between bites of his cheeseburger, Data says, "Fucking Khmer construction. Worthless!"

* * *

Levi's are made in Cambodia, but they aren't officially for sale there. Cambodia is not a Levi's country. England, New Zealand, the United States, and most of the other countries that we *farangs* come from are Levi's countries. Cambodians are Levi's producers, and we are Levi's consumers.

The hardest adjustment coming from Bangladesh to Cambodia is the presence of others from Levi's countries. It's not just the English teachers. There are over a thousand NGOs in Cambodia. Land Cruisers with snorkels and pretty much every combination of three- and four-letter acronyms plastered to their doors patrol the streets of Phnom Penh. A local journalist told me that Cambodia was a sort of modern experiment in nation building. In a sick way, this seems to be facilitated by the Khmer Rouge's Year Zero. They wiped the slate clean, and NGOs and humanitarians have come to help, bringing with them democracy, capitalism, and a sort of self-righteous colonialism. As opposed to the economy being based on communist farms, it's now based on the production of jeans and other garments. If you are Cambodian and you aren't making garments for a Levi's country, you are probably working for an NGO from a Levi's country or servicing tourists from Levi's countries as a guide, driver, or translator. According to the CIA's online *World Factbook*, the apparel industry accounts for about three-fourths of the country's exports; foreign aid contributed nearly $700 million in 2007; and the tourist industry is growing rapidly.

I don't do nightclubs. I'm unable to hear over loud music, and my voice isn't strong enough to talk to anyone. I can count the times I've been to a nightclub on one hand. But when I was invited to tag along with a group of foreigners to the Golden Boss, the experience sounded too cheesy to pass up.

It seemed like a good idea at the time. But now that I'm in the bathroom and everything is going horribly wrong, I realize it wasn't.

I had to go, sure; but I also saw this visit to the bathroom as an escape from the loud music and plush overdoneness of the joint.

The bathroom attendant, wearing a large red bow tie, greeted me with a bow. I reciprocated with a half-bow/half-wave and made my way to a urinal in the back corner.

And just when I was about to take care of business, the shoulder massage began.

"What the . . . ?!"

If there is one rule that I've strictly maintained my entire life, it's that I don't urinate if someone is touching me. Especially if that someone is giving me a shoulder massage. And *most* especially if he is wearing a red bow tie.

I look over my shoulder as he kneads away. My face is twisted with violation. I shake my head "No" and then nod for him to back off, not that I would be able to do anything if he didn't. I'm kind of in a vulnerable position.

He gets the hint.

I'm relieved.

Many of the garment factories in Phnom Penh are owned by Chinese and Taiwanese businessmen—and the Golden Boss is where these men come to get their groove on. The front entrance is lined with local girls in prom dresses, faces caked with makeup like they are participants in a second-rate beauty pageant. They even wear numbers. The businessmen hire girls to dance with them.

Planets hang from the ceiling. Laser lights beam onto the floor. The singing is at such a high pitch and amplification that people dance with their hands over their ears and still manage to stay on beat. Everybody, that is, except for the Chinese businessmen.

I rejoin my group sitting on a black leather couch wrapped around a glass table. They are all members of the Hash House Harriers. I read about the group in the *Cambodia Daily* classified advertising: "Running and walking outside Phnom Penh." What the classified failed to mention was that the group is a drinking club with a running problem. They would pile in the back of an old grain truck, drive into the countryside, and run through people's backyards in the rain following a trail marked by white spray paint. Imagine if you were sitting on your back porch and 20 muddy foreigners in running shorts ran by hooting and hollering. This is the Hash House Harriers.

The group gathered after the run to drink beer and sing songs loaded with sexual innuendos and childish double entendres. I don't know anyone by their real names. They all have nicknames, like Just Add Beer, Blah Blah, Flacido Domingo, and Mr. Tinkle.

Tokyo Joe, His Exalted Excellency, steps out of his role as "Religious Advisor" and tells me about an experience he had had during the run that showed how life in Cambodia has improved. "When it started to pour, I sought shelter beneath a tree next to a local boy. We had a completely clear conversation in English. He asked me what I was doing. We talked about the weather, and he told me that he has to take a boat to school during the rainy season. When it started to storm, the boy advised me to not stand beneath the tree, and we moved to his nearby porch. A few years ago, kids out here in the country wouldn't be attending school. They wouldn't be able to carry on a conversation in English. If it weren't for foreign aid coming in, Cambodia would not be where it is today. Even factories and organizations that are corrupt, at least most of the money stays here. We [members of the Hash House Harriers] run through people's lives. We see the real Cambodia, and it has changed for the better."

I sit at the Golden Boss and watch as the Hash's Sexual Tourism Director (STD), an Englishman, dances with a 28-year-old Cambodian girl recently married to the European sitting across from me. What her husband doesn't know is that she is in love with STD, but STD will not marry her. Like the English teachers, STD isn't in Cambodia to settle down. The girl married the European not out of love, but because she wants to live the lifestyle of someone from a Levi's country. Soon she and her European will return to his homeland, and she'll be living the lifestyle she wants, but will miss her family. But for now she dances, and he sits and watches. She's torn between two worlds.

"Do you want to dance?" Hit On Me asks. She's a small Cambodian girl with a face that lights when she smiles, but is ultra serious when she doesn't.

"I don't know," I say, trying to play cool. Secretly I love to dance, but I rarely do it in public. I've been caught doing it in private. My college roommate once walked in on me busting a move to Harry Connick Jr.'s album *When My Heart Finds Christmas*. He did one of those knock-and-enter-at-the-same-time things, and there I was in the five-square-feet of room that was danceable, breathless, busted, embarrassed. "Sure, why not?"

Off we go, joining STD, his secret lover, and the Chinese businessmen and their escorts.

If I had to critique my dance style, it would be that I overemphasize the beat. Also, I can't continue to do the same little dance step for too long or I get bored, so I constantly try to invent new moves largely based on everyday ordinary tasks such as mowing the lawn or shopping for groceries. But no matter how poorly I dance, I am disgracing my family way less than the Chinese businessmen who have no rhythm whatsoever.

Nine people are on the stage, half of whom are skimpily clad girls who don't play any instruments or sing. The back of the stage is decorated with Christmas garland and silver letters that say HAPPY NEW YEAR, even though it's June.

We do some form of traditional Khmer dance that involves flowing hand motions that resemble screwing in a light bulb. I've been in Bangladeshi mosh pits that were more enjoyable. When the singers break into *Suzy Q*, I'm giddy with relief. The lead singer plays air guitar and occasionally unleashes uncontrollable screams of rockdom. We make eye contact, and I point to him to let him know that he rocks. He points back. We all rock.

The music slows down, and Hit On Me asks me to slow dance. I've never danced with someone so short. On one side, we go hand in hand, while the other side is utter awkwardness. Her hand is on my waist, mine between her shoulder blades. We start to make conversation, and I'm surprised about how much we have in common. We both studied anthropology in college, and she's a certified SCUBA diver, although the seasickness limits her enjoyment of the sport. She's a sweet girl whose boyfriend lives in Switzerland. They met on a Hash event and spent two weeks together, but she hasn't seen him since. They talk every once in a while, and he's always making excuses why he can't visit her and why she can't visit him.

Things might be improving in Cambodia, but its young people are still looking for a way out.

Outside the Golden Boss, our group says their good-byes. I'm standing beside Mr. Tinkle, and we watch as STD propositions one of the escort girls.

"So how does that work?" I ask. "Is that purely a transaction?"

"The rules are different here." Mr. Tinkle says.

"How so?"

"Basically, the girls don't have premarital sex," he says. "You don't have much of a choice if you are here alone. You either get married, or you get a hooker. I'm completely fine with getting a hooker now. Nothing wrong with it. They are good people, better than most. So yeah, that is a transaction. Really, they all are. It's all about money."

Levi's aren't for sale in Cambodia, but love and sex are.

In Cambodia, producer and consumer collide.

CHAPTER 15

Those Who Make Levi's

The door is slammed in my face, and the giggling from behind it won't stop.

I thought she signaled for me to come in, but sometimes I get the signals for *come here* and *go away* mixed up in these parts. I didn't see anything, honest.

Okay, I saw a little. A few girls were squatting in front of a basin wearing sarongs and a few others were standing on the bed gathering things or primping their hair in a small mirror hanging on the wall. I saw enough to know that eight girls getting ready with only one spigot of water and one bathroom was a challenge they'd mastered.

Embarrassed, I sit on the curb in front of their small apartment and a long stretch of many just like it—chipped white paint, metal doors, blue shutters. I watch the early morning goings-on as the citizens of Phnom Penh rub the sleep from their eyes. The traffic is all foot traffic. The street is more of a sidewalk, and the sidewalk more of a front porch. Beside me, a mother bathes her daughter in a green tub using a red pitcher (Figure 15.1). Water rushes down the girl's face, but she doesn't flinch. She just stares at me, her hair matted to her head, her eyes piercing.

The metal door creaks open, and a girl wearing a tie-dyed Tweety Bird shirt leads me in and motions for me to sit on the mattress-less wood bed.

The room is 8′ × 12′ with a squat toilet walled off in the corner. The water spigot empties into a basin that serves as a combination washroom/kitchen/laundry. A pile of dirty dishes sits next to a pile

Figure 15.1   A garment worker bathes her daughter in the street.

of to-be-washed clothes. And even though there is no shower, plastic shower caps hang nearby on the wall. If the door to the apartment isn't shut, passersby could watch them bathe from the street.

Privacy, if that's what you want to call it, is found at the back corner of the bed at which a sheet hangs from a sagging cord. This is the changing room.

A few girls sit on the floor while the others put the last-second touches on their outfits. I scratched their names in my notebook when I first visited a few days ago. Chuuon, my translator, has a sister who lives nearby, and he knew that most of the girls who live in this neighborhood work at the nearby garment factory that makes Levi's. I try to match names with faces without luck. After stumbling around, one of the girls sits beside me to help.

"Nari." She points to herself. Nari is wearing a lot of makeup, and her outfit—cargo pants and a thin sweater over a T-shirt—makes it look as if she knocked off a back-to-school sale. One by one, she points to the girls and announces their names. The girls do one of two things: stop what they are doing and smile at me, or shyly "Oh shucks" at the floor.

Once the primping is done, we just sit in uncomfortable silence. I'm about to explain further what I'm doing here when Nari starts petting my arm. I'm about as tan as I get, and the blond arm hair, bleached white, gives my arms a weird glow.

My face growing red, I try to make some conversation.

"Don't you get hot?" I say, pointing to Nari's sweater.

"The sun makes me dark," she says. "We all want light skin," she looks from my arm to my face, "and blue eyes."

"How about a big nose?" I ask, pointing to my long and pointy schnoz.

We all giggle.

"The people in the USA want dark skin," I say.

Really? They can't believe it. *Dark skin . . . why would anyone want dark skin?* We laugh at the world.

"Cinderella, huh?" I point to a faded poster of Cinderella hanging on the wall with *Cinderella* written backwards as if it was the negative for the actual poster.

"We don't know who that is," says Ai, the girl in the Tweety Bird shirt. "We had an empty spot on the wall, and we got a good deal on the poster at the market."

"Snow White?" I point to a Snow White poster.

She shakes her head "No." I'm guessing she doesn't know who Tweety Bird is either.

"Do you have a girlfriend?" Nari, by far the boldest of the bunch, asks.

"Yes." I pull out my cell phone and show her pictures of Annie.

They crowd around *oohing* and *ahhing* and tell me that she is very beautiful. I field questions about how we met, what she does, and our wedding plans. All girls love a wedding—no matter where they are in the world.

I realize that there's no way all eight girls crowded around me can sleep on the bamboo bed. It's big, but not that big. I ask about their sleeping arrangement.

"Four sleep on the bed and four on the floor," says Phoan, in between bites out of a brick of uncooked Ramen noodles. It's breakfast time, and she's the only one, for lack of a better word, eating.

"Who decides who sleeps where?" I ask.

They point from one girl to the other and collectively relate to me who sleeps on the floor, who sleeps on the bed, and that the arrangement is permanent and not really discussed.

"I like sleeping on the floor," Phoan says. "The bed might be more comfortable, but the [concrete] floor is cooler."

The average temperature in Cambodia this time of year is a humid 85 degrees, and I can't imagine how sticky it must get with eight people in such a small space.

It's 6:30 AM and time to set out for the factory. One of the girls stands and passes out a bunch of ID badges hanging from a nail in the wall. The badges have pictures of them looking very serious and wearing suit coats and ties.

"Do you ever make these?" I pull out my Levi's and lay them on the bed (Figure 15.2).

They do, and Nari tells me what each girl does during the process. The majority of the girls, including Nari, must iron, the least desirable of the jobs because it's hot. Ai works as a checker, looking for flaws. She claims to check over 10,000 pairs of jeans per day, which seems like an awful lot. Phoan fills in wherever she is needed. They earn between $45 and $70 per week, depending on how much overtime they work.

Other than the bed, the only other piece of furniture is a metal clothing rack that bows under the weight of eight wardrobes. As they shuffle out, two of the girls carry it outside for the recently washed clothes to dry in the sun. They lock the door with a padlock and join the morning's commute, walking into the sun toward the factory.

Figure 15.2 A garment worker examines the author's Levi's.

Last night's seasonal rain has turned potholes into mud puddles, and the group winds their way around them down the dirt road, through vendors selling breakfast, and through their fellow workers wearing frocks, pajamas, Mickey Mouse shirts, and back-to-school ensembles. As we near the factory, I start to drop back, keeping Arifa's lesson of not getting too close to the factory in mind.

The factory is surrounded by stone and brick walls with razor wire on top. Elevated guard lookouts sit at each corner, and another guard at the gate checks the girls' badges as they enter.

I walk away from the factory against the morning rush and turn to look back before it's out of sight. With the sun directly in my eyes, all I can see is a mob of silhouettes slowly dissipating.

The eight girls call a 96-square-foot room home. That's only 12 square feet per girl. The home that awaits me in Indiana is 2,400 square feet for two people, or 1,200 square feet per person. Annie and I literally have a hundred times more space than these girls do. We have two and a half bathrooms; they hardly have one. Our home is filled with modern appliances and furniture our parents gave us. Their room only has two pieces of furniture, but it is filled with giggly energy. It's like being in a crowded room of college freshman coeds, except these girls don't go to class. They go to work and make our blue jeans.

* * *

Levi's Cambodian headquarters is located in Phnom Penh's Parkway Square, a shopping center with a lingerie store, a bowling alley, and a Lucky Burger. I ponder a burger, but think better of it. A friend in Dhaka told me that a businessman tried to open a McDonald's in Bangladesh, but the quality of the hamburger and chicken didn't meet the franchise's approval. I've since sworn off fast food in countries without McDonald's.

The office on the third floor is what I expected—fancy lettering and design on glass doors, a receptionist area, and quietly bustling cubicles.

I'm given a cold Coca-Cola while I wait in the reception area.

Pradip, the country manager, greets me and shows me to his office in the corner. The office has a view, but Phnom Penh isn't much to look at. Pradip's left hand is wrapped in a bandage. He moved from India with his family eight months ago, and he doesn't exactly rave about Cambodia.

"I have twin daughters, and we were worried about finding a good school," he says, "but we managed one we are happy with. Other things here are not ideal—the medical facilities, for one. If it's anything internal, I would go to Bangkok. The doctors here are not very good, even the foreign ones."

I'm completely upfront with Pradip, and tell him that I'm a writer trying to locate the factory that made my blue jeans. I expect him to cut me short and blow me off. He has nothing to gain in talking to me.

I tell him that producer and consumer never meet in today's world, and I'm trying to bridge that gap. As I talk, he presses a button on his phone. I wait for a trapdoor to open beneath my chair, swallowing me. I imagine I'll slide down into a pit full of idealistic, antiglobalization activists. I'll be the only one wearing Levi's and drinking a Coke. Some of them, having been there since the mid-1990s, will be zombielike, and they'll walk toward me all herky-jerky with outstretched arms chanting, "Diet, Cherry, or Vanilla, Coca-Cola is a killa!" Then they'll eat my brains, because that's what zombies do.

"Could you come here for a moment," Pradip speaks into the phone.

Scratch the activist-zombie pit. Pradip is calling in the muscle to show me the door.

"This is Sreekanth," Pradip says. "He is our sourcing manager and will be able to arrange a visit to a factory."

Sreekanth extends his hand politely. He's from India like Pradip, and neither a zombie nor a strongman, as best I can tell.

Pradip summarizes my ideas about producer and consumer not meeting. Being from a developing country and working for a multinational corporation, they know this better than I do.

Sreekanth writes down some numbers from the tag on my pants and leaves the room.

"Levi's exports $90 million of merchandise per year," Pradip says, "which retails for about $400 million. Only 5 percent of factories meet our standards (in Cambodia). We currently source from 13. Many of the big companies—GAP, JCPenney, Walmart, and Sears—source from Cambodia."

"GAP, my shirt was made by GAP," I say. "I bought it at the Russian Market." The Russian Market is a labyrinth of dark stalls selling jewelry, silk, bootleg CDs, DVDs, and name brand clothes: GAP, Columbia, Old Navy, Polo, Ralph Lauren, and Levi's. The aisles aren't much more than shoulderwide, and passing a fellow shopper is disturbingly intimate. Picture the most crowded flea market you can imagine. Now, multiply the number of stores by 10—and still, the Russian Market has less space. The primarily female shopkeepers float

Figure 15.3   A shopkeeper at the Russian Market counts her money.

above their wares in hammocks soaked in sweat. Their booths don't seem to be made of metal or wood, but solely from blue jeans and polo shirts. It's the only place in Cambodia that sells Levi's (Figure 15.3).

"Everything there are stolen goods from the factories," says Pradip. "There's nothing we can do about it. No laws are in place to stop the sales. Levi's doesn't have a market in Cambodia, so we are not competing with our stolen products. It's more of an annoyance than anything."

"I thought the products there were all overruns or flaws," I say.

"Brand names don't sell off their overruns," Pradip says. "We have our own way of taking care of them. In fact, some companies who were short on their count or on time have gone to the Russian Market to buy their own products back."

"My shirt might be hot," I say. "But at least I bought my Levi's in the good ol' USA."

Sreekanth returns, "We no longer work with factory #890 that made your pants." He tells me that this could be a result of the factory's poor working conditions, inefficiency, or poor price. Regardless, the factory has closed. "I've made arrangements for you to visit another factory."

I thank them for their help. Sreekanth winds me through the cubicles to the lobby. I walk out the fancy-lettered glass door, take the elevator to the ground floor, and walk past the lingerie store, the Lucky Burger, and a sign for the Superbowl bowling alley.

"Hmm . . . bowling. . . ."

*   *   *

Lunchtime outside the factory is hectic. The mob escapes with a lot more urgency than it had in the morning as workers hurry to grab plastic seats beneath canopies. Vendors dish out brightly colored goop from dented, aluminum bowls.

I spot Nari in the crowd and offer to treat her and the others girls to lunch. I've got a lot of questions to ask them, including one very important one.

Nari turns down my offer of lunch and leads me back to the apartment (Figure 15.4) where the stove is already fired up and lunch is on. Phoan and Chendu cook away.

Pork, rice, green beans, some salad, and I'm full. Phoan offers me more rice, and I feel obligated to take it. I sit on the floor and go at the bowl with my spoon, wondering if I'll ever see the bottom.

Chuuon, starts laughing at something one of the girls says.

"What?"

"She says, 'He sure can eat rice.'"

I push out my stomach and pat it.

"When you're done," Nari says, giggling, "you can do the dishes."

"Where are you girls from?" I pull out my notebook and start in with questions.

Most of these girls are from rural areas outside of Phnom Penh. They miss their families and life in the village, but had to move to the

Figure 15.4   The author at Nari and Ai's apartment.

capital to find work. They send part of their monthly wage home to their families.

"How much do you send home?" I ask Chendu.

"[$7.50] per month," she says. That seems like a pretty high percentage since she only gets paid $45 per month.

"How about you?" I turn to Phoan.

"I make [$60], and I send home half," she says.

"Geez," I joke, "I want to have you as my daughter."

Phoan gets serious. "I support 10 people. I have five brothers and five sisters. I have no education. I can't do anything else but work at a garment factory."

The room falls silent.

"What would you tell someone in the USA who won't buy the jeans that you make because they don't think you are paid enough or treated fairly?" I ask.

Phoan, lost in thought, stares at the floor.

"If they pay [$45] for jeans," Ai says, "it helps us. If people don't buy, I'm unhappy because I wouldn't have a job." Ai laughs at the simplicity of the logic.

Is it that simple? Does an uneducated, 24-year-old garment worker hold the answer to how I should behave as a consumer?

To buy or not to buy; that is the question.

Remember the kids in Bangladesh who protested against the boycott of American consumers because they had to work? The boycott eventually led to a surge of street children before organizations and companies stepped in to provide an alternative plan to support them. Cambodia has gone through similar crises, but produced more positive results. A British documentary uncovered child labor at factories producing for GAP and Nike in 2000. Both companies pulled out of Cambodia after they'd been subjected to the bad press that fell upon many global sourcers in the mid- to late 1990s. Thousands of Cambodians lost their jobs as a result, threatening a budding industry. But factories, unions, and international organizations worked hard to correct the industry's problems and now claim it to be sweatshop free.

Ai works for one of the most monitored garment industries in the world today. With organizations such as the International Labor Organization (ILO) protecting her rights, they are, in turn, protecting the big brands' images and our consumer conscience.

Our pocketbooks are powerful things. We should use them wisely.

I have one more very important question for Ai, Nari, Phoan, and the gang.

"You gals ever been bowling?"

* * *

Any time I put on bowling shoes, I have the inexplicable urge to dance.

But these shoes are a little too tight, so I ask for another pair.

I'm at the Superbowl with Nari, Ai, Phoan, Chendu, and the rest of the gang except for two girls who chose to work overtime at the factory. I'm having a hard time matching names with faces. They've changed clothes and are wearing blue jeans—not Levi's—with fancy shirts pinched and folded in the interest of fashion. Chuuon informs me they are wearing their newest clothes.

The shoe guy tries again, and finally I'm wearing a pair that fit. I test them with a little jig. Perfect.

This is supposed to be my day-in-the-life with these workers, and I probably should be sitting on the floor of their room eating rice learning how they unwind after a long day of making Levi's. But I've spent hours there already. I've seen their world, and now it's time to show them a little of mine. Unfortunately, this bowling alley is the closest thing I can find to middle America.

Beyonce's "Crazy in Love" echoes down the empty alleys, off the plain white walls, and back to us. I prefer my bowling alleys to be cheesier—racer stripes on the walls, maybe a few disco balls, or planets, kind of like the Golden Boss nightclub, come to think of it.

We really don't need eight balls for eight people, but hey, if it's your first time bowling, you gotta have your own ball, right? We load up the ball holder with black and purple and red balls of various weights. Thankfully, there's computer scoring because I don't have a clue how to score spares and strikes. I enter my name as Player A, but no one else enters theirs. It's like I'm special. Each time it's my turn, it says "Kelsey." They're just players B through H.

I come from a land of beer-bellied bowlers, a country that invented the thumb warmer to increase ball control, where at any point in time during the day you can catch a bowling match where people applaud professional athletes sponsored by Lumber Liquidators, hardware stores, and restaurants specializing in the Grand Slam. It's time to show these Cambodians how it's done.

Ball under chin, I set my feet and take a deep breath. I lower my focus to the pins. I block out Beyonce.

Three steps . . .

The release . . .

The ball drops into the gutter. So does my next attempt. I curse. The girls giggle.

It's Friday night. On Friday nights at Woodcrest Lanes in Union City, Ohio, all the lanes would be filled, mostly with people I know. Every time I've gone there, it's like an episode of *This Is Your Life*. I played soccer with the guy on lane 2, shared a babysitter with the girl on lane 7, and I saw the girl on 13 vomit in science class. Bowling is a staple of the midwesterner's recreational diet. And the fact that I just bowled consecutive gutter balls is an insult to my roots.

A few pins go down in the first frame but it's not pretty. Rolling a three-holed ball down a narrow wood lane is not intuitive. Balls aren't lowered gently onto the lane, but heaved from the hip, echoing like gunshots. The lane and shoe rental cost me $27, but I'm afraid splintering the floor could cost much more.

I wait by the foul line and give pointers, kind of like the swim coach I once had who couldn't swim. What I lack in actual technical knowledge, I make up for in enthusiasm. When Nari gets a strike, I teach her what I feel to be the most important part of bowling—the celebration, which is part jig, part 80s dance moves, and a lot of high fives and fist pumps.

Some of the girls, like Nari, take to bowling; others, not so much. They walk to the foul line, roll the ball, and are in their seat talking to a friend about their sore arm and broken fingernail before the ball reaches the end of the lane.

Strikes, spares, gutters, smiles, giggles, dances, and indifference, bowling with this group of 20-something girls is like going bowling with 20-something girls anywhere. It's hard to see it sitting in their crowded room talking to them about my Levi's. But here at Superbowl with Justin Timberlake singing over cracking speakers to an empty bowling alley, one floor beneath the Levi's country office where their orders come from, I'm able to see that they aren't garment workers.

They're just girls.

I win with a score of 104. Nari comes in second with a score in the 80s.

"Do you want to play another game?" I ask the girls.

The girls confer with Chuuon. "They don't like bowling," he says. "They say they are tired."

"What would they like to do now?" I ask.

Chuuon starts laughing.

"Kelsey, they want to go dancing."

CHAPTER 16

Blue Jean Machine

"Our main purpose is to maintain the fundamental human rights and fundamental labor rights. Do you know what those are?" Tuomo, from Finland, is the Cambodian director of the International Labour Organization (ILO), an agency of the United Nations.

"Uhh . . ." In my mind I'm thinking life, liberty, and the pursuit of happiness, but I know that can't be right. "No violence . . . no rape," I say, at a loss.

What kind of human right is "no violence"? I might as well have said, "All humans have the right to have no Acme anvils dropped on their heads."

"Not exactly," Tuomo says, likely wondering what kind of journalist I am. "They are freedom of association. No child or forced labor. No discrimination."

I'm at the ILO office, located in a neighborhood that houses a large number of three- and four-letter international organizations. The properties are gated and guarded. The office is very modern and European. So is Tuomo. He's got that slick-shaved baldhead look with glasses and is dressed chic casual.

The phone rings. "Excuse me," he says.

From this end of the conversation, I can tell that he has a team that has stopped at a factory for a random audit, and they aren't being allowed in.

"If they don't let you in today," he says, talking to his team leader, "mark it as a 'No Cooperation.'" He hangs up.

"Does that happen often—factories not cooperating?" I ask.

"No," he says, "now, they understand what we do. We have a list of 500 points that we make sure that they comply with. Eighty percent of the factories do. We only support the minimums as stated in the Cambodian labor laws. Sometimes the unions want us to do more. We tell them, 'Get the law changed.' And sometimes factories want us to do less. By enforcing the minimums, we can point to the law and keep everyone happy."

The ILO runs the Better Factories of Cambodia, a program that monitors about 300 factories and works to ensure that their nearly 350,000 workers are being treated fairly and given a chance to prosper. The ILO's success as an independent monitor is largely responsible for winning back the likes of Nike and GAP in 2002. Like Bangladesh, the Cambodian industry is very worried about competing with China after the lifting of the quota system of the Multi Fibre Agreement (MFA). Therefore they've positioned themselves as a producer of sweatshop-free products, hoping to continue the industry's growth by giving major garment buyers such as Levi's confidence that their brand name won't be tarnished.

"Is there life for the Cambodian industry post-MFA?" I ask.

Tuomo hopes so for the sake of Cambodia. "The garment industry in Cambodia is seen as a miracle because it was whipped up so quickly. Seventy-five percent of Cambodian exports are garments. Cambodia has an abundant and cheap labor force that does good work. Buyers have invested relationships, and they have faith in Cambodia as a country."

Only one case of child labor was discovered in the past six months, and a 2006 survey determined that the incidence of child labor—defined in Cambodia as anyone younger than 15—is below 1 percent.

"There are few incidences of child labor in Cambodia," Tuomo says. "The factories have nothing to benefit from it. In most cases, children [gave] falsified documents to the factory. The factory really can't be blamed for this. Other than maybe their screening process should be better."

This is yet another case of children so desperate to work that they obtain papers falsifying their age. It was pretty easy to demonize anyone who would employ child labor back in Sociology 201; here, where the rubber meets the road, it's not so easy.

Although the Cambodian industry might be close to sweatshop-free, it is far from perfect.

Not far from the ILO office at the Free Trade Union of the Workers of the Kingdom of Cambodia (FTUWKC), an effigy burns in remembrance of their slain president, one of two union leaders killed in the past six months.

"The Union movement is big and fragmented," Tuomo says, "There are 300 garment factories in Cambodia and 800 unions."

Many of the unions are aligned with different political parties—some with the government, some with the factories themselves, and some are kind of independent. The FTUWKC isn't sure who to blame for its president's death. It could have been another union, a factory, or, they speculate, it even might have been the government.

Tuomo tells me that the unions go on strike at a moment's notice due to problems caused by both the manufacturers and the unions. Recently one of the unions that he was working with asked for an $80 per month pay increase. Tuomo thought this was completely unrealistic since the average worker makes around $60 per month—and of course, so did the factory, who awarded a monthly increase of $5. If unions got everything they wanted, the garment business in Cambodia would fold, and the work would probably go to China.

"The unions need to be responsible and know the market in addition to labor rights," Tuomo says.

Freedom of association is something the ILO fights for, but it is also a threat to the industry in Cambodia. Eight hundred unions means 800 agendas.

"The worst thing a factory can do is favor one union over the other," Tuomo says.

Perhaps the international community's coalitions and organizations have rubbed off on Cambodia a bit too much. Even the Boy Scouts are overorganized. There are two scout organizations in Cambodia, but the World Organization of the Scout Movement recognizes neither because they require a country to have a single group. Each has offered the other to join their group, but since they are affiliated with opposing political parties, it's doubtful that either will budge.

There are many issues facing the garment industry and Cambodia as a whole. Tuomo tells me, "You have to put these issues in context of the democracy and political situation in which they exist." And the context isn't a good one.

The United States Agency for International Development (USAID) released a report in 2004 stating that corruption in Cambodia had reached pandemic proportions. The report is filled with statements like "state-owned enterprises have been taken over by officials or their cronies" and "police and other officials demand small bribes" and "students across the school systems pay unofficial daily fees to supplement salaries of teachers and administrators" and "no one with patronage to the state is punished" and "bribes" and "exploitation" and more "bribes."

You get the idea. How can we expect businesses to run efficiently and fairly when the government—and everything else—doesn't? How can workers possibly get a fair deal when getting ahead in Cambodia depends on an individual's—or company's—ability to grease palms? The people who make our Levi's don't have this luxury.

"Between the unions and the corruption, do the workers get paid enough?" I ask.

"It's not a nice life for garment workers in Cambodia," says Tuomo. "They start working when they are 20. They work for around seven years and then are seen as old. The average factory worker provides for a family of seven, [and they] get by with the minimum. Maybe they buy a nice thing here or play a video game there, but they send most of their earnings home." He says they might live on $25 for rent and food.

Levi's factories moved to Cambodia under the pressures of globalization, and now Cambodian workers have the same fears the American worker once had.

"What if people stopped buying MADE IN CAMBODIA apparel, or China takes the market?" I ask.

"There would be major setbacks," Tuomo says. "Currently, about $24 million per month in remittances are sent back to villages."

We discuss the closeness of families and the lack of financial assistance or social care for the elderly or handicapped, and about how it's nearly impossible to grow financially as a garment worker. The US and Finnish governments help meet the special needs of children or elderly parents. However, Cambodian as well as Bangladeshi families are so tight-knit that there is no room for growth. Workers support their parents, brothers, sisters, and grandparents.

"The bottom line is that poverty needs to be abolished," Tuomo says. "There needs to be more rural development, something for people to invest their money in."

"We are lucky," I say. "We don't have to support so many. Our governments have safety nets for us if we fall on hard times."

"Lucky? That could be a philosophical debate," says Tuomo. "We may have these things, but our families aren't as close. Which is better—family or financial freedom?"

And with that, Tuomo summed up the life of garment workers in Cambodia. Essentially, their jobs might be located in the city, but their hearts are in the villages.

*   *   *

"My boss would like to dry your pants," Violet says.

"Huh?"

"Your pants." She points at my Levi's on the table. "They are wet."

"Sure," I say. "That'd be great."

Have no fear, I'm wearing other pants—a pair of Old Navy cargos. I washed my Levi's earlier this morning, and they aren't anywhere close to being dry, but I had to bring them.

Violet is the manager's assistant at the Roo Hsing Garment Factory. She's from Guangzhou, China, and has worked here for five years.

"I live in a nice dorm here," she says, "and we are fed food similar to what I would eat back home." Like the Cambodian workers at her factory, she sends home much of her wages to support her family.

"I miss them," she says.

Violet's boss Kan Chin Chen answers all of my questions and seems genuinely enthusiastic that I've come to visit. He examines my blue jeans and finds a spot of gunk that's been on the back of the right leg since Bangladesh. He scrapes at it with his thumbnail and says something to Violet.

"My boss thinks that he can get that spot out," she says.

Kan Chin Chen presses a button on the conference room's phone and makes some demands. Soon, an employee whooshes in, and out my Levi's go.

* * *

There is no such thing as a Levi's factory anymore. There hasn't been since the 2004 closure of their last domestic plant in San Antonio, Texas. The company no longer produces jeans or any other type of clothing. They are a brand only, one that designs products, places orders with factories like the Roo Hsing Garment Factory (Figure 16.1), and markets these products to you and me.

If you read much about Levi's, you'll come across a lot of flowery red, white, and blue language such as Karl Schoenberger's in his book *Levi's Children: Coming to Terms with Human Rights in the Global Marketplace* (New York: Atlantic Monthly Press, 2000): "Levi's represents raw American individualism."

And don't even get people started on blue jeans: A president of the denim council said jeans are "a magnificent flag that says 'USA' to the world at large"; designer Charles James said, "Blue denim is America's gift to the world"; James Sullivan, author of *Jeans*, wrote, "Jeans are the surviving relic of the western frontier."

America is in love with the blue jean. Jeans represent a come-as-you-are, I-don't-give-a-damn sort of individualism that our country prides itself on. Levi's makes jeans, and we made Levi's into the world's largest apparel brand.

Levi Strauss & Company has always tried to do right by their employees. When the 1906 San Francisco earthquake devastated their factory, office, and store, the company kept their employees on the payroll. When their orders plummeted during the Great Depression, they found other work for employees to do instead of laying them off. But globalization was unlike any force, natural or economic, that they had experienced before.

The 1990s saw major retailers like JCPenney and Sears launch their own brands of jeans. Calvin Klein, Tommy Hilfiger, Lucky You, and Guess came out with high-end designer jeans. And, of course, there was Bugle Boy jeans, which my mom pretty much kept in business buying outfits for me. Then The Gap and its successful spin-offs—Banana Republic and Old Navy—sourced their clothing overseas and stole the title of the world's largest apparel brand from Levi's.

Levi's had become uncool for the first time in their history, and they scrambled to fight back. They hired urban networkers to infiltrate cultural groups in major cities around the world to learn what was cool and how to best market to their tastes. But rediscovering cool was only half the battle. The company had more competition than ever—competition that was taking advantage of cheaper labor in the developing world while Levi's wasn't.

Levi's was one of the last major US garment manufacturers to cave in to the forces of globalization. Tens of thousands of jobs manufacturing Levi's in the United States disappeared. A company statement addressing the job cuts said, "Virtually every major apparel company has eliminated, scaled back or never owned manufacturing facilities." While Levi's had tried to maintain a North American manufacturing presence, competition would not allow it. Levi's workers at the San Antonio factory were getting paid $10 to $12 per hour before their jobs disappeared. Now Levi's doesn't pay garment workers. They pay factories. And those factories, such as this one in Cambodia, pay their workers barely $12 per week.

*   *   *

"Is it possible to take a tour of the factory?" I ask.

From the conference room, Violet and Kan Chin Chen lead me toward two mirrored glass doors. My image grows as I approach, and soon all I can see is my own reflection. When they pull the door open, I disappear into an endless room of workers and sewing machines, a veritable Blue Jean Land. Wires and tubs hang from the ceiling, which seems low because the room is so expansive. Trolleys of material are pushed. Needles chatter. A thousand workers are wearing hairnets colored according to their duty. Most of them wear baby blue, but there are a few yellow ones and even fewer pink, which I'm told are the line supervisors.

We begin at a pile of cut denim and start walking. On each side of us, young women fold and pinch fabric, lining it up before squeezing off a few bursts on the sewing machine. Fold, pinch, burst, repeat. Their hands are fast and efficient. Pairs of jeans slowly start to take shape as we walk down the line.

At the end of the line, we stand next to a pile of ultrastiff Levi's bound for washing and blasting. These aren't like the jeans we know today, but old school jeans that require a wearer to bathe in them, beat them, and to wash them over and over again before they are comfortable. I remember these stiff jeans from when I was a boy, having to do a few squats before I could walk in them.

"How many people have a hand in sewing a single pair of jeans?" I ask. I didn't count as I walked the line, but I know that it must be a lot.

"Eighty-five," Violet says.

"Eighty-five!?"

"Yes," Violet says. "And that doesn't count the others."

"The others?"

"Please, I'll show you."

*   *   *

Levi's prides itself on its strong ethics. When many jeans were made by prisoners in the nineteenth century, Levi's advertised that their jeans were NOT PRISON MADE. In the 1960s, they integrated their factories in the American South before the passage of the Civil Rights Act. Whites and blacks didn't share bathrooms and water fountains in public, but they did while working at Levi's. They even considered doing business in the booming market of South Africa, but decided against it and waited until the end of apartheid.

In the face of globalization, Levi's established their groundbreaking Global Sourcing Guidelines. From their website:

In 1991, we were the first multinational company to develop a comprehensive code of conduct to ensure that individuals making our products anywhere in the world would do so in safe and healthy working conditions and be treated with dignity and respect. Our Terms of Engagement are good for the people working on our behalf and good for the long-term reputation of our brands.

Many other companies have established similar guidelines today. In 1993, Levi's cited their Guidelines as the reason for beginning to pull out of China. China had too many human rights violations to meet the standards Levi's had set in their Guidelines for Country Selection.

Levi's chose human rights over business wrongs—that is, until the business itself was threatened. Five years after phasing out operations in China, the company succumbed to market pressures and softened their standards. Schoenberger explains, "The company has to survive as a viable profitable business before it can carry out its ethical mandate to the hilt." They were back in China by 1998 because, as company president Peter Jacobi stated, "You're nowhere in Asia without being in China." China's human rights situation hadn't gotten any better, but Levi's competition had gotten that much more heated.

Schoenberger writes:

> *Unfortunately, a cautious and quiet Levi Strauss—succumbing with resignation to the amoral tides of globalization—leaves the international business community without a beacon of strong leadership at a time when it needs positive models of ethical policy more than ever. . . . If the flame goes out, it would be a devastating loss for the world. Because if Levi Strauss can't do it, then maybe nobody can.*

But let's not extinguish the beacon just yet. It was Levi's corporate office in San Francisco that told me to contact Tuomo at the ILO. It was Levi's that arranged this factory tour for me.

Levi's sources from over 40 countries. While I can't say how the conditions are at all the factories they buy from, this one in Cambodia is what I would expect a garment factory in the United States to look like. This might be a result of Levi's maintaining their standards, or of the ILO maintaining its well-run Better Factories of Cambodia program; I'm not sure. But the ILO's strong presence ensures that Cambodia's garment factories are monitored. Organizations like CARE, United Nations Development Fund For Women (UNIFEM), World Vision, and Oxfam support and educate the workers. For better or worse, there are a lot of unions in Cambodia teaching workers about their rights.

USAID funded a six-part soap-opera-styled drama produced by the ILO, titled *At the Factory Gates,* to educate workers about everything from their rights to staying healthy. It's in Khmer. I have all six episodes with English subtitles. If workers don't have a DVD player, which they probably don't, comic books are available. I would be surprised to learn of any other developing nation's garment workers being supplied with comic books or DVDs.

But here's what gets me: If Cambodia has the most regulated and well-run garment industry regarding human rights, everywhere else must be at its level or below. And while I can wear my MADE IN CAMBODIA Levi's and be pretty positive that the workers were treated fairer than most, it's likely that my other Levi's, made in one of the other 40 countries Levi's sources from, were made by workers whose lives are even tougher.

*   *   *

"My boss says that this machine cost $20,000," says Violet. A woman in her late twenties, who probably won't make that much money in her lifetime, adjusts a denim pocket on the machine. She presses the button, and the famous Levi's pocket design—a child's drawing of a bird within an upside down pentagon—is stitched in less than two seconds. Levi's is currently suing competitors for infringing on the trademark of their back pocket design, but I highly doubt this woman cares.

This is about as automated as the jean-making process gets.

In a smaller side room, the walls are lined with motorized grinding stones on workbenches. I watch as a young woman picks a pair of jeans from the denim pyramid at her side and starts grinding the cuffs and pockets of a perfectly good pair of jeans. Another woman grinds a hole in a knee and then holds it up. I imagine her thinking, "Will the Americans think this is a cool hole?" Happy with her job, she adds them to a smaller denim pyramid. In a way, these women are the Queens of Cool. They take a regular pair of jeans and bestow upon them just the right amount of imperfection. Since we're too lazy to break in jeans, they do it for us. They are not machines. They have names.

At another station, a man sandblasts jeans with a sand gun. It's noisy, and sand piles up at his feet. He wears glasses and something that looks like a blacksmith's apron. Levi's will eventually ban sandblasting after a 2010 study in Turkey discovered an epidemic of the deadly lung disease silicosis among sandblasters. But for now, these are sandwashed jeans, and this is the sandwashing guy. He is not a machine either.

There is no such thing as a blue jean machine.

The laundry room has big washers that can wash 60 to 80 pieces at a time depending on their size. To stonewash, the workers throw in small pumice-like stones. The place smells of bleach and other industrial chemicals. By the time we leave the room, I'm used to it.

Is it harmful to breathe these chemicals? Who am I to say? I have faith that the excellent monitoring system in place in Cambodia ensures that areas like this are relatively safe and healthy working environments. In fact, the logbook I signed to enter the factory today showed that a member of the ILO had signed in earlier. The garment industry has such a historically bad reputation that many people hear the words "garment industry" and think the worst—yet a lot has changed because of this reputation. Today, the most common types of injury are ergonomic ones like carpal tunnel syndrome.

We enter another vast Blue Jean Land. A worker approaches and hands me my washed-and-dried, gunk-free jeans. Kan Chin Chen smiles and taps his watch. We've been walking through the factory for an hour, and he probably needs to get back to his business.

"My boss says it is time," Violet says.

"Time to go?" I ask.

Before she can answer a voice comes over the speaker, and a thousand workers step from their stations. Club music pounds a rhythm in the background over cracking speakers. The voice directs calisthenics. The workers stretch their arms, necks, and legs before shaking them out. The voice stops after a few minutes, and the workers get back to making our pants.

If there were a blue jean machine, it probably wouldn't need a break.

CHAPTER 17

Progress

Nari and Ai are from small villages near Kompong Cham where they eat fried tarantulas. This may seem weird, but it wouldn't if you lived here.

A few days after we went bowling, Nari and Ai accepted my offer to visit their home villages for a day. Unfortunately, the girls don't get to go home very often—mainly due to time. Their villages are an uncomfortable, five-hour, $3 minibus ride from Phnom Penh. A six-day workweek making blue jeans does not allow them sufficient time to make a trip home and back in a day.

Like most Americans, I can't imagine a one-day weekend. According to Witold Rybczynski, author of *Waiting for the Weekend* (New York: Viking, 1991), the American two-day weekend has its roots in the textile industry. In 1908, a spinning factory in New England adopted a two-day weekend to accommodate the Jewish Sabbath, Saturday, to accompany the Christian Sabbath, Sunday, which had been observed for some time. Henry Ford took up the cause from there. Ford thought that the additional day off would increase consumer spending and, specifically, increase automobile travel. Weekend road trips were good for business.

If I only had one day off each week, I definitely wouldn't spend 10 hours of it sitting in a crowded minibus, so I can't blame Nari and Ai for not visiting their families more. And, although $3 doesn't seem like a lot, a roundtrip expense of $6 is over 10 percent of the girls' monthly income.

Like all the garment workers in Cambodia, Nari and Ai only get two holidays off—the Khmer New Year and a holiday in October—so they make the journey home twice a year. They'll visit three times this year, because taxis are quicker than minibuses—and I've hired one for the day.

Nari and Ai represent Cambodia's competitive advantage—cheap labor. They are the stereotypical garment workers—twenty-something, uneducated girls from a rural area. Ai is shy and does a lot of staring at the ground when I talk to her. Nari is anything but.

"I paid $50 to get my job at the factory," Nari says from the front seat as she directs our driver to hang a left. "The man told me, 'If you pay me, I'll make sure you get the job.'" The "man" she refers to was a translator for one of the Chinese bosses at her factory. In labor rights circles, this man is known as a labor shark. He uses his position to take advantage of individuals like Nari who need the job. Fifty dollars is a month's wage for Nari, and it took her three months to pay him. She has been with the factory for three years and says that it was worth paying to get the job, especially now that she is using the job to fund her dream.

"I want to own a beauty salon in my village," says Nari. "I have borrowed money to go to school. Now we are studying makeup." I think back to our night bowling and how some of the girls were wearing eyeliner and lipstick and their hair was done—which must have been Nari's work. "I just bought an iron that I will use in my salon."

"Could you start your career as a beautician working for someone else?" I ask.

"The workers at beauty salons make less than garment workers," she says, "but I will be an owner and make more." She stops, as if imagining herself in her beauty salon, her customers chatting while she counts her money. "How much does a manicure cost in the USA?"

"I'm not sure . . . maybe $30." I guess, never having had a manicure or even ever speculated about the cost until this very moment.

"Thirty dollars! Whoa!"

Maybe I shouldn't have said how much I thought it cost. I do my best to avoid sharing what must seem to be the gaudy expenses of life in my world. Actually, I try not to think about them whatsoever because it just leads to guilt-ridden comparisons. A manicure in the United States is a half-month's wage in Cambodia. My monthly house payment is a year-and-a-half's worth of wages for a garment worker; my camera and lens is five year's worth of wages in Cambodia.

"In Cambodia it costs [$1.75] to get your hair and nails done," she says. "How about extensions? How much do they cost in the USA?"

"I'm really not sure," I say. "I haven't touched a brush to my hair in 10 years. I don't know much about that kind of stuff."

"How do you brush your hair?" she asks.

I take both hands and flatten my hair from crown to forehead and then make a pass down the sides starting at the temples. "That's it."

Nari rolls her eyes and says something that isn't translated. I suspect it's something like, "Slob."

The taxi driver has remained quiet up to this point, besides the occasional throat clearing that sounds remarkably like a horse snorting. Apparently, all of this talk about the United States got him wondering. He asks, "Do women wear underwear in the USA?"

There is a pause as the car waits for me to hear the translation, and then we erupt in laughter.

* * *

Cambodians don't hug. So when Nari steps from the taxi, she greets her mom with a respectful bow. I follow suit.

Their wood house sits on stilts. Inside, there is very little furniture, and everything is well kept. As is typical of houses in Cambodia, the open area beneath the house acts as the kitchen and hangout. Hammocks are strung from the house's stilts and occupied by Nari's family. Nari's mom offers me a seat on a bamboo bed, and her father swipes off the top of a coconut with a machete and hands it to me. I try to drink the coconut without juice pouring down my chin, but am unsuccessful. Nari hops on the family scooter to get me a straw.

"What do you think about your daughter working in Phnom Penh?" I ask.

"I'm worried about her safety, but Nari has to work in the city," says Nari's mom. "She helps support our family. There are no jobs here. When I was her age, there were no jobs in the city, so I worked at the nearby rubber plantation."

When Nari's mother was her daughter's age, life in Cambodia was at its toughest—mines, bombs, genocide, *Year Zero*. Not far from here, the Khmer Rouge loaded 30 or 40 villagers at a time into trucks. They told them that they were going to a "new village." When they arrived, they were told to line up, and then a firing squad executed them, and then dumped their bodies into a hole on top of other bodies. When the hole was full, the soldiers covered it with dirt and dug another. Nari's mother had a choice: either work in the fields or die in the killing fields.

Today the exodus is from the village to the city, and families decide to send their girls to the city to make our blue jeans while their boys stay at home on the farm.

Nari's father can't grow enough rice to support his family. So Nari sends home nearly $20 per month to help her family of seven.

"I visit Nari twice per year," says Nari's mom. "I was in the city on Thursday . . . you just missed me. I come during the fruit season to bring Nari some from the village. The fruit in Phnom Penh is just not the same." She offers me a piece of jackfruit. I pop the sweet yellow pod in my mouth. It tastes like pineapple, but meatier and less juicy.

"Nari was a big help," Nari's father says, as Nari returns on the scooter. He's a chiseled man with a strong face. "She fed the pigs and worked in the fields." His face softens. "We miss her. We are proud of her."

Plates are piled with rice, salad, chicken, and pork. It's all delicious. When there is something that I'm not sure what it is, I ask Nari's mom and she points to a tree in the yard, a coop beside the house, or a pen in the back. This is about as fresh as food can get.

"Would you like to see my village?" Nari asks.

*　　*　　*

We walk down the dirt road from Nari's house. The neighbors are surprised to see Nari home and ask if everything is okay. Nari explains my presence to them, and then they invite us under their house for tea. She politely declines, again and again. Thanks to the villagers' hospitality, it's a slow-going stroll.

Chuuon tells me that this is the middle class of Cambodia. The houses and roads are well kept. The people wear nice clothes. "I live in the same type of house," he says, "and we eat the same kind of food."

Nari points out two beauty salons that don't look like beauty salons whatsoever. They sell snacks and odds and ends.

"Most of the salons here are only used on special occasions like weddings so they sell other things," she explains. This is her future competition.

"How will your shop be different?" I ask.

"I want my customers to trust me," she says, adding no explanation of the untrustworthiness of the other salons in the village.

We hop a rickety bamboo fence, wade through a sunlit stream as warm as bath water, and eventually arrive at one of Nari's father's fields. He doesn't measure his land in acres, but in meters.

We look out onto a not-quite-geometric expanse of rice fields. In the midwestern United States, farmers outline their land with a wave of an arm, claiming hundreds of acres in one fell swoop. Nari counts plots back to her father's with a finger. "That one over there is my father's," she says.

We stand at the edge of the fields, watching farmers navigate the worn narrow dams between plots on their way to or from their own field.

We turn from the rice fields and walk through a grove of fruit trees.

Ai hands me a medieval looking fruit—red with green spikes—that she picked from a nearby tree. She tears off the soft outer shell with her thumb, plops a white ball into her mouth, and smiles. After a little chewing and sucking, she spits out a marble-sized seed and tosses it at Nari.

We turn from the field and walk through a grove of the medieval fruit trees. Eventually, we come to a small field of corn. "Field" might be a stretch; when I was young, we had gardens with more corn. Nari hollers into the tall, green rows that begin to rustle before spitting forth one of her brothers and then the other. She greets them as she did her mother, but far less formally.

They seem to be pretty jovial fellas—smiling as I'm introduced and laughing when I realize I'm standing on an anthill. No matter where you're from, ants in your pants is funny.

They are strong guys in their twenties. The older one has a chiseled face like their father and a hint of a moustache. The younger one isn't as well built, but is taller. He easily reaches up into a tree and breaks off a small branch full of fruit.

We walk past a Buddhist monastery colorfully painted and decorated with cobra heads and spires rising to the sky from a multilevel roof. Prayers, chants, and incense spill out of the windowless windows and doorless doors. Nari tells me her family doesn't come here as much as they should, but do come on special occasions.

As we continue our walk, we toss seeds at one another. Out here in the quiet of the village, laughter and prayer are the only noise.

Nari says her good-byes, we say our thank-yous, and we all pile back into the taxi and head to Ai's village.

*   *   *

Ai's life is more difficult than Nari's.

Her house isn't as nice. Her neighbors are drunk. Her family's clothes are more threadbare. One of her brothers died of malaria, and another killed himself. She earns $55 per month and supports her family of six with money she sends home. But her job at the factory isn't secure. She doesn't have a contract, which means that she has no rights. She could show up for work tomorrow, and they could get rid of her for absolutely no reason.

We find her family sitting beneath their house retreating from the heat of the day, and I ask them about life in the village compared to life in the city (Figure 17.1).

"I have always lived in this village," says Ai's mother. "I will never live anywhere else. But there are no jobs here, so I have to send my daughters to Phnom Penh to work."

"So it is a mother's decision?"

"Kind of," she says. "I asked my daughter to go to the city to help our family, and she agreed to do it."

It's hard to have much of a conversation with Ai's mother because her grandmother keeps chiming in. She has a big round wrinkly head and only a few teeth. She talks like she's telling a joke. I can't help but smile at her as she speaks for the first time. It's not until the translation comes that I realize she's not being funny.

"Life in the village is difficult," she says. "It's not like it used to be. Our buffalo was stolen two weeks ago. I was the only one home, and someone put something in my tea that made me sleep. When I woke up, the buffalo was gone."

Figure 17.1 Ai (right) and her family.

This amazes me. First off, that someone would actually drug an old lady to steal her buffalo, and secondly, because this is a small village. How can someone steal a buffalo and everyone not know it?

A crowd of neighborhood children has formed. We are officially a spectacle, and whatever intimacy we had is lost.

"How about some Frisbee?" I ask the children.

Ai has a nice open yard between her house and a creek. It would be harder to play if there were a buffalo in the middle of it, but we don't have that problem.

First, we form a circle and just toss it about. Two of Ai's drunken neighbors join us. It reminds me of something Tuomo of the ILO said: "It would be interesting to learn how much of the money these girls send home gets spent on booze or gambled away."

Life in the provinces of Cambodia is no longer sustainable. The shift from countryside to city and from farm to factory is underway. Jobs and exports might be progress, but at what cost? Families are being separated.

Back in the taxi heading for Phnom Penh, before we all fall asleep exhausted from the long hot day, Ai tells me what she misses the most about life in her village.

"I miss working and talking in the rice fields," Ai says. "At the factory, we aren't allowed to talk. The Chinese bosses want us to work as quickly as possible."

She tells me that at the factory the workers are broken into teams of 70 and overseen by two Cambodian managers, and one Chinese boss. "The bosses are almost never kind," Ai says. "If a worker doesn't meet their quota, they are very mean to the worker."

According to an ILO report, more than a third of workers are verbally abused by a manager, making it a tough transition going from the field to the factory. It is the first formal job for three-quarters of the workers that migrate to the city. Out here in the fields, there aren't colored hairnets or scheduled breaks, management levels or ID badges; there are brothers and sisters and fathers and mothers. There's a hot, unforgiving sun, sure, but there is also camaraderie, a sense of community, and horseplay. And there's talking.

A girl could get ahead in Cambodia if she moved to the city to make jeans and kept all of her earnings or put it toward an education, but she doesn't. She sends chunks of it home to support her family. When you don't have much, family is everything.

Tuomo and I discussed this at his office. Parents in the United States are legally responsible for their children until the age of 18.

After that, it is legally and socially acceptable to cut all financial support. I was lucky that my parents helped me through college and, on occasion, chipped in on down payments for apartments. But many in the United States are not as lucky. Some turn 18, and are on their own. They get a job or an education and move far away. There are calls made on birthdays, visits on holidays, but lives that were once intertwined are now separate. The ties that bind become untied. Medical emergencies and catastrophic events are, in theory, covered by insurance companies. At the end of their working lives, parents are—again in theory—supported by retirement funds and pensions.

I remember learning in college that hunters and gatherers had a lot more free time to spend with their families. Agricultural advances led to a surplus of food that allowed people to do other things besides farm. Trades such as blacksmithing and weaving popped up. If you needed bread, you went to the baker, if you wanted meat, you went to the butcher. If you needed clothes, you went to the weaver. You handed money to the person who produced what you were buying, whose employees and assistants were probably family members.

Today in the United States, family farms and businesses are threatened, unable to compete with the purchasing power of large companies. They are consolidated and bought, while a growing number of people work for someone else. Sons and daughters rarely follow in their parents' footsteps.

In the quiet darkness of the taxi, we travel from the village to the city at 60 mph. Before I fall asleep, I have two thoughts:

1. This is progress.
2. This is progress?

Treasure and Trash

At the Phnom Penh city dump, it's difficult to distinguish the people from the trash.

Black boots, standing and waiting, look like discarded trash bags. Hands in yellow rubber gloves, picking and sorting, look like slimy banana peels. Green shirts look like rotten vegetation, red ones like the torn backpack at my feet.

A truck approaches and is swarmed by scavengers. They don't push and shove because there are etiquette and rules for everything, even this. The truck's bed lifts, and the garbage spills out. This is fresh, never-been-picked-through garbage—the most valuable kind.

The race is on.

Most of the scavengers are completely covered in layers of rags, but one fella—who must be new—is wearing shorts. They have magic wands with hooks on the end that they wave through the trash. They immediately shove anything plastic into their woven bags that once held rice or cement or flour. They consider anything else of interest for a moment—treasure or trash?—and then discard or keep. Time is of the essence, because here comes the excavator.

The long yellow arm stretches out with its shiny metal bucket. It moves as if it were surrounded only by inanimate trash, ignoring the injury that it could inflict. The scavengers take notice, and move if their area is targeted. The arm crushes and pops and lifts and turns to deposit its load at the top of a steep mountain of trash. A few scavengers are up there, too—brave or stupid. They stand knee deep in loose

Figure 18.1   At the Phnom Penh city dump, it's difficult to distinguish the people from the trash.

trash, hoping the arm will dump near them so they can find something the others missed (Figure 18.1).

A few trips of the arm, and the pile of fresh trash sits on the mountain. Another truck approaches. The race continues and, given the line of waiting trucks, will continue for some time.

This is no existence for a human. But these humans sought out this existence. Many of them were farmers unable to provide for their families and had heard about the opportunity at the Stung Meanchey Municipal Waste Dump. They chose to leave their villages where the air is fresh, the space is vast, and the options nil. Two thousand farmers turned freelance scavengers live here and earn less than $1 per day collecting recyclables. They live in makeshift shacks at the edge of the 11-acre dump. They pay rent to live in the shacks. They chose to come here, seeking a better life. I wonder if this is it.

There's fire; smoldering trash spills forth acrid smoke. There's brimstone. This is hell on earth. But there are different levels of hell, which causes me to wonder: What amount of hunger and suffering and desperation did they experience before *choosing* life here?

We worry about the lives of the people making our blue jeans. But what about the souls wasting away at the dump? I've never heard about them before. Ill-treated workers are blights on our conscience for sure, but poverty on this level is magnitudes worse.

The smell is demon-like. It doesn't stop at my nose, but crawls its way down my throat and fiddles with my diaphragm. The smell burns my eyes.

The sight and the smell are nauseating and tear wrenching. I could puke. I could cry. I fight the urge of both. As I walk away, I don't cover my nose. I don't want to outwardly show that I'm sickened by what they do and where they do it.

I walk with my head down because I'm done looking. My Levi's cuffs are caked with black sludge. A yellow doll with red hair is on the ground in front of me. It's covered with the same black sludge and is sprawled out like a homicide chalk outline. A truck track runs the length of the doll's body. It seems so wasteful to throw away something like this that could make a little girl smile.

I look up the bank of trash to my left and see that I'm being watched by a group of kids. One boy wears only pants—no shoes, no shirt. They sit in trash surrounding them and pick idly at it with their own magic trash wands. I walk up to them and invite them to do the only thing that makes sense—play Frisbee.

After a short demonstration of how to throw the disc, I toss it to the barefoot shirtless boy. The wind carries it over his head, and it rolls across the ground on its side past a rusted metal tube sticking from the ground.

The wind makes it hard to throw accurately, but I'm thankful for it all the same. We are upwind of most of the trash and all of the burning piles. If I were a scavenger in need of a break, this would be the place to do it. There are mostly kids picking through old trash up here on the plateau of garbage. The chances of finding something of value are limited. The kids average about 25¢ per day in recyclables. But it's safer, the air is better, and there aren't trucks and heavy machinery moving about.

The boy limps after the disc. When he gets to it, he sits down and examines an old cut on his foot. It's stained around the edges, and he scrapes out black sludge with a dirty finger.

What can I do? This is a question that I find myself asking again and again. What can I do for this boy's foot? I could at least clean it and bandage it if I had my first-aid kit, but I don't. What can I do for these children of the dump?

Scott Neeson, a Hollywood producer who visited the dump during a backpacking trip between the production of *X-Men* and *Minority Report*, thought the same thing. As a man with the means to do something about it and a lifestyle of luxury and excess that I couldn't imagine, the question must have really hit home with him—because he sold his Porsche and his house, and moved to Cambodia. He established the Cambodian Children's Fund and rescued kids from the dump. He houses, feeds, and educates 700 of them.

"The problem is, how do you say no," Neeson told *ABC News*. He said that when he visits, kids come to him and say, "Please take me to school."

It's really all about luck. This boy was born to parents that were lucky to live through Pol Pot's *Year Zero*. He was unlucky to be born into a country that is one of the world's poorest. He is lucky if he finds 25¢ of recyclables; his parents—if he's lucky enough to have them still—are lucky to find enough to feed him. He is unlucky to have cut his foot. He would be lucky if Scott Neeson took him to his school or if one of the many other NGOs in Cambodia focused their help on him. But he's unlucky that there are so many other children like him.

He cleans out the cut and tosses the Frisbee to the girl across from him. The disc hangs in the warm, smelly breeze. She alternates between stretching her arms out in anticipation and holding onto her bucket hat. Her eyes are bright and sparkle when she flashes her perfect smile. She doesn't make the catch, but is quick to pounce on the disc as it wobbles to a stop.

She's about to throw the Frisbee upside down, and I signal for her to flip it over. Strands of hair stick to her sweaty face, and a long unkempt ponytail blows in the breeze. She's about 11 and in a few years will be of legal age to work in Cambodia, but it's not like she won't be working hard until then.

She tosses the Frisbee, and it blows behind her. One of the boys says something to her, and she throws her head back and laughs. She still has the innocence long ago lost by the adult scavengers below. Hers is the only laugh or smile I've heard in the past hour. Her eyes aren't vacant; she knows hunger, but not war. There's still hope in her.

Being one of 85 people sewing blue jeans or giving them that cool look at the grindstone or sandblasting them, while working six-days a week, and getting paid $50 a month—half of which you have to send home so your family could eat—doesn't sound like much of a life to me. But it's a life that this girl would be lucky to have (Figure 18.2).

This isn't something I would have ever thought before this trip, but I hope that someday she's given the opportunity to make blue jeans.

Figure 18.2 After a game of Frisbee with the author, the girl gets back to work.

I hope she doesn't have to bribe a labor shark. I hope she is paid a fair wage and educated about her rights. There are far worse existences than that of the garment worker.

At the dump, one person's trash is another's treasure. And in Cambodia, one person's sweatshop is another's opportunity.

The Faces of Crisis

" If they pay $45 for jeans," Ai said to me in 2007, "it helps us. If people don't buy, I'm unhappy because I wouldn't have a job."

Turns out that Ai was right.

We, the almighty American consumer, stopped buying so much stuff, including jeans, that the impact was felt around the world.

When times were good—when we were buying lots of garments back in 2007—Cambodia's GDP was experiencing over 10 percent growth and lifting 1 percent of Cambodians out of poverty each year. But all of that came to a screeching halt when the global financial crisis hit. According to an ILO commissioned survey's final report, *Understanding the Impact of the Global Economic Crisis on the Cambodian Garment Sector*, 70 factories had closed and 70,000 workers were out of work by December of 2009.

I tried to keep tabs on Nari and Ai through one of my translators, but their numbers stopped working a few months after my visit. My translator told me that I shouldn't be worried; people change phone numbers all the time. I could only guess what their lives might be like from news about Cambodia and garment workers. And that wasn't good.

"The global economic crisis has a human face," said Douglas Broderick, Cambodia's United Nations resident coordinator, in a press release from his office. "In Cambodia it's not just people's livelihoods at risk—it's people's lives."

The April 2009 release goes on to say:

Early indications show that many unemployed workers are returning to their villages, where livelihood opportunities outside subsistence agriculture are severely limited. To survive, more and more Cambodian women and children may find themselves in the informal economy for lower wages, poorer conditions, and greater risk of sexual exploitation and trafficking.

I read that and thought about Nari's dream to be a beautician. I hoped that she finished her training and was spending her days primping and curling hair and doing nails back in her village. If not that, I hope she still had her job at the blue jean factory. If not that, I hope she had found something else to do other than working as a prostitute. But the fact is that countless girls like Nari and Ai, who had supported six or seven family members back in their villages with their wage as a garment worker, have turned to prostitution. Losing your job is a good excuse for why you aren't sending home money any longer; but no excuse will pay for your grandma's medicine, your brother's schooling, or food.

Short of traveling to Cambodia myself and making the trek from Phnom Penh out to their villages, where it is likely their families still live, I wasn't sure what to do. I contacted a friend at the University of Cambodia who put me in touch with a student, Sima, who was willing to make the journey in my stead.

To my joy, she found them!

*   *   *

Nari left the job at the factory in 2009, five months before it closed. The job made her dizzy.

Mass faintings of workers at garment factories in Cambodia aren't rare. In 2011, 1,500 workers were reported to have fainted on the job: ". . . investigations found numerous causes for the fainting incidents, ranging from poor ventilation and toxic chemicals to 'mass psychogenic illness and unhealthy lifestyles,'" reported the *Phnom Penh Post*. "Union leaders, however, pointed to low wages and excessive overtime, explaining that the workers, primarily young women from villages, were supporting entire families on a basic wage. . . ." Essentially, eating less means you can send more money home. A bite of food you don't eat is a bite of food for your family.

Nari moved back in with her parents and began working toward her dream of owning her own business as a beautician. She opened her shop in 2010; but it wasn't profitable, so she had to close it.

She married an elementary teacher and spends her days looking after their nine-month-old baby boy and selling candy, shampoo, and cake from a small shack in front of their house. Tucked in the shack is a barber chair surrounded by mirrors.

She's not giving up on her dream; she still wants to become a famous beautician.

*　　*　　*

"Ai was so friendly with her smiling face every time she spoke," Sima reported. "We sat in the room and chatted happily."

Sima traveled back to Ai's village. Ai had come and gone. When the blue jean factory closed, Ai got a job at another factory working as a checker. Her new job required that she stand all day, causing her legs to ache. She was 27, a year past the prime age for a garment worker, and decided to return to her village to help with the farming.

At the end of 2010, she heard about an opportunity to work at the Lucky Star Hotel. Rooms run $15 per night and are equipped with flatscreen TVs and free Wi-Fi. Ai cleans the rooms and sleeps in what Sima reported as a "squatter's area." She works eight-hour days, seven days a week. The hotel hosts weddings in the evenings, which she works and gets paid overtime. She earns $70 per month—$20 more than what she earned as a garment worker in 2007, but only a few dollars more than the average worker earns in 2012. She's often sick and can't afford medical attention.

"I think it is enough," Ai told Sima, "compared to my factory work."

"Finally," Sima wrote in her report, "she was very surprised to hear from Mr. Kelsey. She hardly believed that she was remembered."

IV

My Flip-Flops: Made in China

PO'ed VP

June 2007

"Every step of the way you've been deceptive and lying," says Pat, thus ending my run of good luck with factories and brands.

Pat is the vice president of Global Sourcing for Deckers Outdoor, parent company of UGG boots, Simple shoes, and Teva, which made my flip-flops. I'm at Deckers' country office near Guangzhou, China, and Pat . . . well, I'm not exactly sure where Pat is. I imagine him sitting in his spacious home office in California, tie loosened after a long day of wheeling and dealing, sipping on a crystal cup of gin, face turning red with anger as he talks into his cell phone. One thing I can be sure about is that Pat doesn't like me.

"You visited the factory," he says. "Who gave you the address?"

"Your Teva office did. I called them last week, and the guy who answered the phone asked his manager and they gave it to me."

"Give me a name," Pat says.

"I don't know his name. I've talked to no less than eight people at Teva and Deckers in the last week."

"No one would give out that information," Pat says. "It's not supposed to be public."

"Well, they gave it to me. The other companies I've been working with have their factories' addresses public. I don't see why visiting the factory is such a big deal."

"That's the dumbest thing I've heard all day—not caring if some *tourist* shows up at a factory," he says. "We don't cater to tourists. We don't make our factories' info public."

"I'm not a tourist."

That's all I can say. I want to explain to him that visiting factories in Bangladesh, Cambodia, and China isn't much of a vacation; that I had been a tourist in Honduras who took a day from his vacation to visit a garment factory. But now, after having napped at Arifa's, played Frisbee at the dump in Phnom Penh, visited villages in Cambodia, I am most definitely *not* a tourist. This trip has nothing to do with my enjoying it. I took out a second mortgage to come here. I'm missing planning my own wedding—which doesn't entirely disappoint me. However, going on a vacation alone during this stage would make me a complete jackass. "Have fun planning the wedding, Annie. I'm going on vacation with money we don't have. See you in three months."

"I've been in this business for 30 years, and I've seen a lot of things," Pat says. "I know when I'm being lied to."

Pat is pissing me off. I feel my face redden. The only thing worse than getting tossed around the corporate phone chain is getting tossed around the corporate phone chain and then bitched at and called a liar and a selfish tourist when you acted on what (very little) information and help you were given. Before I booked my ticket to China, I had made multiple phone calls to Deckers trying to reach the right person. The process went something like this:

Call to describe quest: "Hello, I'm a writer going to all of the places where my clothes were made. I have a pair of Teva flip-flops that were made in China, and I was hoping you could tell me where in China they were made."

"Hold please" or "Let me transfer you."

Describe quest again.

"Hold please" or "Let me transfer you."

Eventually, I would get "accidentally" disconnected, put on hold indefinitely, or transferred to voice-mail.

Hang up. Call again.

Finally, a fella named Brice told me they were made in Guangzhou, which was enough for me to make my travel plans at the time.

When I arrived in Guangzhou, I faced another, even more daunting game of corporate phone chain. I needed the factory's address, and, more importantly, I wanted to speak with a representative in the country to try and arrange a visit or at least an interview. In Honduras, I just showed up and was given a pretty cold reception. In Bangladesh,

Dalton fabricated a lie, and I uncomfortably played along with it. But arranging a factory visit with the country manager, as I did in Cambodia with Levi's, was definitely the way to go and a method I hoped to replicate in China.

I called Deckers' California office from my hotel in Guangzhou and learned Brice no longer worked there. I was put on hold and cut off while some lady whose name I didn't get asked her manager about my request. I called back and spoke with Robert. His manager gave me the factory address, but no contact information for their China office. I was told to call Jaime at an extension they couldn't transfer me to. I hung up and called Jaime, but she wasn't there and I got her voice-mail. I called back and talked to Steven, who said he would speak to Jaime.

Days went by without a response from anyone. I sent e-mails and left voice-mails. When I finally reached Jaime, she gave me Pat's information. I sent a round of e-mails and voicemails to Pat complete with links to my blog that has interviews I had done about the quest and posts about visiting factories in Bangladesh and Cambodia.

I had spent hours and more money on long distance than I cared to think about and got absolutely nowhere. All I wanted was a name and number of somebody at Deckers in China with whom I could meet. They could decide for themselves, in person, whether or not they were willing to help me.

I got the feeling they were just waiting for me to disappear. But I didn't come all this way to disappear. I visited Deckers' website and read: "Our on-site supervisory office in Pan Yu City, China, serves as a local link to our independent manufacturers in the Far East." This led me to believe that the Deckers' office might be located at the factory I already had an address for, which was located near Pan Yu City. So I went.

I explain all of this to Pat, along with how I've been trying for months to get the appropriate contact information only to repeatedly get the runaround. I ask him what he would have done in my situation.

"I'm the one asking the questions!" Pat says, as I imagine him slamming down his recently emptied cup of gin.

What followed weren't questions but accusations about how I cleverly manipulated and deceived everybody—as if I had used Jedi mind tricks on Deckers employees and factory workers.

"You told them you knew me and I had invited you to visit," he said.

"Pat, that's not how it happened."

*   *   *

Figure 19.1   Outside the flip-flop factory.

"In China, when you go to a place like this you should have a letter of introduction," said my translator, Angel.

The guards at the factory wanted nothing to do with us; they said they had never even heard of Deckers. A woman filling out some paperwork at the guard shack approached Angel. She had heard of Deckers; she worked with them. In fact, their office was just up there, she pointed (Figure 19.1).

"What is the nature of your business?" the woman asked.

I tell her.

"Whose permission do you have to be here?" she asked.

"Nobody's, I have not been invited," I said, not exactly Jedilike by any means. "But Deckers did give me the address here. I've spoken with Steven, Jaime, and I've been trying to reach Pat."

As the woman called her boss, I asked Angel if the woman recognized any of the names, and she had—Pat's. Who of course was the only person in the entire Deckers' staff with whom I *hadn't* spoken.

So, I suppose Pat does have a legitimate beef with me using his name; but what part about my saying "I have not been invited" didn't anyone understand? I even repeated it. There were no lies.

The woman guided us past the guards and a retractable metal gate to a factory that seemed more like a campus, complete with tinted windows and AC units dripping onto the pavement below. Buildings are connected by a skyway, and a lone palm tree stood in the shade. A loud generator hummed somewhere in the distance.

We entered the nearest building through a room full of paper pushers at desks, perhaps designers, looking at shoes. The place smelled good—that perfect blend of leather and glue that makes you want to buy those new shoes even more. We were shown into a room lined with glass cabinets, floor-to-ceiling, displaying Teva and Simple shoes.

After a few minutes Mr. Huang, the woman's boss, entered and asked, "Whose permission do you have to be here?"

"Nobody's. Deckers gave me this address, and because they are busy with an upcoming project," I said, repeating one of the excuses I had been given for their lack of communication, "I have been unable to get through to them recently for more info. I was hoping you could help us."

"This is a very secret area—research and development," Mr. Huang said. "We can't show just anyone around, or they may steal industry secrets."

Apparently, the "on-site supervisory office" is not Deckers' Chinese headquarters, and Mr. Huang works for the factory, not Deckers. I try to assure him that I just want to learn about my shoes just the way I learned about my pants in Cambodia with Levi's and that if he could help me reach the appropriate Deckers people, I would appreciate it.

Mr. Huang repeatedly asked me if I had been invited or if I knew Pat. I repeatedly confirmed that I hadn't, and I didn't; although, to hear Pat's account of the visit as related to him, you would think I had told Mr. Huang, "Yeah, Pat and I are buds. He told me to come to the factory and you would show me around."

Mr. Huang left the room and came back with some business cards. He read the info to Angel.

"Here's the number for the Deckers office in Pan Yu," he said. "You should contact them. I can't tell you anything here until they give me permission. Sorry, I can't give you the address. You'll have to call and set something up on your own."

Now does that sound like something Mr. Huang would say if I misled him about my relationship with Pat and Deckers?

I apologized for just dropping in unannounced and thanked him for his time.

*　　*　　*

"I've tried to do the right thing every step of the way," I tell Pat. "I'm sorry if there has been some kind of miscommunication or mistranslation. Thanks for . . ." I hesitate. Thanks for what? Calling me a liar? "Thanks for your time." I hand Dindo, the Deckers country manager, his cell phone back.

Dindo has a one-sided conversation with Pat and says several different forms of "yes" before hanging up. It seems that whatever Pat told him was the exact opposite of what and how Pat told me. He apologizes for the misunderstanding and says that Pat told him to answer any questions I might have.

Dindo couldn't be nicer. It seems that we are now brothers-in-arms. I had faced the wrath of Pat, and he probably had too, many times. He tells me about his life. He was born in the Philippines and moved to the United States when he was five. Now he spends three months here and one month at home with his wife and 17-year-old son in California. We talk about SCUBA diving. The Philippines is a short plane ride from here and offers great diving.

Eventually, I get back down to business and consult the list of questions in my notebook. "Walk me through the process of making my sandals," I say.

"All of the material comes from China," he says. "We pick the suppliers and approve all of the components that the factories use. We choose the design on the webbing and the material for the outsole and insole."

I take off my smelly sandals that have been with me every step of the quest and even before that and hold them above the table.

"Make sure you don't touch them," I say. "They're nasty."

He points at the individual pieces with my business card, explaining that the webbing comes in huge spools and they cut it to length before stitching the pieces together. It's then anchored by washerlike things at the toe and each side of the foot where it meets the footbed. The insole and the outsole are made of foam created by Teva. They didn't patent the material, but they are about the only ones who use it. It's a type of memory foam. The soles are stitched together and glued. I would have never guessed that any sewing was done on a flip-flop.

Flip-flops are simple to make, and it only takes about five people: a cutter, a sewer, a gluer, a buffer, and a boxer. Workers can pump out 2,000 to 3,000 pairs in one day. Compare this to the 50 to 80 people needed to make a typical tennis shoe, for which the daily production rate is about half of that of flip-flops.

"Will hands ever be replaced by machines?" I ask.

"The technology has existed for 15 years," he says, "but it's just not the same. [You have to work with] each piece of leather differently. A machine would not know what to do. Reebok has a line of machines, but stitching machines are the only ones that we use. The workers line it up and press a button. A few seconds later the stitching is done."

Figure 19.2 A woman at Guangzhou's Metropolis Shoe City sits amid walls of shoes.

"So how is the shoe business?" I ask.

"It's good. Sales just keep getting higher (Figure 19.2). My question is who is wearing all of these shoes? Nike produces 20 million shoes per month, Reebok 10 million. We produce around 8 million pairs per year."

"Wow, that's almost as much as Reebok," I say.

"That's 8 million pairs per *year*, not month," he says. "We have five factories that we work with in Pan Yu district. We used to have factories in Macau and Thailand, but we can control and monitor everything better in one place. Flip-flops like yours are made at the Irofa factory in the Pan Yu district."

"Would it be possible to see the production line?" I ask.

"Your sandals are out of season right now," he says—"NO" #1.

This makes sense; it's June, and they are probably producing their fall and winter shoes right now.

"Any shoe line would do," I say. "I expect normal shoes being manufactured would be much more interesting to see anyhow."

"Unfortunately," he says, "the factory that makes your sandals is currently shut down because of no power. In the Guangdong province, there are scheduled blackouts. Some of the factories run generators, others just shut down." This is "NO" #2.

I'm guessing Dindo likes his job; if he wants to keep it, there's no way I'm getting into any of the factories with which Deckers works. He's just being polite about it.

"Maybe next week?" I ask.

"Maybe next week," he says.

*   *   *

To Pat's credit, who comes to China to see where their flip-flops were made? I'd be suspicious of me, too. Plus, I don't have any credentials. I don't work for the *New York Times;* heck, I don't work for anybody. It's hard to take me seriously until I show up on your doorstep and then you no longer can ignore me.

But what is wrong with me, a loyal Teva customer, wanting to know where my flip-flops are from?

I'm sure the realities of the shoe business, like the realities of the garment business, aren't pretty, and Pat doesn't want us to think about them. This is why Pat doesn't like me. But there is one thing Pat should know: I like wearing shoes. I like not having sharp objects poke my feet. I like having a little arch support.

Pretty much every piece of footwear I own was made in China. I'm guessing yours was, too. Who am I to damn the brands and the factories that make my shoes?

Pat doesn't want us to think about our shoes. He wants us to buy them, wear them out, and buy another pair. Pat doesn't want us to think about the people who make our shoes and what their lives are like. But no matter how much control Pat has over his global supply chain, he can't stop me from meeting the people who made my flip-flops.

CHAPTER 20

Life at the Bottom

Flip-flops are the most fun thing you can wear. And of all the things you can wear, flip-flops is the most fun thing to say.

They go flip-flop on your feet, so they're called flip-flops. Simple. Nice. But have you ever really thought about this? They don't go flip-flip or flop-flop or even flop-flip. They always go flip-flop.

This is about as deep as my thoughts go when I'm wearing flip-flops. As I'm walking, I hear the left always going flip and the right one always going flop, and I consider it for a second or two and then I stop thinking about it because a flip-flop day is always a good day, and I've got better things to do.

It's warm when I'm wearing flip-flops, at least 75 degrees. I'm not worried about objects crushing my toes or sharp things cutting my feet. I'm not one of those who wear them year-round or during every activity. In fact, maybe I'm a bad person because of this, but when I see someone wearing flip-flops in winter, a little bit of me secretly hopes that they get a touch of frostbite to teach them a lesson. Or when I see someone wearing them during any sport or physical labor, I just want to go up and step on their toes.

My love affair with the flip-flop began in Key West. I would wake up, put on a T-shirt and swim trunks, and pedal my bike down palm tree–shaded streets to the dive shop where I worked. I would help customers get their gear ready. They were on vacation, happily whistling Jimmy Buffett songs, and wearing flip-flops, too. When everyone had their equipment, we would board the boat and kick off our footwear without having to bend over.

For the next four hours, we wore fins and chased colorful fish around the reef, or we were on the boat, barefoot, eating fresh pineapple. At the trip's end, we would slide back into our footwear—again without the inconvenience of bending over. The customers would flip-flop off to the nearest bar for a fruity cocktail, and Ralph, Roy, or Rusty (it seems all of the captains' names started with R) and I would search the ice chest for a couple of cold ones to nurse as we washed down the boat. Then I would pedal back home in the shade provided by the opposite row of palm trees. I would kick off my flip-flops just inside the door, and there they would wait until the next morning, ready to do it all over again.

Unfortunately, this isn't the lifestyle of those who make our flip-flops.

Far from it.

*   *   *

In front of the flip-flop factory, the flip-flop fabricators wear flip-flops.

As much as I would like to associate flip-flops with Margaritaville, there are magnitudes more poor people right this very minute wearing flip-flops than there are islanders or beachgoers or vacationers. Flip-flops are the footwear of choice in developing countries, mostly because they're cheap—often less than $1—and repairable. All of the workers I've met up to this point wear flip-flops to work, and Chinese workers are no different (Figure 20.1).

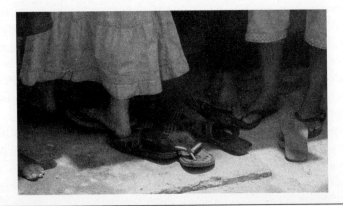

Figure 20.1 No shoes allowed inside, workers in Cambodia slip off their flip-flops before entering their room.

It's 5 PM, and the workers stream out of the space between the retractable gate and the guard building in front of the factory. The majority of them cross the street and enter a narrow alley. Angel and I follow them until the alley intersects with another. This is where we'll wait.

"Okay," I say, "this looks good. Ask them if they mind chatting and if they manufactured Tevas."

Some of the workers ignore us, while others take a wide berth and stare from a distance. I don't blame them. I'm getting somewhat used to this, after having done similar things in factories in Honduras, Bangladesh, and Cambodia, yet I still feel a bit like a survey taker at the mall trying to impose on others.

But the randomness of the experience is exciting. I'm in China because my sandals were made here. I'm in front of this factory because they make Tevas. I found the factory because someone at Deckers slipped up and gave me the address. The workers walk by with their stories waiting to be told. Who will share theirs with me?

Angel stops a woman wearing a green badge. Zhu Chun is shy, and doesn't want to talk with us. Rings of onlookers begin to form. A man with a flat-top haircut and a confident step pushes his way through them all and encourages the woman to talk.

"Are you a couple?" I ask.

The man named Dewan gives Zhu Chun a half smile. "Yes, we are married."

"Do you make these?" I point to my flip-flops.

They nod.

"Where are you going right now?" I ask.

"Back to our room," the man says.

"Can we join you?"

"Yes."

We follow them through narrow alleys. I try to keep my directions, but it's pointless—everything looks the same, and the sun, lost beneath the smog, is no help in guiding me.

We climb a set of concrete steps that stick out from the side of a brick building, and Dewan unlocks the door. The steps turn in to the house and are met by metal steps, like a fire escape's. I have to duck as I enter the doorway and enter the community kitchen. There are five unattended woks that smell of warm oil. The second landing is theirs. We come to a wood door that has "305" scrawled on it in permanent marker along with Chinese characters I can't read.

The room is just wide enough for the bed, which takes over half of the limited space. A rice cooker and TV/DVD player sit on a shaky table. Speaker wires run from the TV to speakers in the corners. I'm not sure if surround sound is needed in such a small room, but you have to appreciate the effort.

Dewan, 36, and Zhu Chun, 31, are on a break. On a normal day, they work from 7:30 AM to noon, break for an hour and a half, work from 1:30 PM to 5:00 PM, and after that, they can choose to work from 6:00 PM to 9:00 PM if there is work to be done. Today, they have chosen to work the extra hours. On a normal day, they work between nine and twelve hours—or so they tell me.

The hours don't seem too unreasonable, but I wonder how much of a *choice* the overtime really is. I don't ask because I don't want to lead them down that road. If someone came up to you and immediately asked questions about how rotten your job was, you would initially be somewhat insulted—as if the questioner were above your rotten job— and would likely only talk about the negative aspects of the job if you even bothered to answer.

"Do you have any children?" I ask.

"Yes," Zhu Chun says. "We have one son, Li Xin. He is 13."

"Thirteen!" I say, "You look too young to have a child 13." She does, too. I'm not trying to win any points here. There's hardly a wrinkle on her face.

Dewan laughs, and Zhu Chun shyly lowers her head, hiding a smile.

"So he lives with you here?" It doesn't seem as though there is enough living space to add a 13-year-old boy and his trappings. There's barely enough room for the four of us to sit. Zhu Chun sits on a plastic stool in the middle of the room, and Dewan, Angel, and I sit on the bed hip to hip. The room seems smaller than it is, if that's possible. There's no window, and a fan circulates stale air. Our foreheads are moist with sweat.

"No," Zhu Chun says. "He lives in our home village."

"Where's that?"

"We are both from the Sichuan Province," Dewan says.

I pull out my guidebook and open to the map of China. Dewan points just west of Chongqing.

"That doesn't seem too far," I say.

"It takes 30 hours by train," Dewan says.

I reexamine the map trying to get a sense of the size of China. It's about two inches from Guangzhou to Chongqing, and that's about . . . 600 miles as the crow flies.

"We haven't seen Li Xin in two or three years," Dewan says.

It's not easy to read the emotions of people speaking a language you don't understand, but they both seem kind of emotionless. I scan the room for a picture or a drawing or any signs that they are parents. Nothing. The walls are lined with newspapers and posters. One of the posters says something about Jesus being born and has a picture of Santa on it.

"The walls aren't good," Dewan says.

"Huh?"

"The walls." He lifts up a corner of a poster and shows a pockmarked, crumbling concrete wall. "They are bad, so we cover them."

"Oh," I say, not sure if I should believe they actually have a son. Two or three years—I just can't get over it. "Who does your son live with?"

"My father," Dewan says, again, emotionless.

"What does he want to be when he grows up?" I ask, digging for some type of reaction.

"The last time we saw him he wanted to be a police officer," Zhu Chun says, in that brushed-off "oh-kids" kind of way.

I'm just not feeling it from these two. Something isn't right.

I decide to change the subject to my flip-flops. I squeeze past Zhu Chun and grab one of mine among the pile of flip-flops at their door. I hold it up. "I was told that my sandals were made in a different factory."

"Right now we are making shoes," Dewan says, "but we make those."

"I sew the strap on and the nametag," Zhu Chun says.

"And I paint them," Dewan says.

We talk more about their jobs. They are happy with their pay—about $140 to $225 per month—which seems quite good compared with the other apparel workers I've met.

"Do you like your job?" I ask.

"Of course," Dewan says, "we are very happy to have this job."

They start preparing dinner, and Angel tells me that we should probably go. I thank them for their time and slip my flip-flops on without bending over.

*   *   *

Later that night, I review my notes and photos trying to make sense of my time with Dewan and Zhu Chun. They've been separated from their son for three years and yet everything seems hunky-dory. They seem content living in their tiny room, far from their family, making my flip-flops. I just wasn't buying it.

As I scroll through photos of their room, I zoom in looking again for signs that they are parents. Still nothing. But something does catch my eye: a piece of packing tape on the door looks familiar.

Keen Footwear—IF THIS TAPE SHOWS SIGNS OF BEING BROKEN OR RESEALED . . . DO NOT ACCEPT. ADVISE SHIPPER IMMEDIATELY.

It has been a few years, but I used to accept many packages sealed with that tape.

I sold women's shoes.

Now, I don't mean any disrespect to women or shoes, but I'm about to make some generalizations about both. It's not my intent to be chauvinistic or antifootwear, but in the shoe-selling business—as in the wild—generalizations are key to survival. As with sharks in the ocean, I approached all women in the shoe section with care.

Technically, the store where I worked was an adventure outfitter. I would help customers select exciting, outdoorsy gear like sleeping bags, tents, water purifiers, stoves, and backpacks, some of the time. But mostly I sold shoes to women.

I would not recommend this to anyone, even other women.

For one thing, women lie about their shoe size. If they say they are a size 7, they are probably an 8.5. I quickly learned that it was in my best interest to say, "These shoes run small."

One day a woman brought her sandals back complaining that they smelled. I wanted to tell her that mankind can build skyscrapers, we can send a man to the moon, we can explore the depths of the ocean in submarines, we can destroy our world with a press of a few buttons, but we will never, ever, invent a sandal that does not stink. But instead, I acted surprised. Her petite feet obviously would not perspire the slightest bit causing them to stink, so, there must be something wrong with her sandals. And then I instructed her on how to wash them.

After a year of selling shoes, I thought I had seen and heard it all until one woman truly stumped me.

"Do you have any hiking boots that weren't made in China?" she asked.

"I'm sure we do," I said. "Let's look."

How blissfully unaware I was. China produces 9 billion pairs of shoes per year, which is over half of the world's production.

We had a good selection of hiking boots at the store—maybe 15 or 20 styles—and we only had one pair that wasn't made in China: Garmont Vegans made in Slovakia. They fit her ethics, but they didn't fit her foot. She left the store bootless with the intention of ordering some boots online that were made in Vietnam. I expanded the search to the rest of our shoe inventory. It was slim pickings. Better to have a customer come looking for pink, nonstink, plantar-fasciitis-friendly sandals than a shoe not made in China.

What did this lady have against China?

I thought back to my college days and Sociology 201. During our lectures on the evils of globalization and sweatshops, our professor introduced us to the concept of the race to the bottom. Companies would go wherever labor was the cheapest, and often that was wherever the people were the most desperate. He told us that China was winning the race as evidenced by the majority of our stuff being made there, and, as trade became freer, it would continue to lead the race to the bottom.

He told us China has better roads and ports than the other developing countries. They have lots of resources, including the largest population of any country ever, giving them a near limitless supply of workers who lack the fundamental rights that we Americans hold so dear: freedom of expression, freedom of association, and freedom of religion. He told us there's hardly a dictator that the United States stands against that China doesn't support, and yet we support China's economy, which supports the government.

There were plenty of reasons the woman could have been shopping for boots not made in China.

China was the bottom then. China is the bottom now.

I figured the plight of the Chinese workers must be similar or worse compared with the workers I've already met. The other workers offered up complaints about their jobs or the struggles in their lives and their lack of options without my pushing them. But Dewan and Zhu Chun didn't. Their wages are higher than any of the other workers'. They have surround sound. And, this is the strangest part, they seem content even though they haven't seen their son in three years.

I expected the bottom to be different.

* * *

"How's your day going?" I ask.

I'm treating Dewan and Zhu Chun to lunch near their factory. It wasn't easy to arrange. They've been working a lot of nights recently and have been using their lunch breaks for naps.

"I'm tired," Zhu Chun says. "We worked last night, again."

"How late?" I ask, as I lift a peanut to my mouth with my shaky chopsticks.

"Until 11:00," Dewan says, laughing as my peanut zings across the room.

They seem different today—less formal and more open.

Dewan orders a bottle of beer, pours some into my tiny glass and some into his. We tink our glasses of beer—mostly foam—together, and he gives me a wink.

After another zinging peanut, Zhu Chun adjusts my chopstick technique. Dewan signals the waiter to bring me a spoon.

"Tell me again, how many hours a week do you work?" I ask.

"Eighty to 100," Dewan says.

A hundred hours! That's 16 hours per day, if they work the government maximum of six days. But they don't, because they work every day. Is that better or worse? Would you rather work six, 16-hour days or seven, 14-hour days? They tell me it has been over a month since they've had a day off. This sounds a little more like the bottom I expected to find.

"It is a very difficult life," Zhu Chun says.

"Do you get paid for the overtime?" I ask.

"Last night," Dewan says, "I got paid until nine, and then our boss told us to clock out and come back to work."

The basic unit of communism is the worker. Everyone works for the greater good of society. But the greatest good of 1.3 billion people can lead to hundreds of millions of people getting crapped on. The Chinese lawmakers pride themselves on the labor laws that they've established to protect the worker. They set the workweek at 40 hours. Overtime is allowed, but in 2007 no worker should work more than 203.4 hours in a month. Such precision makes the law look exceptionally empty and foolish since the average worker works far more hours per month.

In China, there's the law, and then there's Dewan and Zhu Chun, who tell me it's not rare for them to work more than 400 hours in a month. They would lose their jobs if they complained about the hours or not being paid for overtime, and they can't afford that. They took out a loan to build a two-story home in their village. Shortly after the home was finished, Dewan's mother became ill and died after racking up expensive medical bills.

There's no one to fight for Dewan and Zhu Chun. Government officials caught up in a booming economy don't want to do anything to hinder local businesses and foreign investments. The labor union is run by the Communist Party, which makes the laws that aren't enforced. Given that public gatherings are prohibited, unions aren't exactly going to sprout up on their own. NGOs are restricted, and other international organizations such as the ILO struggle to get anywhere with labor rights. Deckers' on-site supervisory office may ensure quality and production efficiencies, but they, along with everyone else, don't seem to do much for Dewan and Zhu Chun.

"Why has your story changed?" I ask. "Before, you told me that you worked a maximum of 12 hours per day and that you were happy with your job."

"We thought you were a customer of our factory," Dewan says. "Not a writer." Apparently, Angel didn't get this point across the first time, or they didn't believe it.

Like most of their coworkers, Dewan and Zhu Chun are migrant workers. They come from the other China, not the one that business people and tourists return from, marveling at the change, the growth, the modernization. Their China hasn't changed as much or grown as fast. If you go to McDonald's in the cities, a smiling girl wearing McDonald's blue jeans will take your order on a PDA that will wirelessly transmit your order to the register. You can check your e-mail at Starbucks on your laptop. You can ride on a modern metro system or in a cab where the driver presses a button and a voice welcomes you in English.

In the villages, they farm terraced fields by hand.

"Daily life in the village is better," Zhu Chun says.

"We will definitely move back once we save enough money . . . maybe in five years," Dewan says.

"I wish I could be with my son," Zhu Chun says, "and with my family and we could play cards. Here, we have to work every day. We are not free."

The people who make boots or sandals in China aren't free. They, like most of the people who make our apparel, are bound to their work because they don't have any other options.

Although they live and work in the city, everything they live and work for is in the country hundreds of miles away—so I ask Dewan and Zhu Chun if they want to go with me to their village. I would pay.

"We have to work," Dewan says. But he gives me the address and tells me I can visit on my own, if I want.

"Is there anything I can take to Li Xin for you?" I ask.

They can't think of anything, but I can. I pull out my camera and tell them to smile.

Dewan eyes the clock and pats his belly. They both thank me for lunch. Side by side, husband and wife, mother and father, two of 200 million migrant workers, walk back to the same factory with the same goal: earn enough money to move back home and be with their family.

Growing Pains

A man in pink flip-flops puts a tiny fish into an umbrella, which has been turned upside down and filled with green water. If the fish gets a swimming start, it can make it part way to the edge of the umbrella and freedom before sliding back down. Eventually the fish gives up.

The fisherman's pole, like a 12-foot blade of grass, is all rod and no reel. He baits the hook with a grub and flicks his line out into the water and waits. I've never seen a pole so long, and I've never seen a fish so small caught on a hook. Normally, fish this size are caught with a net and used to catch bigger fish. When I was five, I used to catch bluegill 10 times the size of these fish at the pond across the road with my Snoopy fishing pole.

The fish must taste good, though, because fisherman line the rocky bank. They all have similar poles and use a variety of buckets, cans, jugs, and jars for their bait and catch.

A stream trickles between the rocks and into the river. Fish splash in buckets and umbrellas. It's a peaceful day to be fishing on the world's third-longest river, the Yangtze, until the cranes fire up.

The cranes sit on barges and lower their grapples into the water. The grapples emerge with fingers full of sediment that is dumped into a nearby barge. Naturally flowing rivers don't need this type of maintenance, but this is no naturally flowing river. In fact, there is nothing natural about anything around here. The cliff sides are scarred by dynamite, the banks covered in concrete, the sky filled with haze, and even the boulders the fishermen stand on are too uniform in size

Figure 21.1   Fishermen are dwarfed by the world's largest dam, the
Three Gorges Dam.

and shape to be natural. But all of this pales in comparison to the dam
(Figure 21.1).

The Three Gorges Dam, with its multilevel tiers, is a chorus
of concrete. I'm not as impressed by the dam as I thought I would be.
I expected a huge sloping wall of concrete like the Hoover Dam that
stretches to the sky. The Three Gorges Dam is the world's largest
dam, but I think that its largeness is lost a bit in its width. Although, to
be honest, I'm not easily impressed by concrete; and if this dam, which
is almost a mile-and-a-half long and 607-feet high, doesn't blow me
away, no concrete structure will.

The construction of the dam started in 1994 after decades of
planning interrupted by revolutions and "leaps forward." The concrete is in place, but the generators won't start turning for another
few months. The $23 billion project will supply seven provinces with
power, including Guangdong Province—where my flip-flops were

made. This means that if I come back in 2009, Deckers would have to find an excuse other than the factory's not having power to deny me a tour. I'm sure they would think of something.

According to a placard at the project's museum, the dam is a great success that we probably wouldn't understand because we weren't there:

> *Without self-participation, it is hard to understand the complicated technology and arduous construction involved in the river closure. [The closure] . . . set up several new records in the world river closure history, demonstrating the capability, resolution, and wisdom of the Chinese people to harness rivers.*

And just in case we weren't quite buying the historical significance and ubergreatness of the project:

> *The great feat of the river closures . . . by the Chinese people on the Yangtze River will surely be written into the water development history of the world as a brilliant example.*

Yet some Chinese people don't feel that the project was done *by* them, but *to* them. In 2006, the government boasted about the world records the dam set. Not only did they list its size and its capacity to produce electricity, they highlighted the sacrifice their people made to have it built. The rising waters of the Yangtze have displaced 1.4 million people—the most ever—and are expected to displace 4 million more. In fact, the water in which the fishermen now fish probably covers their homes.

I guess you can look at the relocation of over 5 million people as an accomplishment, if you're impressed by the amount of authority a country's government has, or how obedient its citizens are.

To help sell the project and to populate the gift shop, the dam has two mascots—one smiling skipping boy and one smiling skipping girl. They both wear hard hats and overalls. The ponytailed girl carries a banner that undoubtedly says something along the lines of: "I (heart) dam." Their level of happiness about a giant wall of concrete is creepy.

The project is done for the Chinese people and by the people, and it's also done to the environment. Water quality has declined since the natural flow of the river has been stopped. The dam is blamed for contributing to the extinction of the Yangtze River dolphin and threatening the Siberian Crane. The fish population doesn't seem to be thriving, either.

The Chinese government hopes the positives outweigh the negatives in the long run. They'll be able to control the Yangtze's floodwaters and prevent their damage, and they need more power due to growing populations, cities, and industries. The majority of their power currently comes from coal, which is largely responsible for the haze seen in many of the major cities. The dam, and the hydropower it will produce, is a part of the country's goal to have 15 percent of its electricity come from renewable sources of energy by the year 2020.

I leave the fishermen to their long poles and tiny fish in the shadow of their big dam, and I head to the nearby city of Zigui to learn what the locals think of the world's largest public works project in their backyard.

* * *

Zhou Zhi owns a tiny restaurant on the banks of the Yangtze. She has freckles, her hair is dyed red, and she seems genuinely happy that I stopped in for a bite. She pours me a cup of hot tea and sits across from me.

The walls are bare cinder block and the floor concrete. Everything is in its place and clean.

"Where did you live before the dam was built?" I ask.

She points out the door, across the road, and down into the water.

"Your house is now underwater?" I ask.

"Yes," she says, as she plays with the gold heart hanging from a chain on her neck. "My family grew oranges. This area used to be very famous for oranges. Now all of the fields are covered by water. But life is better thanks to the dam."

"What was it like when you first heard you had to move?" I ask.

"No problem," she says. "The dam is beautiful for development."

"But surely," I say, "you were a little disappointed."

"I didn't want to move far from my family," she says. "The government gave each person [$10,000], and my family built this restaurant. Our life is better. The road is nicer. The transportation is more convenient. The electricity is more reliable. I miss nothing."

The conversation continues in this vein, and my notebook fills with notes of how the dam is a "good thing" and that "life is better." Her family's land of three generations is 60 feet below the river's surface, and she doesn't seem to have a tinge of regret that she had to move. Like the dam's mascots, she couldn't be happier.

I find Wang Kai, a muscular fella with gray stubble on his face, outside of his house a few places down from Zhou Zhi's restaurant.

He was moved here 10 years ago and points toward the water with a crooked thumb when I ask where he moved from.

He used to be an orange farmer, too, and now works as a handyman.

"I loved being a farmer," he says, "but. . . ." He holds up his hands as if to say *what can ya do*. And then he talks about how good the dam is, repeating many of the same points that Zhou Zhi had and adding that now the phone system is better. "Life is better; . . . the dam is good; . . . the future is more promising now; . . . we benefit from the dam; . . . it is good for the country; . . . I am happy to make the sacrifice."

I can understand why the locals think the dam is better. Their fields and former way of life are gone, but a new one has arrived. The government built up the local infrastructure, introduced many modern conveniences, and provided money to rebuild and relocate. I have no doubt that life is better for the citizens of Zigui who live with the dam in their backyards.

However, reports of people living in isolated villages also flooded by the dam aren't so great. They tried to relocate their farms on steeper, higher ground where erosion washed away their crops, but the government didn't provide sufficient funds or assistance to do so. The *New York Times* reported that one family lost their home and now live in a tent on a terrace that houses a monument "celebrating efforts by local officials to improve the environment."

Even though life may be better in Zigui, it freaks me out that no one has anything bad to say. I understand that the Chinese people are reluctant to speak negatively about anything the government does— especially to a foreigner—but I still expected to pick up on a negative vibe. I come from a world where change is good—if it takes place in somebody else's backyard. But change in your own backyard gives you the right to bitch. If the United States government says they'll be flooding your land and you should probably move, you—and your lawyer—will be on every news program from sunup to sundown. And even if your ranting doesn't do any good, it'll make you feel better.

And, really, isn't that what the right to bitch is all about?

The good and the bad of the Three Gorges Dam are heavily debated even within the Chinese government. It is likely that no one will know for sure all of the good and all of the bad and if it was worth the time, the money, and the hardships until many years into the future. For now, the project is just one of many growing pains China faces.

We faced them too.

* * *

"Okay, go, Dad," I said with a high-pitched Mickey Mouse–like voice. I was seven.

Dad pushed the throttle forward, and the boat started to pull me through the water. It didn't take much for the boat to plane out my skis. I was doing what I was told and "making like a lead butt": squatting on the back of skis that weren't much bigger than the ones you see those squirrels use on the Internet. Like the squirrels, mine were tied together. And, again, like the squirrels, I had a big bucktoothed smile.

I didn't weigh enough to pull the 100 feet of rope taut, and it sagged into the water. I waved and flashed my big buckers as we passed boats whose passengers would holler and toot their horn. I was beyond excited. Not only was I officially a water skier and presently the center of attention, but Dad had also promised to buy me a teddy bear if I got up that day. I named the bear Skeeter.

This was just one of many memories that I have from Lake Cumberland, located in southern Kentucky.

Lake Cumberland was our family getaway. We would go there several times a summer. To me, it meant Cheetos, grapes, canned cheese, sunburns, splinters, wipeouts, faceplants, and boatfuls of good times. Whenever I smell sunscreen, I think of Lake Cumberland.

But there wasn't always a Lake Cumberland.

Lake Cumberland was created by the damming of the Cumberland River. Completed in 1950, the Wolf Creek Dam provided hydroelectricity and flood control down river.

But not everyone was happy about it.

Several small towns were flooded in the process—one of which was Rowena, Kentucky. According to a 1943 story in Louisville's *Courier-Journal* written during the dam's construction, the locals varied on the subject of the dam.

There were those who said things like:

"The dam will develop our town."

"Industry will come to the valley."

"It's swell."

And there were those who thought the dam was somewhat less swell, including L. C. Humble, a 74-year-old farmer who owned land bisected by the dam.

"The dam is the worst thing that ever happened to Kentucky," said L. C. (not-so) Humble. "Folks up the river don't have to move out for two or three years. We've got to move out right now. We've got no idea at all where we're goin'."

Humble and his wife had raised 12 kids in the two-story house, where, to quote the article, "(Humble and) his little gray-haired wife observed their golden anniversary in 1939."

His wife Thenora didn't look forward to leaving the land either. "We've been tryin' to hold out until we find out what to do with our dead," she told the paper, which reported her voice was "almost a sob" and there was "a little quiver in her sun-browned cheeks." "We've got a son and two girls buried in the cemetery 'round back. We want to get them out before the Government takes bids and gives somebody money to do it. . . . It hurts me most givin' up this house. It was built in 1847, long before we came here. I reckon it hurts the men most givin' up the cattle. . . . Everybody thinks we'll get big money from the Government," she added. "But what's money to comfort?"

The citizens of Rowena weren't the only ones hoping to get money from the loss of their land. My great-great uncle and his wife, who lived in Highway, Kentucky—also threatened by the dam—were in the same situation; that is, until they got into trouble for making moonshine and moved to Mississippi. Once the dam was built, they returned to Kentucky and attempted to claim the government payout. However, the government said that since they had received the land in a land grant, they had to occupy the land to claim it. They were out of luck.

I'm not exactly sure where Highway is, but there's a good chance I've water-skied over it.

Over time, the Wolf Creek Dam is said to have saved hundreds of millions of dollars in flood damage. In addition to this and the electricity it produces, the boater's paradise of Lake Cumberland has become a major source of income in southern Kentucky. So far, so good for the Wolf Creek Dam; that is, until the scare in 2007 when the Army Corps of Engineers discovered the dam was leaking and was in danger of collapsing. The Corps is working to remediate the problem, but if the dam were to give way, the resulting damages are estimated at $3 billion—which would erase much of the economic benefit to date.

Many dams popped up across the United States in the wake of the Great Depression. Each came with its own good and bad; each was a growing pain experienced by a growing country.

Dams are just one of many growing pains in our history; garment and apparel factories are another.

The Northeastern United States was once the bottom. Young girls subjected to prisonlike conditions worked at garment factories and textile mills. Their rights were few, and their struggles many, including the Triangle Shirtwaist Factory fire tragedy. As workers attained more rights, the bottom moved to the South and eventually jumped overseas where it fought communism and cut the price of our clothes.

The business community, economists, and developing countries argue that those who focus on the evils of the race to the bottom forget that many of the developed countries today, including the United States, were once the bottom and that the garment and apparel industry were essential to their development. I can understand this logic in a way. I can see how the garment industry is giving Amilcar, Arifa, Nari, and Ai—or at least their children—a shot at a better life. However corrupt their countries are politically or economically, they live in democracies that allow foreign organizations to educate workers about their rights and, hopefully, lift the bottom as they go. But what about Dewan and Zhu Chun? They are in a one-party communist regime that does not allow any of this.

So, when the business community, economists, or the Chinese government say that workers being paid little for working a lot in less than desirable conditions is all part of the growing process in China, I have trouble believing it. Who's to say that human rights and worker's rights in China will improve? Levi's took a stand against China, hoping to source elsewhere—until the Chinese government changed their approach to human rights to meet the Levi's company Code of Conduct. But instead of China improving their human rights, Levi's, under competitive pressure to source in China, lowered the requirements of its Code of Conduct.

James Mann, the author of *The China Fantasy* (New York: Viking, 2007), calls this approach the "Soothing Scenario." He says that we think trade has some sort of magical quality to it that will lead to human rights improvements in China and eventually to democracy. He wonders what if it doesn't. What if China maintains its one-party, repressive system and an open economy? Where does this leave Dewan and Zhu Chun?

The labor wrongs in the garment and apparel industry are just the tip of the wrongness iceberg in China. A June 2007 investigation rescued 450 brick makers who were badly beaten, burned, and broken spiritually and physically. A June 15, 2007, report in London's *Guardian* said that the workers "were locked for years in a bare room with no bed or stove, allowed out only to work in the red-hot kilns, from where they would carry heavy, burning loads of newly fired bricks on their bare backs. Many were badly scalded. Fifteen-minute meal breaks consisted only of steamed buns and cold water." One worker had been beaten to death with a shovel, and others had starved to death.

Like the Three Gorges Dam compared to Lake Cumberland's Wolf Creek Dam, this growing pain—one of many in China—is on a whole other level. And the brunt of the pains is often forced upon the rural villagers like Dewan and Zhu Chun. Hopefully, they won't be passed on to their son, Li Xin, whom I'm on my way to visit.

I grab a bus to the dam's ferry terminal where I'm to catch a ride to Chongqing, near Dewan and Zhu Chun's village. The bank that was lined with fishermen is now being attacked by violent surf. A gate on the dam is open, and water roars out into the river.

The ferry isn't a boat; it's a hydrofoil that rides on two skis at 35 mph. It's a long tube of riveted metal, completely enclosed. It was built by the Soviets. I feel more than a little like James Bond as we ski by and above what were once the homes of 1.4 million people.

The Real China

I can feel the fresh air in my lungs, and it feels good. I can smell flowers and juicy greenery. This is the countryside, and I haven't felt this at home since I arrived in China.

I'm a country boy, and I don't like big cities.

Guangzhou was a sweaty hustle and bustle. Getting on a bus or on the subway involved pushing and shoving, mostly me being pushed and shoved by people two-thirds my size—a speck swallowed by a raging amoeba.

I had never heard of the city of Chongqing. I expected it to be a small city, if not a village, and a relief from Guangzhou.

This is how little I know about China.

Chongqing has a population of 31 million. That's nearly double the population of Ohio and Indiana combined. It is one of 100 Chinese cities with a population over 1 million.

People spit a lot in the cities; they have to. The air is a chemical weapon that pushes the body's mucous manufacturing to the limit. Spitting is healthy; you either ingest the air or spit. People do it everywhere—on the train and in the bank, on carpet and on tile.

But you don't need to spit out here.

With the help of my translator Huang from Chongqing University, I've followed Dewan and Zhu Chun's directions from Chongqing to the city of Yongchuan to here in front of China's second-largest zoo, which appears abandoned.

The directions from here are fairly vague: We're supposed to ask someone to take us to the "Shuai family" on the "sixth team." That would be all well and good if there were anyone around to ask, but the countryside is every bit as abandoned as the zoo.

A bus roars around the corner and stops in front of us, and a denim-clad lady exits with a teenage girl. They are both loaded down with sacks of groceries.

"This is the foreigner?" she asks, and Huang confirms the obvious. "Follow me."

She leads us across the road. I offer to carry some of the groceries, but she declines. We follow a narrow path up a steep bank of grass and weeds. The path, moist enough that our shoe prints squish in with each step, skirts the edge of terraced fields.

The woman is Dewan's sister, Lin Chang, and she's wearing blue jeans and a jean jacket. Overall, it's a bit too much denim, but I suppose she would fit in at most grocery stores in the United States on a Saturday morning. Her daughter, Dai Gan, is tall and thin and wears purple jeans embroidered with flowers and a white jacket. She wouldn't be out of place hopping off a school bus in the suburb of any American city.

As we walk, voices greet us from the fields. Sometimes they are below or above us, and other times they are hidden in the corn. They address Lin Chang, but she doesn't stop to talk. She doesn't have to; it's quiet, and she can carry on a conversation as we walk from one small valley to the next. The next valley brings a different set of voices and conversations.

Eventually, after winding our way up, over, and across several terraced valleys, we come to a house atop one of the hills. The two-story home is faced with white tile, and its barred windows are outlined with arches of red tile. It's a small castle overlooking green fields of corn, potatoes, rice, and a large pond.

A boy peeks out from the shadow of the door, and Dai Gan runs to him like an excited puppy, not sure what to do when she reaches him. I know it's Li Xin, Dewan and Zhu Chun's son (Figure 22.1). I can see his father in his strong face and pointy chin, but mostly in his eyes, which are aware and hint at mischief. A similar face emerges from the door. Where Li Xin's face is a younger version of Dewan's, this face is an older, more tired one. This is Dewan's father, Zuyang.

Zuyang gives a slight bow, a smile, and motions for us to come in. We sit at a wood table on wood benches that aren't much wider than a pair of old saw horses. He excuses himself and walks into the next room. I peek around the corner and watch as he stokes the fire beneath a cauldron filled with some sort of sliced roots. He gives the contents a stir. This is the kitchen. There's no running water, but there is a garbage

Figure 22.1   Li Xin and the author.

disposal—two of them. Two hogs lie sleeping on the other half of the kitchen behind a wood gate. Zuyang is cooking for his hogs.

Li Xin stands in the corner with his right arm hanging from his left shoulder, like he's giving himself a half hug. It appears he is having one of those uncomfortable, I-don't-know-what-to-do-with-my-arms moments. He's relieved when a neighbor enters the room, and then another neighbor, and then another. Soon the room is full of neighbors sitting on small wood stools of the size adults in the United States would only sit on if they were clowning around.

They ask me my age and if I'm married.

A slight gasp circulates when I tell them I'm 28 and not married. The spokesperson of the group, Dewan's uncle—whom I'll call Uncle Randy because he possesses that unique quality of shamelessness that my uncle of the same name has—says, "You should be married by now. In the village the common age to marry is 17 or 18."

They aren't so much appalled that I'm not married as they are bemused. I'm a silly foreigner who can't find a wife.

I assure them that I'll be married soon, but I get the feeling they think I'm making this up to appease them. Now that the important stuff is out of the way, Uncle Randy asks me what I'm doing here.

I tell him I'm a friend of Dewan and Zhu Chun, and I pull out the picture I took of them at the restaurant and hand it to Li Xin. He reluctantly takes it and for a moment is lost in the picture before recognizing that it's the center of the room's attention and quickly passes it on to a gray-haired couple. They are Zhu Chun's parents.

"She must be eating well," Zhu Chun's mother says, expressing the cross-cultural concern of every mother who hasn't seen her daughter in a long while. "She's fat."

The group chuckles, and now they all want to see the photo.

Dewan and Zhu Chun have both put on a lot of weight since they last visited the village. It's a commonly held truth that the food in the city is better and more abundant.

The picture is passed from aging farmer to aging farmer. For the most part, the room is missing a generation. A grandma holds her baby grandson, and when he pulls the woman's hair next to them, she slaps him on his bare, dimpled butt. There are grandparents and there are grandchildren, but other than Lin Chang, there is nobody in between.

"How many of you have children who work in the city?" I ask.

Heads nod, and hands go up. They all do. Their children make garments, shoes, computers, and toys. The workers send money home to care for their parents and their children.

The middle class is growing in China, but so is the disparity between rich and poor. The rich are getting richer faster than the poor are getting less poor. Seven hundred million people live in the vast Chinese countryside. They earn less than $600 per year and are nowhere near to becoming middle class. The middle class in China have a household income of at least $10,000 per year and work as professionals in the major cities. Conservative estimates put the size of the middle class at around 5 percent of China's 1.3 billion people. The China that we see on television, that we visit, where our stuff comes from is not the China that the majority of people live in.

This is that China.

They are China's farmers, brick makers, and factory and construction workers. They are China's rural poor who love the countryside, but dream of the city.

The photo is passed to Zuyang.

"Do you know what your son does at the factory?" I ask.

He shakes his head no.

"He paints shoes," I say. "He works hard."

"My son," Zuyang says, "has been gone for three years. He earns better money in the city. I'm sure that life is better in the city than in the village, but each has its good and bad."

"Is village life happy?"

"It depends on how you define happiness," he says.

Uncle Randy, not one to stay quiet, jumps in. "Here you can do whatever you want. You don't have a boss."

"In the village," says Zuyang, "the air is fresh, and the sun is strong. In the city, you can buy many things, but you can't buy fresh air."

Zuyang tells me that life is better since the government gave him his farm in 1985. Before that, the government collected his crop, but now he can feed his family with his own crop and sell what's left over.

"We eat most of it," Zuyang says. "I earn about [\$140] selling the rest."

"When you stop farming, who will take over the field?"

He looks around the room and sighs. "Young people don't want to be farmers." Then he slips off to care for the hogs.

"What do you do?" I ask Lin Chang—the only representative of the missing generation between grandparents and grandchildren.

"I'm a farmer now," she says, "but I used to work at the same factory as my brother. I worked there for four years, but quit to take care of my daughter."

"Was it a good job?"

"I was homesick when I was there, but the food was better," she says. "Guangzhou is much more developed, and the living conditions were okay. I worked 15- to 16-hour days depending on the workload. It was easy to save money because I was always working. Life is much better in Guangzhou."

"How many hours a day do you work in the village?"

"Two or three," she says.

"Wait," I say, "if I had a choice between living in a tiny single-room apartment while working 16 hours per day, six or seven days per week in a crowded city far from any of my friends or relatives, or working 2 or 3 hours per day while living in a two-story house in the clean-aired countryside with all of my friends and family, I would choose the country. Why is life better in Guangzhou?"

"It just is," she says. "The pay is better. Guangzhou is modern."

"Why don't you move back?"

"My daughter can't speak the language in Guangzhou, and she would have trouble in school," she says. "Maybe when she is out [of school], I can go back; but now, I must take care of her."

China is roughly the size of the United States, but its regions have been historically and linguistically isolated. The government assigned people to rural areas in the 1950s to produce food for the cities. This delayed an exodus from the fields to the cities, until the system was lifted in the 1980s. The surplus of labor, once prohibited from seeking jobs in the cities, then flocked to the factories.

It was this seemingly endless supply of docile, uneducated rural labor that has led to China's manufacturing success. The restricted movement of its people has also maintained strict language barriers. Cantonese is spoken in Guangzhou, while the villagers speak a dialect of Mandarin. Students in Guangzhou learn in a different language from Dai Gan's.

Who am I to say whether modern is better? I can live in the United States far from any city and have access to reliable electricity, banks, and medical care. I can watch satellite television and get a college degree online. The countryside is modern in the United States. Maybe modern can mean something other than items of luxury and conveniences. Maybe modern can mean being a part of the future. And everyone knows that China's future is not in the countryside, but in the cities.

Dewan and Zhu Chun talked as if they want to return to the village to be with their family and friends. But do they? I want to think that they want to be with their son and that they prefer the peace of the countryside over the commotion of the city. But if their opinion is anything like Lin Chang's, this isn't what they want at all.

The grandparents holding their grandchildren seem to know this all too well. The life they know is ceasing to exist. Their children have left and may not return. Who knows what kind of life awaits their grandchildren?

"Young people want to live in the city," Uncle Randy says breaking the silence. "Someday I'll move to the city."

Zuyang emerges from the kitchen with a twinkle in his eye. "You've been saying you were moving to the city for the last 60 years. It will probably be another 60 years before you do."

Eight of us sit at the small table for lunch. I don't think there is going to be enough room for our bowls or plates or whatever we'll be using. Out come the dishes, one after the other. It's amazing what comes from the small kitchen. Some of the dishes are simple—just beans. But others have multiple ingredients. It's hard to believe they whipped it up so fast.

"Beer?" Zuyang asks.

"Sure."

Zuyang hands the bottles to Uncle Randy, and he pops the tops off by hooking the lips of the caps on the table and pounding the tops with his fist. I'm about to take a swig from the bottle when everyone starts pouring their beer into their bowls. We drink warm beer from bowls.

Eating is not easy. We do so by grabbing food from dishes that might be located at the end of our reach and transporting the bite over the other dishes and arms of our fellow eaters to our mouths. We don't have plates to load or bowls, other than those holding our beer, to fill. My first awkward attempt at a potato on the other side of the table causes them to question whether I need to use something other than chopsticks; but I eventually win their confidence.

This type of eating requires too much strategy and timing. If I want to go for the pig heart across the table, I have to wait until all arms and sticks are clear. (By the way, I don't know it's pig heart until Huang tells me. After that I don't eat any more.)

When everyone is finished, Uncle Randy gets a funny look on his face and says, "Want to play a game?"

"Sure."

"A drinking game?" he says with a grin.

I hate drinking games, but nod "yes" anyhow.

He takes a long drag from his cigarette, puts it out, and then rips the butt off.

"I will hold out a hand and you say if it's in there or not," he says. "Okay? If you are right, I drink. If you are wrong, you drink."

"How much are we drinking?"

"An entire bowl!" he says, laughing.

He smiles and puts his hands behind his back, which causes him to lean out over the table. He giggles and slowly holds out his right hand. I stare him in the eyes and then look at his rough farmer hand swollen from years of hard labor.

I shake my head and wave my hands that it's not in there.

He doesn't reveal it right away, but works the crowd prolonging whatever drama can be had at a midafternoon drinking game.

He reveals his hand—empty.

I win. He chugs a bowl.

The second round, he holds out his left hand. I guess wrong. I grab the bowl with two hands and tilt it back and start chugging. Beer drips from my chin. Everyone laughs.

After a few more rounds, our game ends, and the neighbors leave as quickly as they came. Zuyang throws our leftovers to the hogs/garbage disposals, and Li Xin reluctantly agrees to show me around the house.

The bedroom is opposite the kitchen. Li Xin and his grandpa share the room. A mosquito net is draped over the lone bed, and a heap of blankets are undoubtedly in the same position as when they were thrown off. The room is larger than the one Dewan and Zhu Chun have in the city, but messier. This is obviously a bachelor's pad.

I point to the corner and ask about the TV that is missing a speaker.

"I'm fixing it," Li Xin says proudly.

There are two rooms upstairs. The first has shucked ears of corn piled in the corner and the second, two wood beds pushed together. The outside of the house is shiny, white, and new; it's only seven years old, after all. But the inside is dark and depressing, almost prisonlike with its simple wood furniture and undecorated, concrete surfaces. It doesn't feel like a home at all.

"Nobody has stayed in this room for a long time," he says. "This is my parents' room."

We stand on the second-story porch outside of the rooms and look out over the valley. Birds splash in the pond. Wisps of smoke rise from similar homes. An old farmer pulls some weeds at the edge of a field of corn.

I imagine the optimism the family shared in 2000 when the house was built. I'm not sure what their previous home was like, but it was probably far less permanent than this. You don't borrow money and construct a house of concrete if you aren't of the mind that "this is where we'll spend the rest of our lives." In 2000, Zuyang's wife was alive and well. Li Xin was six. I'm sure they had plans for every room: This is who will sleep here, and this is how we'll decorate it. The beds will go here, maybe a dresser there.

Dewan and Zhu Chun likely knew of neighbors who had gone to Guangzhou to earn money and made plans to go themselves. After a few years of making shoes, they would have the house paid off and would return home to be with their family. At least, that was the plan.

But Zuyang's wife became ill and died, and the medical bills added to the debt they had acquired to build the house. A few years in Guangzhou turned into a few more, which turned into even more. I suspect something else unexpected happened, too: They began to like living in the modern city.

Seven years have passed since the home was constructed for the family of five, but only two remain. Zuyang and his family have farmed the land for decades. He's seen droughts and floods. He's seen the communist government relinquish its control over his crop. He's seen revolutions. But he probably never thought he would see the day when he was a single grandparent of a 13-year-old boy.

If you think the cities of China have changed a lot over the past eight years, you haven't looked at the lives of Zuyang and his family.

CHAPTER 23

On a Budget

I can't afford breakfast this morning. Today, I'm eating on a budget. Not my own, but Dewan and Zhu Chun's. After they pay their rent and send money home to Zuyang and Li Xin, they have a little less than $3 per day with which to eat, buy necessities, and pay off their debt. So my goal is to spend less than $3 on food today.

Guangzhou's Shamian Island is not a good place to try this experiment. It is an island of western comfort that caters to couples from the United States adopting Chinese babies. They eat at places like Lucy's diner, which serves cheeseburgers, apple pie, spaghetti, and a host of other western dishes, where a meal costs nearly $10. The boulevards are leafy and peaceful—everything that the rest Guangzhou is not.

So I'm heading off the island to find cheaper food. I walk past small markets that sell dried sea horses spread out on the sidewalk in front of their shops, meat on hooks, and unfamiliar fruit.

I come out onto a shopping strip. I count eight different versions of American Eagle–like stores. Hip teens and college-aged kids clap their hands and try to lure me in. They play music at speaker-cracking levels or they shout into a microphone. Their marketing tactics do nothing but repel me.

There aren't too many places in the world where you can buy a pig's head and a chicken foot, and walk around the corner to buy brand-name jeans and shoes. Guangzhou is one.

I pass a McDonald's, a KFC, a Pizza Hut, and another McDonald's. I'm okay with walking by, but there is something comforting about these places. I know what to expect, but today they are too expensive.

177

I walk past a restaurant selling New York–style pizza by the slice. I haven't had pizza in months. I consider dropping the whole budget thing, but I stay strong. I'll go there tomorrow.

I turn off the shopping row down a narrow alley when I spy a man toting some Styrofoam boxes—a telltale sign that cheap street food is ahead.

For 50¢, I get a bowl of rice and my choice of two dishes. I pay a woman at a school desk, and she hands me a ticket. The ticket woman joins another lady in a Plexiglas room and then asks for the ticket she just handed me. I point at the scrambled eggs mixed with tomatoes and then at the green beans with some kind of meat; I think it's fish, but it could be pork. No matter what dishes I select at places like this, they always taste the same to me. I just try to choose things without bones and ones that aren't domesticated animals that were once "cute." The woman dishes out my food and hands the Styrofoam container through a little banker's slot in the Plexiglas. I find an open seat on a plastic step stool.

I'm not the first person to attempt living on a worker's budget. My attempt is really kind of pathetic when compared with Jim Keady's, especially when you consider I almost caved for a slice of pizza.

In 1997, Jim was a graduate assistant soccer coach at St. John's University studying theology. For one of his classes, a professor asked him to do a project on theology and sports. He chose to look into Nike's labor practices in developing countries. At the same time he began his research, St. John's University, the largest Catholic University in the United States, was about to sign a multimillion-dollar contract committing their coaches and players to wearing nothing but Nike shoes, clothes, and gear. Jim, who refused to wear any Nike products, received an ultimatum: "Wear Nike or you're out." Jim's career as a soccer coach came to an end, and his life as a labor activist began.

Along with labor rights activist Lisa Kretzu, Jim traveled to Indonesia where he lived on the daily budget of the local Nike workers, $1.25 per day, for an entire month. They lost a combined 40 pounds and, as Jim wrote in an article for Doctors of Global Health. He described how they lived "in a 9′ × 9′ cement box, with . . . two thin mats to sleep on . . . in a neighborhood lined with putrid open sewers, riddled with piles of burning garbage, and pollution you could cut through." The experience left them even more impassioned to raise awareness about the workers, writing, "they are fellow human beings, our brothers and sisters. We will strive to give them a voice, to let the world know that they are suffering and in need of justice."

Jim called the experience an act of solidarity.

Is mine?

I think about this as sweat drips from my brow into my Styrofoam box heaped with rice, eggs, tomato, beans, and fishy pork or possibly porky fish (I'm still not sure which). There is no way I'm going to eat it all.

Solidarity isn't a word that gets thrown around on a daily basis—except among labor activists. There were solidarity claps, the solidarity chant against Coca-Cola, and discussions that often turned to the need for solidarity between the workers and us consumers at the Minnesota SweatFree Conference.

French sociologist Emile Durkheim wrote about the necessity for organic solidarity in an advanced society. He claimed that as specialization of labor increases, the parts of a society rely more heavily on one another like organs in a body and therefore create stronger social bonds among them. For instance, a hunter/gatherer in 10,000 B.C. could make his own tools, clothes, shelter, and anything else he needed to get by. But I can't. I eat meat someone else killed. I drive a truck that someone else built. I wear clothes that someone else made. If I were responsible for making my own clothes, I would probably wear rags stapled together or trash bags taped together. But somebody also made the rags and the staples and the tape.

I'm helpless.

So if we consider the world's population as our society, what role do I play in it?

It's easy to see what role the workers I've met on my quest play. They make stuff. They actually contribute something concrete to our world. I write quirky little stories about faraway places that appear in a newspaper one day and line a bird cage the next. As social organs go, I'm the appendix. I'm here collecting the gum you swallowed, and you really won't notice me unless I rupture.

Jim Keady ruptured big time. You may have noticed him being interviewed by ESPN, HBO, the *New York Times*, among other programs and publications from here to Australia.

I would say some of the attendees at the Sweatfree Conference were ruptured social appendixes, or at least in a stage of becoming ruptured.

But me? I'm no ruptured social appendix.

My experiment eating on Dewan and Zhu Chun's daily budget isn't an act of solidarity. It's just about fulfilling my curiosity about how far $3 will go in China.

Is solidarity possible? The world was a much different place as Durkheim's idea of solidarity began to take hold at the turn of the twentieth century. The labor movement in the United States was fighting for a minimum wage and a 40-hour workweek. Workers rioted at Chicago's Haymarket Square. Labor Day was created. The country was collectively appalled by the Triangle Shirtwaist Factory fire. The workers fighting for their rights were our countrymen. We shared a flag, a language, a culture, and a passion for baseball. Workers' lives weren't much different from other Americans'. It wasn't hard to imagine what the lives of the people who made our clothes were like. In a sense, they were us. Producer lived with consumer.

But we share little with the people who make our clothes nowadays. We're divided by oceans, politics, language, culture, and a complex web of economic relationships. It doesn't affect our daily lives if they are overworked and underpaid as it did during the turn of the twentieth century. So we don't think about them much, and they don't think about us much. We hardly seem to belong to the same organism.

I stare at the bottom of the Styrofoam box with only a few grains of rice scattered about. I can't believe I ate all that. Then it hits me: Maybe my sole function in our global society is to consume.

Maybe, by not eating or buying what I want when I want it, I'm not upholding the only function I have. I'm tearing at our social solidarity.

It's not a happy conclusion, but I can't seem to find any other at the bottom of the box of rice. I'm a mindless voiceless consumer wearing the clothes of mindless voiceless producers. But it just doesn't seem fair that Dewan and Zhu Chun have to work so hard for so little and I, who serve little function, work so little for so much.

A small street-side restaurant where a heaping plate of lunch costs less than a videogame at Chucky Cheese just doesn't seem like the right place to ponder my consumerhood.

But I think I know a better one.

CHAPTER

24

An All-American Chinese Walmart

This isn't your typical all-American Walmart. For starters, it's in China. Foshan's Walmart Supercenter is located a short bus ride from Guangzhou. After devouring my lunch, I decided to come here on a little pilgrimage. As the world's largest retailer, there might not be a better place than Walmart to ponder the gap that exists between Chinese producers and American consumers.

If it weren't for the familiar blue-and-white sign on the side of the building, I would have no idea that this was a Walmart. There's no parking lot filled with cars and RVs, and no trampolines or inflatable figures lining the sides of the building.

I pass beneath the sign and enter through glass doors that don't open automatically.

"Nihou," says the young girl, wearing blue jeans and a blue sash with a yellow smiley face on it (Figure 24.1). It's the Walmart smiley face, and she is a smiling Walmart greeter. But this isn't Walmart. It's a three-story mall with clothing and jewelry stores. The speakers play mall music, and the place smells of clean floors and mall perfume. There's a McDonald's and a KFC.

"Walmart?" I ask.

She points to the far end of the room where I see another blue-sashed greeter.

Figure 24.1   A greeter at Foshan's Walmart Supercenter.

"Nihou," says greeter #2. She stands at the top of an escalator that carries shoppers into the basement.

At the bottom of the escalator, I am met by Walmart greeter #3. Like the other two, she's a young woman. None of them would make it as a greeter in the United States. We like our greeters old and friendly. The girls aren't unfriendly, but it seems as if they've been stationed in a spot and given strict orders to smile. They're a bit stiff. I doubt they've ever ruffled a youngster's head of hair or pinched a baby's cheek.

"Supercenter" seems like an exaggeration. The ceiling is too low, and the aisles are too narrow. We have Kmarts larger than this in the Midwest.

A man handing out samples of some drink motions me over as a family of three walks away. The little boy stops and stares, and his parents urge him along until they see what he is staring at—me—and then they join him. I suppose seeing an American in a Chinese Walmart is akin to seeing an NBA star at your local gym or the pope at your church. The man hands me a paper cup. I ham it up for the family by giving the contents of the cup a sniff and then raising it to their health. Bottoms-up. It's a type of aged apple cider with the unexpected kick of whisky. Part of it goes down the wrong pipe. Thankfully, there's a moment before the choking starts, and I'm able to make the proper laryngeal preparations to keep it from squirting out my nose. It's like watching that NBA player at your local gym miss a wide-open dunk or hearing the pope at your church say, "Oh shit," when he drops a host.

I cough my way over to electronics and admire the flat-screen TVs that cost over $1,000. Who buys these? "Rich people," I think to myself, somewhat disgusted.

In Bangladesh, anyone with a car was rich. In Cambodia, I rolled my eyes at the residents living in gated mansions with guards. I always questioned how they earned their money and whom they had to step on to get it. I always seemed to forget how much more I had in common with the upper class of these countries than the workers with whom I spent my time. I'm an average American, and the workers are average Bangladeshis, Cambodians, and Chinese; but our averageness isn't relative.

One of the first things Annie and I purchased upon moving into our new home was a flat-screen TV. Our house has a large, open living room, and Annie's 19-inch TV that's been with her since her college-dorm days looked kind of silly sitting in the corner. It's been months since I've seen the new TV, and I have trouble remembering how many inches it is or if it has a LCD or plasma screen.

And all of it seemed so important at the time.

This might sound silly and shallow, but looking at these TVs makes me a little homesick. I don't miss the TV, but I miss lying on my end of the couch and Annie lying on hers, our legs tangled together in the middle, both of us falling asleep.

Annie has kept me up to speed on what I am missing on the TV. Jordin Sparks won *American Idol* while I was in Cambodia. I didn't miss *American Idol*, but I missed rushing home to watch it, critiquing contestants, and Annie and I sharing a glass of grape juice and a bowl of popcorn. I missed the NCAA Men's Basketball Final Four while I was in Bangladesh. I didn't miss the game as much as the conversation Dad and I would have had as we watched it in his basement. I missed having to wake him up for unbelievable plays and key moments.

In the appliance section, I marvel at how small the fridges are. The largest fridge in the store is about two-thirds the size of the one my parents bought us as a housewarming gift. I miss the ice and water the fridge dispenses and how Oreo, our cat, would come running to beg for a few ice cubes in her water dish. I miss baking frozen pizzas when we were too lazy to cook and too tired to eat out.

I don't miss the *things*, but I miss the lifestyle and the relationships that I've built around them.

I never expected Walmart would make me homesick. While there's a lot that looks familiar, there's a lot that doesn't.

For example, there is only one toy aisle, a quarter of which is taken up by Barbies—all Caucasian. We have Asian Barbies at Walmarts in the Midwest, but they don't have them in China. The hardware and automotive section is only half an aisle.

The fish tanks aren't in the pet section, but in the produce section. A pathetic looking grouper bumps a pair of dead snappers out of the way as it tries to nibble at some food on the surface. A four-foot alligator is on ice, scales and all, displayed like a pig at a feast. A customer waits while the butcher cleaves a hunk of flesh from it.

Snakes slither at the bottom of a dry aquarium. The only thing that might bite you at a Midwestern Walmart is an unruly toddler on a sugar high, not the meat.

In the dairy section, speakers blare remakes of "Who Let the Dogs Out?" followed by "We Will Rock You."

In the back corner near the paint, a group of employees wearing yellow smiley faces chant and clap. I've heard about this. In high school, my buddy John worked at Walmart and before his shift, his shift leader would get John and his coworkers pumped up with a group chant—a Walmart chant of solidarity:

"Gimme a W!" their leader would say.

"W!" They would respond.

"Gimme an A!"

"A!"

For the punctuation between the *Wal* and the *Mart*, the leader would say, "Gimme a squiggly!" and they would shake their butts. At the end, the leader would ask, "What's that spell?!"

"Walmart!" They would respond.

"Who's number one?"

"Customers!"

John told me, "There are a lot of things that I have done in my life that I have tried to forget—and having to shake my ass in that cheer is one of them."

"Hello, sir." A clean-cut man approaches. "I'm Tony. How can I help you?"

Don't let his name fool you; Tony is Chinese. He is every bit as Chinese as the translators who have helped me out here in China. I always enjoy the English names they take on. There was Angel who had the patience of one. There was Pink—a petite girl. And there was Luther, whose rugged manly name contrasted completely to her shyness. All of this reminds me of Spanish class in high school where all of the girls wanted to be Margarita and all of the boys Jesus.

"Where's the shaving cream?" I ask.

"Right this way, sir."

Tony is the store's manager, and his English is excellent. He's been to the United States to train and soon will be visiting a Walmart store in Texas for more training. I tell him that I never knew there were Walmarts in China and ask if it is the largest retailer in the country.

"We are eighth or tenth, but growing," he says. "When I started four years ago, there were 40 stores; now there are more than 100," he says. "This store opened in April. All of our stores are in metro areas. It's not like the United States."

I confirm this statement. We don't have alligators and snakes in the United States, and we do have parking lots.

"Most of our customers come by bus and taxi," he says. "We are introducing them to American-style one-stop shopping. Their habits are much different. In America, customers come to Walmart maybe once a week and buy a lot. Here, our customers might come every day. They come to pick up a small item or two."

As Tony speaks, I grab a bottle of Gillette shaving cream. It was made in China and costs more than my budget of food for the day. I think about that and consider putting it back.

"In the United States," I say, "most things sold in Walmart are made in China. How about here?"

"Of course," he says. "Ninety-nine percent of our products are made in China. We have some exports, but they are often expensive and don't sell well."

"Some people back home won't shop at Walmart because most of their products are made in China. Do people in China not shop at Walmart because it is an American company?"

"Not really," he says, and then relates a story about a customer complaining to a customer service rep. "The customer was trying to return something, and he wasn't happy with the answer the rep gave him. The customer said, 'Why do you work for an American company? I'm your compatriot. You should help me.' And the customer rep told him, 'Sir, this is my job. This American company gives me money to do it. The better question is why you give your money to an American company.'"

Tony smiles, "I think that was a pretty good answer."

I try to learn about the man behind the manager and ask Tony if he is married and has any kids. He says he does and quickly moves on to how exciting Walmart is. He is a man on a mission—and like any missionary, his job is conversion.

Today, the Chinese middle class is roughly 100 million people, but experts predict that by 2020, it will have more than 700 million members—twice the current population of the United States. Sometimes, experts refer to them as the "consumer class." There will be more stuff made in China, more stuff sold in China, and, with dedicated missionaries like Tony converting people to consumerism daily, there probably will be many more Walmarts in China.

"We want shopping here to be a real experience," Tony says. "We have karaoke contests and parties. We like to introduce Western culture to our shoppers. For example, each Halloween we have a party with costumes and pumpkins."

As more and more Chinese move from peasantry in the villages to consumerism in the city, Tony, Walmart, and countless other Tonys and Walmarts will be here to show them the way.

"One last question," I say. "Do you have apple pie?"

Tony smiles. "Of course."

I thank Tony and buy the shaving cream. Walmart greeter #3 smiles and bows as I step onto the escalator with my smiley-faced Walmart bag. In front of me, a woman is weighted down with arms full of bulging plastic bags. So is the woman behind me and everybody else going up. We've prayed at the altar of consumerism.

As much as I hate to see a way of life dying in the villages, I can't help but hope that in 2020 when experts are counting China's booming middle class that Dewan, Zhu Chun, Li Xin, and Zuyang are among them. I hope they can afford to buy a cheeseburger at McDonald's and maybe a nice hunk of alligator with a side of snakes at Walmart.

CHAPTER 25

The Chinese Fantasy

There is big money to be made in the flip-flop business. Pat, my buddy who scolded me on the phone, is the vice president of Global Sourcing for Deckers Outdoor. It is his job to think about the places that make our shoes. He is paid a base salary of $200,000, plus an incentive bonus and stock compensation to do the job.

Pat makes in three days—on base salary alone—what Dewan and Zhu Chun make individually in an entire year at the factory gluing, stitching, and painting flips-flops for Pat to sell to you and me.

When I tell this to Dewan and Zhu Chun, their eyes get big and their jaws drop.

"Whoaaaaaa," Zhu Chun says, followed by, "sheesh."

"Tsk . . . tsk . . . tsk," Dewan says, shaking his head. "We are just small workers in the factory. We had no idea."

"Our salary is too low," Zhu Chun says, "but we can't improve it. This makes me upset, but we don't have the ability to earn that much money."

When I found Pat's contract with Deckers Outdoor on the Internet and discovered his salary, my first reaction was *not* to tell Dewan and Zhu Chun. Maybe it is best if they don't know. And then I thought about it some more and realized that not knowing is the problem—and exactly what Pat wants. The ignorance-is-bliss theory never improved anyone's life. Knowledge is what Dewan and Zhu Chun and the other workers I've met are lacking. You don't know when you are being treated wrong unless you know how you are supposed to be treated.

I feel that I've been somewhat selfish throughout this entire journey. The workers tell me about their world, but I've been guarded when talking about my own. I've done the math in my head while I compare how much I paid for my possessions with their monthly or annual wages.

But this is it, the last night of my quest, and tonight, I'm confessing.

"How much did it cost you to fly here?" Dewan asks.

I tell him.

"Your house is very beautiful," Zhu Chun says when I show her the photo on my cell phone. "How much did it cost?"

I tell her about my first mortgage, and then I tell them about my second mortgage. I tell them about our furnace/AC unit, which just died and the expensive new unit that Annie had to replace it with.

Dewan smiles and pats me on the back. "We are the same—both in debt."

If solidarity, or something like it, is possible in our world of globalization, it is a two-way street. The reason I never discussed my world in depth with the other workers was guilt. But guilt does nothing to inspire change or to help Dewan and Zhu Chun. Guilt is something that we have to move beyond.

I used to think that buying stuff made in China was bad for Americans, but now I wonder if it is bad for the Chinese. The corporations that source in China have a unique influence on the Chinese government. More than anything, China wants to do business with the United States. The big story in 2007 was the MADE IN CHINA toys painted with lead-based paint. There was recall after recall in the United States. The American public was outraged that the Thomas the Tank Engine toys our three-year-olds were slobbering on were toxic. There was also recalled toxic fish and the MADE IN CHINA dog and cat food that killed our pets. To save face, China executed a former chief of their food and drug agency, as if executing a former bureaucrat would remedy the damage done. It was a harsh form of PR: "Look America. We got the guy. Please don't stop buying our stuff."

It's hard to argue with China's results. Over 400 million people have been lifted out of poverty by the fast-growing economy. I suppose not being hungry and not being impoverished are the most important types of freedom—the freedom to survive. But there are other freedoms that the 1.3 billion Chinese don't have.

Teng Biao is a lawyer in Beijing. He has represented activists and farmers stripped of their land. Along with activist Hu Jia, he penned a letter speaking about the Olympics and China's failure to improve human rights as they had promised the international community they would. They wrote:

> *When you come to the Olympic games in Beijing, you will see skyscrapers, spacious streets, modern stadiums, and enthusiastic people. You will see the truth, but not the whole truth, just as you see only the tip of an iceberg. You may not know that the flowers, smiles, harmony, and prosperity are built on a base of grievances, tears, imprisonment, torture, and blood.*

After he wrote the letter, police grabbed Teng Biao in front of his apartment, put a bag over his head and detained him for two days. They warned him to stop speaking out and gave him a taste of what awaited him if he didn't. Hu Jia wasn't as fortunate. He was imprisoned.

I worry that the China Fantasy—economic prosperity yields democratic freedoms—won't become a reality. I worry that Dewan and Zhu Chun will never experience the freedoms that they should, and that the people who speak out for Dewan and Zhu Chun will continue to be repressed.

Today is Sunday. Normally on Sundays the people who make our flip-flops only work until 5:30. I tried to arrange an evening out with Dewan and Zhu Chun to have a little fun—maybe some karaoke, a movie, pizza, and some drinks. I haven't been able to do anything with them but sit and talk, and I always kind of feel like I'm intruding on their nap time. If I worked 16-hour days, you would have trouble getting me to do much of anything.

They declined my offer because Dewan had an appointment to visit a doctor about a pain he was having in his throat. They couldn't go out, but they invited me to visit them for dinner.

Dewan showed up late for dinner. I assumed he had been seeing the doctor. I was wrong.

He had visited the doctor, but then returned to work to finish an important order of shoes. When he returned, he wasn't allowed to clock in. It isn't rare for the people who make our shoes to work for free, as if making our shoes is a privilege. They either work for free, or they lose their jobs. Like all of the other people who make our clothes, they don't have much of a choice.

Zhu Chun leaves the room to retrieve our dinner cooking on the community stoves on the stair landing. Dewan and I laugh and pal around. Later, I won't remember all that we talk about because I've put my notebook away when I started talking about myself. Besides, it's full—the last pages documenting my trip to Walmart. In a way, I'm glad.

The interviews are over.

Like the buyers, the sellers, the middlemen, the brands, the oceans, the continents, the guilt, and the Pats, the notebook was just one more thing standing between Dewan and me. Now there's nothing. It's just him and me—two fellas who couldn't be more different.

And some things don't require a notebook to remember.

After dinner I reach into my bag. "I have something for you," I say to Zhu Chun, handing her a framed picture of Li Xin (Figure 25.1).

"Oh," she says, her voice and expression changing, "he is far too skinny."

It's been awhile since she's seen him, and she loses herself in the photo for a second or two before passing it to Dewan. He smiles and makes a remark about the green scenery in the background before handing it back to Zhu Chun. She puts the photo in a plastic bag and slides it behind the bed, as if it is there to stay. I brought the photo

Figure 25.1   Li Xin and his cousin Dai Gan.

because I noticed on my first visit that there were no photos of their son, which I found odd. Now I wonder if this is on purpose, and if there are other photos of Li Xin tucked away in the nooks and crannies of their room only to be looked at and then put away again. The photos are reminders of what they are working for and, at the same time, painful reminders of what they are missing.

"One thing is for sure," Zhu Chun says. "I don't want him to come here to work in the factory. I just want him to study, because people like us who don't have the knowledge have to work very hard."

"Will you write about us in your book?" Dewan asks.

I don't have the heart to tell him that right now there is no publisher, no book deal, just an idea, but no book, that I hope to give them the voice they've never had, but I can't make any promises. So, I lie.

"Of course I will."

"Do you have a Chinese name yet?" Dewan asks.

"No, I tell people to call me Tim because no one can pronounce Kelsey."

Dewan wrestles with the pronunciation of the L in my name before giving up. "I think your name is very difficult for Chinese people to pronounce. You need a Chinese name."

"Sure."

"How about Xiong Di?" Dewan says.

They walk me through the pronunciation of my new Chinese name, and then I ask, "What does it mean?"

Dewan puts his arm around me.

"It means Brother."

Migration

Each Chinese New Year the biggest migration of humanity on the planet takes place. The stats of the annual exodus are colossal. I can no more imagine what they mean than I can imagine a dinosaur peeing hundreds of millions of years ago.

In 2012, more than 3 billion plane, train, boat, and bus tickets were purchased as 200 million workers made their way back to rural villages to celebrate the New Year.

These workers wait days for tickets; if they are lucky enough to get one, they cram into standing-room-only cars. When they arrive, they embrace the children they've left in the care of older relatives.

"I have been working in Wenzhou for over 10 years," wrote Huang Qinghong, a migrant worker from Chongqing, to his local newspaper, "and I have only gone home once every other year because getting tickets is so painful. My daughter is six now, and I wonder how tall she is now, how many words she knows."

The reunited families clean the family home from top to bottom, sweeping away life's misfortunes from the previous year, making room for good luck. They write spring couplets filled with peace, well wishes, and life's renewal in calligraphy with fragrant ink and hang them on the front door.

The 2009 New Year festival was a bit less festive. *Twenty million* workers lost their jobs—which is like every Australian getting canned. And another 5 million were newly unemployed by March of 2009. Even those who still had a job suffered decreased overtime hours and workdays.

The West was suffering through the worst economic recession since the Great Depression, and orders were down. There were more workers than jobs.

A year later, everything changed.

Overseas demand for MADE IN CHINA has returned, but workers haven't. China's economic stimulus, a reaction to the global recession, created more opportunities for workers inland. More young people were enrolling in universities. By this time, there were more jobs than workers, and wages rose as companies fought over a limited labor pool. In 2010, wages in Guangzhou increased 40 percent and continue to rise 20 percent each year.

Some labor-intensive factories such as shoe and garment factories are moving inland where wages and real estate costs are lower.

"Labor may be cheaper, but the added cost of inland transport can wash away those savings," Paul Midler, author of *Poorly Made in China: An Insider's Account of the Tactics Behind China's Production Game* (Hoboken, NJ: John Wiley & Sons, 2009), wrote in an email. "In the end, there is great value in having factories clustered together. You get a network effect in some industries that is difficult to replicate. Consider that the cost of office rents in Omaha is cheaper than Manhattan; [you still] won't see any relocation of Wall Street as a means to lowering costs. When all the factories moved to Hong Kong and South China, the savings were tremendous. Now, the gap in cost from the coast to the inner provinces is minor. We can still expect Guangdong to remain robust as a center of manufacturing, in other words."

This can only be good for Dewan and Zhu Chun, right? If they are still working in the shoe factory, they are earning 40 percent more. If Dewan's boss tells him to clock out and go back to work, he can tell him to shove it, and go get a job at a different factory desperate for workers. Or maybe they found new jobs near their village, which allows them to be the parents to Li Xin they couldn't be when they lived thousands of miles away.

I can only speculate what their lives are like now. I can't reach Dewan and Zhu Chun. Their number no longer works and neither does the number of Dewan's father, Zuyang.

*   *   *

"Is Pat Devaney here?"

I stood in the office at the Deckers Outdoor corporate head-quarters in Goleta, California. It was the spring of 2011.

"He no longer works here," the receptionist said.

For a moment, deep down, I secretly hoped that Pat got fired because of me. I hoped that my book came out and the CEO called Pat into his office. I imagined the scenario.

"Shut the door," said the fictional CEO. "Have a seat. Pat, do you know a guy named Kelsey Timmerman?"

"Oh, you mean the guy from *Cheers*?"

"No, the only other dude in the world named Kelsey," said the imaginary CEO.

"Nope, doesn't ring a bell, but Kelsey is totally a girl's name."

"Pat," the imaginary CEO said, "your name is *Pat*." Then there would be an awkward pause and the CEO would push a copy of my book across his wide desk. "Pat, you were mean to him and hurt his feelings a little bit when you called him a liar. I'm afraid your behavior breaks our 'No Meany' policy and you're terminated immediately."

After the imaginary scenario played out, I felt bad for Pat. He probably has a family and a mortgage. The housing bubble hit hard in California. How was Pat going to pay the mortgage?

It turns out that Pat is fine. In fact, he popped up in my LinkedIn "People You May Know" sidebar the other day. Apparently, I know six people who know someone who knows Pat. I clicked on his profile and learned that he now works for Stella International Holdings Limited, which entered a joint venture with Deckers in 2008—right before they hired Pat—to introduce Uggs to the Chinese market.

"Could you give this to Jaime," I handed the receptionist my book. Jaime was my other contact at Deckers.

A few days later, Jaime emailed me and put me in touch with Mark Heintz, the company's director of corporate responsibility and sustainability. Mark was the first person to hold the position at the company, and he assured me that his hiring was one of many things that had changed since my 2007 visit.

I asked him if Deckers would like to make an official response to the book. Here it is:

We apologize for any difficulties that you encountered while researching your book. As you said, having a customer travel to a factory to see where their shoes are made is an unusual request that we hadn't gotten before and didn't respond as well as we could have.

Our Corporate Responsibility (CR) Program has come a long way since the first edition of Where Am I Wearing. *Since 2007, we have created a CR department and hired a director to help manage our efforts towards minimizing our social and environmental impact. We've also increased our transparency by making our list of factories public, and creating a CR website where you can find information about various Deckers programs.*

Read the full response at www.kelseytimmerman.com/Deckers. The letter goes onto address their CR program's three main areas:

1. *Fair and Safe Factories.* They monitor all of their key suppliers and factories at least once per year and have established procedures to deal with violations of their supplier code of conduct.
2. *Environmental Stability.* They're making efforts to reduce and monitor their environmental footprint.
3. *Community Engagement.* They've donated $2.4 million and 220,00 shoes to charitable organization since 2006.

I appreciate Deckers' efforts to communicate with me, and publicizing the list of their factories is a big step in the right direction. Are their efforts improving workers' lives? I have no idea. But the balance of power has tilted a bit toward the workers in these times of worker shortages.

I like to think that somewhere in Chongqing or Guangzhou, Zhu Chun is stepping into a Walmart, and she's rocking a pair of pink Uggs that my brother Dewan bought her.

PART

Made in America

CHAPTER 26

For Richer, for Poorer

September 2007

My Grandma Wilt had been a garment worker. In the summers growing up in Versailles, Ohio, she had sewn the pockets on Lee bib overalls. "The more pieces you completed, the more you got paid," she had told me. She didn't like the job and—not surprisingly—the money wasn't very good.

Surprisingly, I never knew this. I had traveled around the world to meet garment workers without even knowing that my very own grandma was one.

She's not your typical grandma. For instance, she's seen every *Death Wish* Charles Bronson has made, and she's a fan of *Walker: Texas Ranger*. But like any grandma, she beamed with pride and smiled up at me from her seat in the front row next to my parents on her grandson's wedding day.

Annie's grandmas sat on the other side of the aisle next to her mom, Gloria. Betty remembers the Great Depression; to this day, it pains her to throw anything away. She has enough canned and frozen goods to survive a nuclear winter. Back then, recycle and reuse wasn't an environmental practice, but a purely economic one. In fact, Annie's other grandma, Clara, used to make clothes for her family and herself from chicken-feed bags.

The fountain in the center of the pool trickled. Despite the dry summer, Mom's flowers were big and bright and Dad's grass green.

White chairs filled with 350 of our closest family and friends were spaced out perfectly on each side of the aisle. It was easy to forget our grandparents' simple beginnings standing in my parents' backyard.

I had thought a wedding with 350 guests was a large one, but I was corrected by my friends in Bangladesh. They measured the size of weddings in the thousands, not the hundreds.

I hate dressing up. But really, this was nothing compared to a wedding in Cambodia. Nari, the aspiring beautician, had told me that weddings in Cambodia lasted a few days and required multiple wardrobe changes. Given that the only thing worse than *being* dressed up was *getting* dressed up, I was thankful to have gone through only one round of cuff buttoning, tie tying, and collar straightening.

The heat was oppressive, and the guests were sweaty. My suit was made in the Dominican Republic. I wondered if anyone else there knew where their sweaty dress clothes came from.

I was comfortable, other than the darn suit, until I saw her.

Annie looked beautiful. Her neck sloped gracefully to her bare shoulders. Her coral lips matched the bridesmaid dresses. She walked arm in arm with her dad, Jim, and she stared up the aisle at me.

The muscles in my face and insides quivered. I grinned so hard I thought my cheeks might cramp.

I'm not sure what it's like for people who didn't date for 10 years or didn't know each other before they could drive. Maybe their weddings were exciting milestones in their lives, a major change. But for me, it wasn't. It was a certification that a decade of silly dances, hello hugs, and good-bye kisses were every bit as real and wonderful as they had felt. Annie had been out of the country only twice, if you counted a day trip to Tijuana; yet she had been with me every step of every trip I've taken. For 10 years, regardless of where I was or where she was, she had been my first thought in the morning and my last at night. The knowledge that she would continue to be these things for the rest of my life overwhelmed me with an emotion I had rarely felt—contentment.

I was home.

Thankfully—before I turned into a blubbery, unbecoming blob of emotion—the thunder brought me back.

I tried to pay attention to the preacher, but I couldn't stop staring at the approaching storm clouds. There wasn't a plan B. If the storm arrived, we would have to move into the garage. I pictured Annie, makeup running, hair flattened, dress drenched, standing between Dad's air compressor and workbench. It wouldn't have been pretty, especially considering that the outdoor wedding was my idea and the only one I contributed to the day. "Don't worry," I had told Annie. "September is the driest month of the year."

The question wasn't *if* it was going to rain, but *when*. The preacher talked about love, marriage, and commitment—things that preachers can ramble on about for days.

"Do you, Kelsey . . ."

I saw a flash of lightning in the clouds and began to count. I remembered learning in the Boy Scouts how to tell how far away a storm was. Every five seconds equals one mile. This is especially important when you're hiking in the mountains where lightning is lethal. Like knowing how to start a fire with two sticks or how to make a life vest out of your pants, it isn't the type of knowledge you want to use on your wedding day.

". . . for richer, for poorer . . ."

"That's kind of relative isn't it? Richer than whom?" I thought. According to the United Nations Human Development Report, 40 percent of the world's population lives on less than $2 per day. If our homeowners' association allowed it, Annie and I could open a lemonade stand and support a life richer than most of the people who make our clothes.

The gap between the world's rich and poor is a relatively new phenomenon. Our grandparents can relate far more closely to the lives of the people who make our clothes than Annie and I. We've never gone without and probably never will—mostly because our grandparents *did*. Our life is built on the hard work and prosperity of the previous generations.

Compared to the rest of the world, Annie and I will never know "poorer."

". . . in sickness and in health . . ."

I lost three of my grandparents to Alzheimer's. I've seen what it means to love in sickness and in health, and how difficult a commitment it can be. Annie's family has a history of cancer. However unfortunate these diseases are, they are ones normally associated with old age. They are the main causes of death in the United States.

The main causes of death in developing countries like Bangladesh and Cambodia are diseases and illnesses that are rarely lethal here, such as pneumonia, tuberculosis, malaria, and diarrhea. Whatever illnesses Annie and I would suffer, it's unlikely that we'll have to watch the other die from an easily treated or prevented disease.

As the pastor finished up his business, Annie got my attention with the widening of her eyes. Through all of the wedding planning—the cake shopping, the entrée tasting, the photographer and DJ interviews, the dress shopping, the scheduling, the song selection, the rehearsal— Annie forgot to plan for perhaps the most important thing—The Kiss.

She did her best to relay her intentions using her eyes, nose, and mouth, but I was lost. Was I supposed to go right? Was I supposed to go left? Was she asking me to really lay one on her?

"You may kiss the bride."

Our journey of 10 years was sealed with an awkward kiss, not unlike the first with which it began.

Happy the kiss was over and the storm held in the distance, we bounded down the aisle, past smiling friends and relatives and teary-eyed grandmas, to our life together, which would begin with a traditional honeymoon to Niagara Falls and a not-so-traditional stop at one last garment factory.

*   *   *

"A Wyoming County woman walking from her car to her house felt a small pain in her back," says the voice on the radio. "The police determined it was a small-caliber bullet."

If you are going to choke on French toast, I suppose you would want to choke on the Silver Lake Diner's French toast; it's that good. I do, as I imagine bored police officers not saying, "Holy crap! It's a bullet!" and instead, "After further investigation of that-there hole in yer back, we've determined it was made by a bullet . . . but just a small-caliber one."

"A small pain?" I say to Annie, sitting across from me digging into her pancakes. "They must make 'em tough in these parts."

We spent last night at Letchworth State Park, home of "the Grand Canyon of the East," a feature that I played up in my sales pitch of this side trip to Annie. This morning we drove into Perry past Murph's driving range and Daryl's Pizzeria. We parked across the street from one of the two restaurants in town named the Hole-in-the-Wall and walked into the diner, which we had noted the day before as a place that looked like it would serve a mean breakfast.

Perry, New York, is surrounded by rolling fields of corn and pumpkin patches. The village has a population of 4,000, one of whom is drinking his ritual cup of joe at the diner's bar and another who drives by in a pickup truck. Four thousand seems like an exaggeration.

It's the third day of our honeymoon. On a normal honeymoon, couples, by this time, are probably overstuffed with fresh seafood, sunburned, and thinking about settling into their first argument. At least, that is what I try to convince Annie.

Perry is southeast of Buffalo and *sorta* on the way to Niagara Falls. If you're thinking that it seems pretty coincidental that the place that made my shorts just happens to be *sorta* on the way to our honeymoon destination, between you and me, it's no coincidence. Annie let me plan our honeymoon.

The first thing I did during the planning process was to call Champion USA and asked them for the location of the factory that produced my shorts. I was pretty sure that had closed by now, but I still wanted to know where it was.

"I don't feel real comfortable with this," said Linda, the Champion employee.

"I have that effect on people," I said, and continued to tell her about my quest around the globe.

Eventually, she caved.

With Annie being the traditional girl that she is, I had packaged the honeymoon to her as "a visit to Niagara Falls: America's favorite honeymoon destination," and then I slipped in the bit about the brief day-or-two side trip to Perry, "a small village nestled in northwest New York's rolling countryside," and the part about the Grand Canyon of the East. I thought I was pretty clever.

She saw right through it. Luckily for me, she has an inexplicable patience for my schemes and me.

We pay our bill and drive to American Classic Outfitters on the edge of town.

*   *   *

There are certain things our nation should be proud of: apple pie, rock 'n' roll, Garfield, Scooby Doo, and my shorts. All were made in the USA.

My shorts are 16 years old. Most people don't remember how old their shorts are, but mine have a birthday: July 26, 1992.

On this date during the Barcelona Summer Olympics, the greatest basketball team ever assembled—the "Dream Team"—stepped onto the hardwood wearing shorts like mine. Michael Jordan had a long pair, Larry Bird's were a little shorter, Charles Barkley's shorts were the biggest around, and John Stockton's were about the same size as mine. There were eight other guys who had a pair. You probably know them all. Through advances in media and marketing, the members of the Dream Team were the world's greatest basketball ambassadors. In 1992, whatever country you were in, you wanted to *be like Mike*.

My shorts are blue with red stripes and white stars running down the outside of each leg, and I don't go anywhere without them. They've been around the world with me several times. In Honduras, Bangladesh, Cambodia, and China they were patriotic pajamas. They're a reminder of home and endless summer days pounding out my own hoop dreams on our concrete court.

I lived and breathed basketball in 1992. Wearing my shorts, I watched the Dream Team with pride as they crushed their competition by an average of 44 points. Afterward, like countless other kids across the country, I laced up my Nikes and got busy emulating Magic's no-look pass, Bird's fadeaway, and Jordan's air reverse—minus the air.

But American kids weren't alone. The Dream Team got kids around the world excited about the game of basketball. Somewhere future NBA MVP's Steve Nash from Canada, Dirk Nowitzki from Germany, and Tim Duncan from the Virgin Islands were emulating the same moves.

And thus the globalization of the game began.

"Finally there will come a day," said coach Chuck Daly during the 1992 Games, "I'm not saying it will happen any time soon, mind you, but it's inevitable that it will happen—that they will be able to compete with us on even terms. And they'll look back on the Dream Team as a landmark event in that process."

That day came at the 2004 Olympics in Athens when the USA men's basketball team finished third, after losing three games and finishing with a bronze medal. Lithuania, a country I can't place on the world map, beat us by a bucket; Argentina won by 8; and US commonwealth Puerto Rico beat us by 19.

The United States was no longer the dominant force of international basketball—a painful fact to accept.

Of course, this wasn't the only thing that had changed since 1992. My shorts were quite different. I can no longer play basketball in them, because the waistband is too stretched; they fall around my ankles if I jump or run. Sixteen years is a long life for a pair of shorts.

Recently, my brother bought me a new pair of team USA basketball shorts, but they won't replace my favorite shorts (even though they don't fall to my ankles when I jump). They haven't been anointed with years of sweat. They don't remind me of a time of youthful innocence when I thought each dribble and free throw put me that much closer to a career in the NBA. Besides, the new USA shorts weren't made in the United States. They were made in China.

My shorts mean a lot to me, but they also mean an awful lot to the workers in Perry, New York, who made them.

*   *   *

As we pull into the Perry Commerce Park, home of ACO, Curves, and a nonprofit organization that assists disabled people and their families, I immediately recognize that this garment factory is different from all of the others I have visited. The 200,000-square-foot building sits beyond a sprawling parking lot. Though I doubt any research has been done on it, my guess is that 99 percent of the world's garment workers don't own a car. However, they do here. Cars occupy the two nearest rows of parking spaces, leaving most of the lot empty. Knowing how kids from small towns think—having been one myself—I would bet that this is the best place in town to do high-speed donuts in the snow when winter comes.

The sign in the lobby says: "American Classic Outfitters Welcomes Kelsey and Annie Timmerman."

It's the first time we've seen Annie's new name in print. It's as if the wedding, the reception, and the heaping truckload of wedding gifts didn't get the point across in the same way this sign did. We are married.

A reporter from the local newspaper named Lorraine greets us, and it's obvious how excited she is that we came all the way to Perry to see where my shorts were made. She doesn't act as if this is a weird thing to be doing at all. She thinks it's neat. I like Lorraine.

A plate of cookies and an ice bucket of soft drinks await us in the boardroom.

"The cookies are made by Archway on the other side of town," says ACO's president Mark, who is sitting at the head of the table.

"I always tell people," Lorraine says, "that the south side of town smells like cookies and the north like manure."

"I'm not sure if it's true," Mark says, smoothing out his gray moustache, "but they say that Wyoming County has more cows than people."

Annie and I, born and raised in rural Ohio, can easily relate to life in Perry. The people are the kind of nice that city slickers don't know—small-town nice. Really, they're not people at all, but *folks*—and Lorraine, the newspaper reporter, and Mark, the company president, are good folks.

Over Archway cookies and chilled Coca-Cola, Mark tells us the story of ACO.

Sara Lee bought Champion in 1989 and began downsizing and making factory consolidations. At its peak, this factory employed 850 people, and the parking lot would have been full. In 2002, Champion left town and moved the production to Mexico. ACO moved into the factory with 11 employees.

"ACO was born out of the ashes of Champion by Sam who owns the furniture store in town," Mark says. "Sam didn't know much about the apparel industry. He just knew when Champion left, Perry took a hard hit. There was a void to fill."

Mark wasn't one of the "original 11." He had worked for Champion for years, but followed the industry to North Carolina where he received a call one day from his former secretary Sue. At the time, ACO's vice president, Ed, was battling cancer, and Sue asked Mark if he would be interested in coming back to run things.

"Ed thought he was going to beat the cancer," Mark says. "Sam didn't have a contingency plan. When I came to visit for the day and saw the same people I worked with in the same office I had worked in . . . that's what did it for me. I came back for the people. Definitely not the weather."

"It's not that bad," says Sue, who pokes her head in the door.

"This past winter was awful," Mark says, through a laugh that trails off. "That thing about not being able to go home again . . . it isn't true."

In 2006, Mark traded in the mild Carolina winters for the harsh environment of northwest New York. ACO had 34 employees when he returned; but now, thanks to a multiyear contract with Adidas for custom uniforms, the company employs 120 and is still hiring.

Mark leads us out of the office and stops to officially introduce us to Sue. She's worked in this building for 28 years—first for Champion and now for ACO.

In the mass-produced apparel game, US garment factories struggle to compete, so ACO found its own niche. As Mark guides us through the factory, he tells us what makes it successful.

"The difference between our product and the other factories is the difference between buying something off a rack and having something made by a tailor," he says, stopping next to a woman sewing the name on Jason Kidd's jersey. "The factories overseas do runs of tens of thousands. They aren't interested in doing a run of two dozen. This is our niche. If a team needs a replacement, we can make it for them and have it to them fast."

ACO makes the uniforms for 16 of the 30 NBA teams, all of the WNBA, 73 colleges, 3 NFL teams, and many high school teams. The Jason Kidd replica uniforms that fans wear in the stands are probably made in a factory overseas, but the one Jason Kidd wears is made right here in Perry.

A man in the corner with tattooed arms traces a pattern with a saw atop a small stack of cloth. It reminds me of watching the workers in Bangladesh cut huge stacks of cloth with what appeared to be gigantic electric bread slicers. The process here is the same for the most part, although scaled down quite a bit. The lighting, the air, the safety markings, and the overall factory conditions aren't that different; but the feel of the working environment is. Employees listen to iPods and have family photos at their decorated workstations. They snack on open bags of chips. They *smile*. At the other factories I toured, I tried not to look at the workers for fear that any interest in them would cut the tour short. They, in turn, focused intently on their work as their boss and I hovered over them. In Perry, Mark greets each employee by name and spends a few minutes chatting with them about their families. He asks them how many years they have making garments, and the number seems to vary between 20 and 40.

We stop beside a woman lining up the numbers of a Buffalo Bills jersey beneath a heat press. Mark waits until she has lowered the press and removed the jersey. "Did you see the Bills game against the Broncos this weekend?" he asks. "It was raining, and the tackle twill was running from the Broncos numbers."

"Glad those weren't ours," she says, as she lines up the numbers of another jersey that she guarantees won't run come next Sunday.

Mark explains the process of cutting, stitching, printing, baking, and pressing, and how it's becoming more complex all the time. One uniform might have several different types of fabric—some that wick, some that stretch, and some that do both. It's not easy matching colors across the different fabrics. He credits ACO's success to the decades of experience that most of the workers have. Many of their competitors focus only on the uniforms for a sport or two, but ACO's workers are familiar with the intricacies involved with many sports uniforms.

Standing beside a machine that looks like a pizza oven with a conveyor running through it, Mark introduces me to a red-haired woman wearing blue jeans and a Notre Dame polo shirt made by Champion.

"This is Debbie. I believe she was here when your shorts were made."

I hand her my favorite shorts, and she examines them with a knowing eye.

"Yep, I remember those. I sewed them," she says and continues on with an explanation of how they were made. She even points to the areas of the factory where each process took place. Many of the areas she points to are unlit. Like the parking lot, much of the factory floor is unoccupied.

In Honduras, I was fairly certain that my shirt was made in Delta's Villanueva factory, but probably not by Amilcar since he had worked there for less than a year. Finding the exact factory in Bangladesh that made my underwear was impossible. The factory in Cambodia that made my jeans had closed. In China, there were several factories that produced flip-flops like mine, so I couldn't be certain where they came from. But here, at last—in Perry, New York—I've found the factory that made my shorts—and the person who made them.

I could hug Debbie.

It's a homecoming for my shorts (Figure 26.1).

Debbie has been in the business for 28 years. The job was supposed to be a filler between college and whatever she decided to do, but the money was good—so she stayed. For years, Debbie and her coworkers worried that each day at Champion might be their last. "They would have had to push me out the door to get me to leave," she says. The day after Champion finally closed their doors, she started working for ACO. If not for ACO, she's not sure what she would have done.

My shorts are passed from one woman to the other. They each tell me what hand they had in making my shorts. Donna has been making

Figure 26.1 The author with Mark, the president of ACO, and Debbie, who made the author's shorts.

apparel for over 20 years. She walks me through the printing process of affixing the stars to the legs of my shorts.

Maxine, the production control manager, joins us. She's worked here for 37 years. "I told my husband that I was only going to work for a few weeks . . . but here I am so many years later," she says, and then after asking my age, she marvels, "I've been making clothes since before you were born."

In a country where what you do often defines who you are in the eyes of others, these women—and this town—have fulfilled a definitive role: to make clothes for others. They've been doing it for decades. Although their way of life was threatened when Champion left, the vision of furniture store owner Sam, the hard work of the "original 11," and a community coming together has made this factory operational once more.

"I'd like to thank you all for making my shorts, but I do have a few complaints." Maxine hands me the shorts, and I pull at some loose threads and point out a place where the fabric is separating. "I've only had them for 16 years and look."

They laugh. They're proud of my shorts. They're proud of the job they had with Champion that allowed them to buy their homes and send their children to school, but they're proudest of ACO.

ACO is growing and looking for the next generation of American garment workers. As the months go by, the parking lot is a little less empty and the factory a little more lit. A new sewer starts out at $8.50 per hour plus benefits. They make more in a single day than Arifa in Bangladesh and Nari and Ai in Cambodia make in a month. In two days, they make more than Dewan and Zhu Chun. The workers aren't wealthy, but they aren't poor either. The people of Wyoming County and Perry are resilient and tough enough to have battled back from the void that globalization left in their community. What else could you expect from a county where a woman gets shot in the back and refers to the injury as a "small pain," as if the bullet were a mosquito and the wound merely an inconvenience?

Before we leave, I ask Mark, "What does this factory mean to Perry?"

He takes a deep breath. I imagine he's considering the Champion years when the factory was hopping and the devastating job loss when the factory closed.

"It means the future," he says solemnly and nods to emphasize the importance of his statement. "It gives the town a future."

Restarting, Again

Believe it or not, Annie and I are still married—even after a honeymoon that involved visiting a garment factory. Some might wonder if their spouse was "the one" for them. I'm constantly reminded by members of women's book clubs, by college co-eds I meet while speaking at universities, by Annie's friends, and by readers that Annie is "the only one" who would put up with me. I'm not quite sure how to take this, so I just say, "Thanks."

I think the lameness of our honeymoon is a testament to our love. We laugh about it every once in a while, and then Annie reminds me that I owe her a real one.

Perry, New York—the home of American Classic Outfitters (ACO)—will always hold a place in the story of our family. Sure, it wasn't the best way to start a marriage, but it was a great way to end the book: the story of a town that reeled after the loss of the Champion factory and rallied around ACO. Small towns that lose their industrial base can fade away these days, but not Perry. They dusted themselves off and moved forward.

I wish this were still the case.

In November of 2009, my brother, Kyle, e-mailed me a link with a note, "Isn't this the factory you wrote about?"

It was a *New York Times* story about how Adidas was pulling their contract with ACO and that for the first time in the league's history, NBA uniforms would be made outside the United States. Some new-fangled material was coming out of Asia, and they were moving production closer to the source.

"It is flat wrong for Adidas to move the production of jerseys worn by NBA players outside the United States when there are US companies that have done this work so well and for so long," said US Senator Chuck Schumer, coming to the company's defense. "And to do it in this economic climate adds insult to injury."

When we were at ACO on our honeymoon, Mark, Donna, Debbie, Maxine, and everybody else was buzzing about the new contract with Adidas. ACO was required to invest $1 million in upgrades and new equipment, and to produce exclusively for Adidas. But German-based Adidas didn't keep their promise to the American factory.

"I think it's a horrible thing," Donna said. "American teams should be wearing American garments made in the United States."

ACO immediately cut workers' hours 20 percent. Sam, the furniture store owner, sold the company to R. J. Leibe, a St. Louis–based athletic lettering company that had worked with ACO for years.

For a few days in November of 2009, the story of Adidas and the NBA abandoning ACO made headlines in regional and national publications. Then, there was silence. Senators and reporters weren't calling. No one pestered NBA commissioner David Stern or Adidas any longer. The headlines ended, and reality began.

A year later the NBA's new uniforms—NBA Revolution 30— were receiving high praise. According to an NBA/Adidas press release, the uniforms weren't just uniforms any longer; they were "basketball uniform systems" that were 30 percent lighter and dried twice as fast. They helped players be one step quicker and jump one inch higher. (If only I had worn this uniform when I played high school basketball, I could've double my vertical leap!) All 30 NBA teams would wear the new uniforms.

Back in Perry, Donna and Debbie kept their jobs, but 100 other workers didn't. Maxine, who had started as a sewer at Champion and then worked her way up to management at ACO, was one of them. On the Monday after Christmas, Jan—with whom Maxine had worked for almost 20 years—struggled to break the news to her and Marty, another long-time employee.

"It was horrific." Maxine described the day to me on the phone. "I worked the same job for 40 years. I was like a drowning soul in the big ol' ocean. I just couldn't believe that I had lost my job. . . . I thought my life was over. I don't even know how I got home because I was absolutely in a state of shock."

Maxine, 62 at the time, planned on working another four years and retiring at 66.

"I try not to think about the place because it makes me very sad. I thought I was going to retire from Champion and they announced on my 50th birthday that was going away. And then I thought I would retire from ACO and they took that away as well. . . . I gave 40 years of my life to that business and they just said, 'Seeya! Bye!' At 3:30 I was in the building, and at 4 o'clock I was going home."

She looked for other work, but couldn't find it. "I needed something to do. Luckily, with my social security and unemployment, I could volunteer." So she did, at the local elementary school. "I was like a hero when I went to school . . . working with the kids has been the biggest joy of my life."

She couldn't believe how many kids, even kindergarteners, were already at risk. It wasn't like that when her daughter was in school. She attributes it to the stability of the home life.

"Do you think the economy has anything to do with that?" I ask.

"Yes, I do. We have a program at school where they do backpacks for kids. Every Friday night at the end of the day they go and pick up their backpacks, and it might have a loaf of bread or a box of cereal in it. How sad is that?"

Some of the kids call her Mrs. Flint and others just call her Max. "You walk out of there and you feel so good and you know that you helped."

She remembered our visit in 2007 and asked about our honeymoon.

"I still owe Annie a honeymoon since we visited a garment factory and went to Niagara Falls, which is kinda of a lame place to go for a honeymoon."

"Oh," Maxine said, "that's where my husband and I went."

"Well," I said, hand on forehead, foot in mouth per usual, I try to recover, "maybe it was nicer back then. I bet there were less wax museums then, because it's really cheesy now."

"That was 40 years ago," she comforted me. "It is a lot, lot, different than it is today."

Maxine is right. So many things are.

Return to Fantasy Island

November 2011

D riving in Honduras is like NASCAR with canyon-sized potholes and horses. It's not the sort of place where a passenger should hang out the window and let the wind blow through her hair, but that's what Karla is doing.

The oncoming cars ignore the solid no-passing lines. There are no rules of the road, only mild suggestions. Physics is the only law that people follow, and even that is challenged by unlicensed SUVs taking sharp curves. I wind my way through the mountains south of San Pedro Sula, Honduras. When I dare to take my eyes off the road, I'm left staring at Karla's too-tight blue jeans with strained seams and zippered-pockets and her bra strap visible through her sheer black shirt that seems straight out of a Michael Jackson video.

My Spanish is a mess—a mix of college Latin and half-remembered, decade-old high school vocabulary lists. I search for a word—Hell. As in, "What the Hell are you doing?!"

Her shoulders jerk. For a moment I think that she has the hiccups and this is some sort of Honduran remedy. I half expect her to ask me to hold her ears while she leans out and drinks a cup of water upside down. It definitely meets the scare-the-hiccups-out-of-you requirement. Another jerk and I get it: she's carsick.

I pull my Smurf-blue Toyota Corolla into a Texaco station, but it's too late.

There she blows. This has to violate some clause in my rental car agreement. Once she gets the door open, she doesn't get out, but simply leans out as if she's checking to see if we have a flat.

I go into the station and get a few bottles of water. Mainly, I want napkins and a plastic bag. Back at the car I get to deliver a line from the movie *Wayne's World* that I've waited years to deliver.

"If you're going to spew," I say, handing her the plastic bag, "spew in this."

We're unlikely co-riders on an unlikely road trip, heading to the village of El Porvenir—or its English translation, "the future."

Yes, that's right. We're going back to the future.

*   *   *

"Let's call it," Gabriel, my translator said.

I read aloud the phone number I had for Amilcar from the notes from my first trip to Honduras six years ago. I had tried the number before, and it hadn't worked.

Gabriel held the phone to his broadcaster's head. His jaw is squared off, his eyes intelligent, his hair perfectly coiffed. Gabriel is studying journalism at San Pedro Sula University and had been offered a job working as a reporter for San Pedro Sula's Channel 6, but he declined it. He wanted to be his own man. I understood what Channel 6 saw in him, though. Good news or bad, Gabriel was capable of delivering it with a straight face.

The phone rang.

"Hang up!" I shouted. Gabriel did. It was too late in the evening to be making such a call.

I couldn't believe it actually worked. My strategy for finding Amilcar was scattered across my bed—two blurry headshots of him and less than 100 words in my notebook describing our first and only brief meeting. Gabriel and I were planning to head to the factory tomorrow like two detectives on *Law & Order*, hold up the 5 × 7's, and say, "Have you seen this man?" Instead, we just prank called Amilcar at 11 PM on a Tuesday night.

When we called back the next day, a woman answered.

I held my breath. Gabriel greeted her and began his spiel. He spoke too fast for me to catch more than just a few words: *loco, gringo, ropa.*

Crazy, white dude, clothes—the three words just might be the best description of this quest that I've ever heard. As the conversation continued, I hung on every "uh-huh" that Gabriel uttered. I gave him a thumbs-up and a nervous grin. He looked at me blankly.

Too lost in the call to respond, he ran his fingers through his hair and leaned forward. The call went on too long to be a wrong number—she must know Amilcar—but it went on too long to be a simple conversation about how he was still working in the factory and things were swell.

Was Amilcar alive? Was there something wrong?

I paced the room.

Gabriel hung up, "Man, you'll never guess."

*   *   *

"This was Amilcar's favorite dog, Duke," Amilcar's mom said as she showed us into her home. "On Fridays Amilcar would come home drunk, but he would still walk his dog."

The woman Gabriel had spoken with on the phone was Amilcar's mom, and it had taken us a while to convince her to meet with us. At first, she thought we meant her harm. Apparently there's a scam in Honduras in which a caller phones you and tells you that they know where you live, where your kids are, and if you don't give them money, they'll hurt you and your family.

Honduras isn't the safest place to be these days. In fact, the day before I left, the *Washington Post* called it the "Homicide Capital of the World." A paper in Tegucigalpa, the country's capital, commented on a decline in homicides "this week." They measure homicides here by the *week*.

Honduras is geographically and figuratively in the middle of the war on drugs escalating in Mexico and in Colombia. There had been a massacre at the airport a month before I arrived in San Pedro Sula. Upon reading about it, I posted on Facebook: "Things u don't want to read about the airport u are flying into tomorrow: 'after the massacre last week . . . a place to be avoided at any cost!'"

Gabriel asked why I had posted this when he saw it. After all, he pointed out, "That was like a whole month ago." Apparently a shooting at the airport in which six people were killed is water under the bridge after a few weeks. In the short time I had been in Honduras, I had a meeting cancelled with a professor at a local university after his colleague was shot and killed leaving a bank. The brother of one of the workers at my guesthouse had his car stopped, was shot 20 times and was now just barely hanging onto life. Perhaps nothing sums up the level of crime and violence better than Garbriel telling me about how he had been robbed at gunpoint while carrying the body of his recently deceased grandfather from his home.

I always tell people that the world is safer than they think it is. Not Honduras. Not now.

"How big of a target is a gringo?" I had asked Gabriel, expecting him to say that tourists were left alone and that it was mainly just gang rivalries, and that a dead or missing gringo is often more trouble than it's worth. You know, that kind of thing.

"A big one!" he said. Very reassuring.

Honduras is a dangerous place. It's the kind of place where people just disappear. It's the kind of place where if a strange foreigner calls you saying they know your son and they want to visit, you do your homework. You Google. You Facebook. You ask for photos proving it.

Eventually, Gabriel convinced Amilcar's mom that we were good guys, and she agreed to meet with us. We drove to her house a few miles down the road from the Delta factory where I first met Amilcar.

Duke greeted us on the porch, held there by a thin, almost decorative chain attached to a thick leather collar. He dutifully barked at us before returning to his rest. Amilcar's mom sprayed medicine on a large gash on Duke's back, and then led us into her home.

Three dogs on the back porch joined in on the barking. Amilcar and his mom were dog people.

She showed Gabriel and me in and invited us to sit on a velvety floral print couch that reminded me of my grandma's. I watched a lot of *60 Minutes* sitting on a couch like that. Amilcar's mom sat in chair next to the door with a white cat curled on the arm. She fiddled with a cough syrup shot glass—a tiny bit of blue backwash swirling the bottom. Karla, Amilcar's older sister, joined us on the couch.

A portrait of Amilcar's father in a plastic black frame couldn't have been hung higher; it was jammed against the ceiling. He died 11 years ago. When I met Amilcar, he told me he lived with his parents—not his mom and the memory of his father. It was a reminder of how little I knew about the man who had become a legend in my mind. All of this started with Amilcar.

I pulled *Where Am I Wearing?* out of my bag and read from the acknowledgments, "Most of all I'm indebted to Amilcar, Arifa, Nari, Ai, Dewan, and Zhu Chun, who let me into their lives and put up with my questions. This book is as much theirs as it is mine."

I handed the book to Karla, and she thumbed through it.

"Thank you," she said. "You are giving it to me, but it's like you are giving it to Amilcar. I'm going to take good care of it."

And then I pulled out the only proof I had of our meeting: a shirtless me giving a thumbs up with one hand and the other resting on Amilcar's shoulder. Amilcar has an arm around my waist, and is wearing my Tattoo T-shirt. We're both grinning like we're long lost amigos, both completely unaware of the paths our lives will take following our meeting.

I showed the picture to Amilcar's mom and told her the story of how I arrived at the factory and asked the beer-bellied guards with pistols down the back of their pants for a tour. She laughed, and her laugh became a cough.

"I was about to give up." I said. "Nobody was stopping. Hundreds of workers walked by me. It's like I was invisible, but then Amilcar stopped."

"I'm not surprised," she said. "He's friendly."

She stood and pulled a Winnie the Pooh photo album off the entertainment center. On top, an Indiana Jones Christmas ornament rattled. She flipped open to a photo of a scrawny little boy—all ears and smile.

"This is Amilcar in sixth grade . . ." she said, coming to life despite her cold. "When he was in school, he would tell me he was going to class, but he would hide his books under a tree and play soccer." Again her giggle turned to a cough. "He was a little rebel. In seventh grade he didn't want to go to school any longer."

So at 12 years old, Amilcar moved from their village near Tegucigalpa, the nation's capital, to Villanueva. He followed in his older sister Denia's footsteps. She had moved to Villanueva at 15 to chase a guy, and eventually got a job at a garment factory. And with her, yet another family began the exodus from farm to factory.

"They moved to Villanueva," she said, "looking for a job. I was worried about my children. So I followed them."

Karla also works at a nearby garment factory—Gildan. If you have a T-shirt collection of any size, chances are good one of them is a Gildan. They are the leading producer of screen-printed shirts in the United States and Canada. The company has a worldwide workforce of 30,000, and even sponsored a college football bowl—The Gildan New Mexico Bowl.

"I've been there for six years," Karla said, "and I'm bored. Gildan has a nice working environment. We work in teams. The more we produce the more bonuses we get. If my team does well, we get [around $65] per week. If bad, we get the minimum [$54 per week, or $1.31 per hour]. Plus we have insurance and retirement deducted. Last week was excellent, but my last shift was bad."

Karla is paid too much.

At least, according to The Honduras Council of Private Enterprise (COHEP). They calculated a minimum living wage in Honduras to be $232 per month. They came to this number by looking at the monthly cost of 32 necessities for a family of six. The worker unions think the minimum living wage should be $333.

Regardless of how much under or overpaid workers are, a 2010 study conducted by the Honduran government in conjunction with the European Union reported that 72 percent of Hondurans— 5.7 million people—didn't have their basic food needs met. Another 1.5 million Hondurans were able to adequately feed their families, but didn't have enough to cover other basic needs like housing, health care, education, and transportation.

Still, wages in Honduras ($1.31/hour) are higher than in Nicaragua (65 cents/hour) and El Salvador (92 cents/hour)—and many fear that the garment industry will leave the country to seek cheaper wages elsewhere. A lawyer at the Committee for the Defense of Human Rights in Honduras (CODEH) told me he thought the garment industry would be gone in two years. This is a doomsday scenario for sure, considering approximately 130,000 people are employed by the industry, but there are layoffs, and factory closings prove that the industry is heading in that direction. Twenty-one factories left for neighboring countries, and 10,000 jobs were lost over a seven-month period in 2011.

In January 2009, Russell Athletics closed a factory in Choloma, Honduras, and put 1,200 workers out of work. The decision to close came on the heels of the workers forming a union. This did not sit well with the United Students Against Sweatshops (USAS), who had fought for codes of conduct—including the right to unionize—in the factories that produced licensed apparel for their schools. The Worker Rights Consortium, an independent monitor formed by labor activists, the USAS, and university administrators released a report calling the closure a flagrant violation of the code of conduct. So USAS sprang to action. They picketed the NBA Finals, knocked on Warren Buffett's door in Omaha (his company, Berkshire Hathaway, owns Russell's parent company, Fruit of the Loom), and, most importantly, successfully pressured universities to drop their licensing agreements with Russell. Duke, Georgetown, University of Miami, Wisconsin, Rutgers, and more than 100 other schools in total announced they were ending their licensing agreement with Russell, because USAS hit them right where it counted—in the pocketbook.

Russell announced less than a year later that they were rehiring all 1,200 workers in a new factory. In May of 2011, the union negotiated a

26 percent pay increase, the purchasing of new equipment to increase production numbers, free lunches, and third-party freedom of association trainings at all of the Russell and Fruit of the Loom plants. This kind of thing doesn't typically happen in Honduras; it shows that when producer and consumer unite and work together, they can accomplish great things. The student movement recorded its largest victory to date.

USAS followed it up with a "just pay it" campaign against Nike. Two factories that produced Nike apparel had closed without paying their workers the severance pay the Honduran law requires based on years of employment. So once again, students protested. The University of Wisconsin canceled their agreement with Nike, and Cornell University threatened to follow suit. Yet another company was getting kicked in the bottom line. Eventually, Nike agreed to pay $1.54 million into a workers' relief fund—despite the fact that they maintained they didn't own the factory and weren't responsible for paying severance to employees of a separate company.

Like most of the workers I talked to, Karla was happy that unions existed, but would never join one. She knew joining would likely help her get paid more and make her job more secure. However, she feared that if she did lose her job, she'd be blacklisted by all of the other companies and unable to find a new one.

"I'm a single mother, and this scares me," Karla said. "[The garment industry] is the only employer here in Villanueva."

I met workers who had recently lost their jobs after a situation very similar to the Russell and Nike ones: the workers started to unionize, and then the factory closed without paying severance owed. Unfortunately, there were no students in the United States protesting this time. The factory produced kids' clothing, and toddlers weren't conducting sit-ins. The parents who bought the outfits were likely too busy with their toddlers to even become aware of the violation.

Parents everywhere concern themselves with being parents. The workers who lost their jobs are no different. They are fighting to get their severance and trying to think of a way to provide for their children. Karla is no different.

She confesses, "I've heard rumors that the jobs are moving to El Salvador and Nicaragua because our wages in Honduras are the highest in Central America. Even if Honduras has the highest salary, I only make [$65] weekly, but I have to pay utilities, telephone, rent, and send my daughter to school."

If you don't work in a union, your job is at higher risk. If you do, you risk not being able to find another job. If you are the average worker or Honduran, you can't even provide enough food for your family.

The "opportunities" in Honduras are barely opportunities. They simply reduce your level of not being able to get by.

"Who's the beauty queen?" I point to a loose photo in the album of a 12-year-old girl being escorted down the aisle by a young boy sporting a clip-on tie. She's wearing a frilly white dress that seems to have been stitched from a cloud.

"This is Amilcar's daughter, Genesis," Karla said.

Amilcar has kids! In fact, when I met him, he had two daughters and a third on the way. He didn't mention any of this to me, but I suppose you don't reveal everything to a shirtless stranger whom you meet for 10 minutes. Genesis, lives in the family's home village, El Porvenir, with her mother, Jolanis.

As I flipped through the photo album, Karla added the verbal captions. This was Amilcar's youngest daughter, Betsabe, five. His middle daughter wasn't pictured. Jolanis, his long-time girlfriend, and Amilcar had separated for a few years and Amilcar fathered a daughter, Karen, eight, outside of their relationship. Here's a birthday party, there's a family gathering, here's a graduation. A life and a family were revealed one photo at a time.

Every once in a while, Amilcar's mom would chime in with an Amilcar story of her own.

Amilcar had a drinking problem, but he was a good dad and brother when he wasn't drunk. He loved his dog and his mom's tortillas. His marriage fell apart, and then they tried to work things out. He was a good worker, but life as a garment worker was not enough.

Too often we objectify people living in poverty. We paint them as two-dimensional characters that we pity. I was guilty of this when I first met Amilcar in the sea of workers rolling out of the factory. I felt sorry for him before I even met him. I was scared of what his life was like and wandered whether my lifestyle was complicit in the state of his. All I learned about him was that he was 25, lived with his parents, and liked to play soccer.

Yet each and every one of us, whether a garment worker or tycoon, is a complex person with dogs and flaws and passions and problems.

After I convinced her that I'm a capable driver, Karla agreed to go with me to visit their family in El Porvenir.

One thing was certain: Amilcar was sorely missed. The family's stories about him often concluded with laughter, followed by sighs. The relived moments gave way to the reality: He was gone.

"He seems like a really good guy," I said.

"He's a good guy," Karla added. The room went silent but for the driving rhythm of the salsa music coming from the computer next to the TV on the entertainment center. "He's a good guy."

I flew all the way from Indiana to track down Amilcar. Gabriel was right; I would never guess what Amilcar's mom had told him on the phone:

"Oh, Amilcar, he lives in California."

He walked there.

*   *   *

I'm not sure that there's anything worse than a carsick backseat driver who has never driven before and with whom you don't share a language.

After four hours of winding our way through the mountains—making several stops for Karla to puke—we arrive in Tegucigalpa. San Pedro Sula is the commercial hub of Honduras, but Tegucigalpa is the capital. The city is sprawled out across narrow, hilly streets that—perhaps as a testament to the effectiveness of the government the city houses—have manholes without manhole covers. I dodge these axle-busting manholes as Karla guides me down a one-way street the wrong way. We're quite the team.

El Porvenir is a two-hour drive north of Tegucigalpa. We pass from city hustle to country tranquility (Figure 27.1). Men on horses wear hats. I guess you'd call them cowboy hats, but that's sort of like

Figure 27.1   On the streets of El Porvenir.

calling a meal in China Chinese food. The hats aren't about fashion; they're about function—block the sun, shelter your eyes from the rain, wave at some cattle, tip at a neighbor. A few men atop their horses gather for a chat where the dirt road meets the pavement. Others trot home on their afternoon commute. The horses pass around potholes and over speed bumps without hesitation. I pass them white knuckled and exhausted in the final few miles of a six-hour drive.

Karla begins to primp herself in the mirror of the visor, so I know we're getting close. We turn off the paved road. She hasn't been back to her home village in two years.

We're a sight to stare at. She nods at pedestrians and shopkeepers eyeing us. That's when it occurs to me what this looks like: Karla returning to meet her family with her gringo husband who didn't have enough sense to rent a truck to handle the sedan-swallowing streets of El Porvenir. She sits up. She waves as though we're in a parade.

I turn into an alley and then into a smaller alley before finally being directed to a stop by a swirling group of bouncing kids. There are cousins and nephews, and nieces of nephew's cousins, and neighbors of aunts' uncles. I lose track of names and where one relation ends and another begins. They all greet us like family.

The front door—a waist-high wood gate—of the cinderblock home is swung open, and I'm shown to the couch and given a fizzing glass of Coke. This is Karla and Amilcar's aunt's house. The living room and kitchen share a long, open room. There's enough furniture to seat at least a dozen, but it's standing room only. Little heads peek over the gate and under the curtains of the paneless windows. Some members of the crowd are simply curious about our arrival, but I get the feeling that this house is the hub of all of Amilcar's family.

I recognize the girl in the back of the room as the beauty queen from the photo in Villanueva. Tight loops of curls sprout from her ponytail and hang down her back. Amilcar's daughter, Genesis, hangs on the arm of a young woman who appears much too young to be her mother. They are both wearing makeup and matching pink shirts. While everyone stares at me with a wide-eyed curiosity, the mother and daughter steal looks in my direction.

"Kelsey," Karla said, "meet Jolanis and Genesis." I stand and shake their hands.

Amilcar called and told Jolanis that a strange American who had just visited with his mom and sister was traveling all the way from San Pedro Sula to meet her. I'm that strange American, and now she's shaking my hand.

Karla, Jolanis, Genesis, and I sit at a plastic table and eat dinner. It's a quiet dinner with not much said other than comments about whether I like the food and Honduras. I give the answers that I always give when I'm asked, regardless of the country: Yes, the food is great, and the people are really friendly.

After dinner, we walk toward the village center down a cobble-stone street. There are no streetlights, but the moon is full and casts shadows of our strolling figures that disappear in the bouncing lights of passing cars. We grab some ice cream and find some benches at a park across the street.

A group of kids chase a donkey off the basketless basketball court and start playing soccer. We eat our ice cream and watch the game. The players are a mix of boys and girls. Some of them are serious about the game, others serious about flirting.

Jolanis and Amilcar were high school sweethearts and neighbors. They went on their first date 15 years ago at this park, holding hands for the first time, their friends likely teasing them. No longer were they playing and chasing and hoping to find that someone to share awkward good-byes with. They had chosen.

"I liked him," Jolanis said. "I made eyes at him." She bats her eyes, and Genesis can't keep from laughing. The thought of your parents flirting is hilarious. "He asked me if I wanted to go out, and I said yes right away. He asked me on a Friday, and we went out on Saturday."

Five years later, they were still together and living with her parents. Soon after, they welcomed Genesis into the world.

Amilcar worked in the fields near his aunt's house with his uncle Jose Antonio, planting and harvesting beans and corn. Jose Antonio said that Amilcar was a good worker. But the early years of their relationship weren't carefree.

"He drank too much," Jolanis says. "He spent too much money on alcohol."

Some nights he wouldn't come home. He would drink the night away and crash at the hotel where his buddy worked. His nights were filled with drunken banter and the clink of empty bottles on concrete. He cheated on Jolanis.

They figured there had to be more than village life in El Porvenir. So they moved to San Pedro Sula where Amilcar worked at several different garment factories. He made clothes for Nike, Puma, and others. The late nights continued. Jolanis and Amilcar separated. He fathered another daughter, Karen, after an evening of drinking with friends. Jolanis and Amilcar reconciled. Amilcar met a crazy, shirtless gringo outside of the Delta factory where he worked. Jolanis gave birth to the couple's second daughter, Betsabe, in 2006.

One of Amilcar's friends had just been deported from the United States back to Honduras and planned to return. His friend had stories about all of the opportunities that await in the United States and that those opportunities were worth risking another perilous journey from Honduras through Guatemala and Mexico. Around this same time, Delta rewarded Amilcar with a $333 bonus for his excellent work in the factory.

He gave one-third to Jolanis, one-third to his mother, and pocketed the rest.

On the morning of March 30, 2007, Amilcar was supposed to meet his three friends at the main road at 6 AM. Instead, he started drinking. He was excited. He was sad. Betsabe wasn't even crawling yet. He hadn't heard her say "papa." Would he ever?

At 7 AM, his friends found him half drunk on the front porch of his mom's house. When Amilcar left, he said good-bye to his family and gave Duke one last pat on the head.

Once he stepped off his mom's front porch, he didn't look back.

"When he left, I felt bad," Jolanis says, sweat, or tears, or both glistening on her cheeks in the moonlight. "He didn't say good-bye to me. [I thought] he's a good man. He'll take care of us."

A lot has happened since Amilcar and Jolanis first held hands in this park.

The basketball court erupts with hollering as a goal is scored. We sit in silence until I break it.

"For Halloween . . . my daughter was a cowgirl," I say, showing them a photo of her on my phone wearing a cowboy hat, a western shirt, and boots with Buzz Lightyear and Woody from *Toy Story* on them. "She looks like she belongs in El Porvenir."

"Oh, beautiful," Genesis says.

"And for my son, we carved out a pumpkin, pulled out the insides, and cut holes for his legs." I show them a picture of my son Griffin inside of a pumpkin. They laugh at the photo, but I'm not sure if they are laughing at the sight or the fact that we stick our children inside of fruit.

My phone intrigues Genesis and her cousin. They sit on each side of me and I introduce them to Angry Birds and then Shrek Kart. To give Shrek a boost of speed, you tap a button that makes him fart. There's not a 10-year-old in the world that this doesn't delight.

"How do you say [I make a fart noise with my lips] in español?"

"*Pedo*," Genesis says, cracking up.

We leave the park and walk to Jolanis's house. Jolanis and Genesis hold hands.

The house is behind Amilcar's aunt's and next to the field of beans in which he once worked. It's constructed of cinder blocks, a tin roof, and a creaky metal door. Inside, a plastic sheet divides the kitchen from the bedroom—the only other room in the home. The toilet is tucked in the corner of the bedroom behind a bed sheet and next to the washbasin. Clotheslines crisscross over the bed and imperfect artwork from coloring books hang on the wall. A TV is tucked in the corner of the bedroom and angled to face the bed covered in laundry.

Jolanis and Genesis live here (Figure 27.2). Betsabe is currently living in Villanueva with family members who have kids her age for her to play with.

This is the house that Amilcar built. The land and the house cost around $8,000, a sum that he could never save working as a garment worker in Honduras.

"The house is finished," Jolanis says, "and now he should come home."

Amilcar sends money home each month to feed, clothe, and send the girls to school. He even sends money to Karen's mother, something that Karla talks about in a way that is above and beyond what the average Honduran male would do.

Figure 27.2 Jolanis and Genesis in their home.

I feel like an intruder in Amilcar's life. Here I sit in the house he's never seen, talking to the girlfriend he can't hold, laughing with the daughter he can't hug. I'm asking Jolanis to reflect on things long forgotten and project a future barely imagined. Amilcar is here in a way he couldn't be if he were actually here.

Outside, bugs hum; a dog barks. El Porvenir is peaceful.

"I'll wait for him for 10 years if I have to," Jolanis says, although she expects he'll return in the next 3.

"What will you say to Amilcar when he returns and you see him for the first time?"

Amilcar and Jolanis have been through a lot. He risked life and limb on an unimaginable journey to get to the United States. She faces each day as a single mom.

Jolanis giggles and looks over at Genesis. She blushes. Thinking of him still brings out the school girl in her.

"I'll say, 'Never, never, never leave again!"

Before I leave El Porvenir, Jolanis hands me a letter.

On the outside of the envelope, she's written, "For Amilcar from Jolanis."

"Please give this to him."

CHAPTER 28

Amilcar's Journey

2007

The Mexican bandits carry machetes and rocks. The American border patrol officers carry guns and radios. Between them, Amilcar and his cousin Edwin stand knee-deep in the Rio Grande with a decision to make: They could escape the bandits by climbing the chain link fence, but be deported, making their two-month life-and-limb-risking journey for naught. Or they could try to escape the bandits and cross another day.

They run for the fence.

Amilcar's fingers lace through the chain links and pull—his knuckles white, his fingertips the first part of him to complete the journey of more than 2,000 miles. He hikes one leg over, then the other, and drops into the United States.

He made it.

The bandits close fast and are climbing the fence after Edwin. Amilcar has known Edwin since before he could remember. He was the one who knew the way to the United States. Tired and weary, they had hung onto the sides of speeding trains, hiked through the desert until their shoes were worn through. They had dodged rocks thrown at them from the residents of Chihuahua. They had experienced unspeakable hardships and unexpected kindnesses. And now the bandits were at Edwin's ankles, trying to pull him back into Mexico and do God knows what to him.

Amilcar grabs a rock. He scrapes it back and forth across the chain link fence. The sound is a metallic zip interrupted only by the howls of the bandits as the rock rakes across their fingers.

Sorry about your fingers, Amilcar thinks, *but he's my cousin*.

Edwin makes it.

They enter the United States just as they had entered Mexico— bloody, afraid, and broke.

The border patrol officers greet them: "Where did you come from?"

*   *   *

This wasn't how Amilcar imagined his first night away from his family in Villanueva would go. The robbers had burst through the door of the hotel room, held a knife to his throat, and started to shuffle through all of his belongings stuffed into his brown backpack. There wasn't much to shuffle through. He had packed one sweater, two pairs of socks, one shirt, two pairs of underwear, and a toothbrush. He was grateful at that moment for heeding Edwin's advice to not bring any ID or photos.

"They'll kill you," Edwin told him, "and call your family and demand money."

All they wanted was money. In an instant the last of Amilcar's bonus money for his good work at Delta was gone, but all he could think was, "Thank God they didn't kill me."

The thought of turning back didn't even cross his mind. He had to make it to the United States for his babies. Genesis, Karen, and Betsabe were never far from his mind. He still cries when he thinks about hugging little Betsabe good-bye that last time.

Amilcar traveled with three friends, all from El Porvenir: Oscar, "Macaron," who earned his nickname for his love of macaroni, and his cousin Edwin, who had been to and deported from the United States once already.

They traveled from Honduras through Guatemala by bus to the Mexican border. Amilcar's friends paid for them to catch a boat past the border patrol.

Once in Mexico, they walked for three days through the jungle-clad mountains. They walked in the late afternoon and through the evening by the light of their flashlights. Amilcar almost stepped on a snake. They ate cans of sardines and tuna. By the second day, they had eaten everything but a bit of fruit. Their water bottles were empty. They came across dried cow tracks holding small pools of water. Amilcar knelt beside them and scooped palmfuls of dirty water to his dried lips.

They arrived in Tenosique, Mexico, on a Saturday to face "the beast": what the migrants call the trains that they hop on and off as they make their way through Mexico to the United States border. Catching a passing train is dangerous. Migrants, young and old, male and female have lost limbs and lives to "the beast."

Amilcar's shoes were shot, and the balls of his feet were giant blisters. There was no way he could catch the train scheduled to pass at 5 PM. They waited until Monday, sleeping on the streets, buying food at the stands set up specifically for the migrants.

"Migrants represent a lot of money," Brother Storm, a Catholic priest who aids migrants, told Spanish-language news channel Univision, "whether it's for the store owner along the railroad tracks, corrupt authorities and immigration officials, or organized crime."

Migrants are blackmailed, robbed, and raped. The drug cartel has made a side business of capturing migrants and demanding ransoms from their family members already in the United States. Mexico's National Human Rights' Commission reported that more than 11,000 migrants were kidnapped during a 6-month period in 2010.

"This is a world economic system that expels and vomits out poor men and women of all ages," Brother Storm said. "The American Dream is a goddamned nightmare."

And for Amilcar and his friends, the dream—or the nightmare—had just begun. "The beast" rolled through town on Monday, and these four men—along with countless other migrants—ran alongside it.

Edwin grabbed onto the train and pulled himself up. Amilcar was next. The beast shook the ground beneath his feet and rattled his insides. He had never been on a train, let alone tried to hitch a ride on a moving one. He gave up. He was too scared. Edwin looked as if he was going to jump off to stay with him, but then disappeared down the tracks.

Oscar had missed the train too, but Macaron zipped by with a look of indecision on his face. He hesitated and then jumped from the train, but his backpack got caught. He dangled from the side of the train as Amilcar and Oscar looked on. He swung wildly toward the wheels—the mouth of "the beast"—but just before he was about to be sucked in, a tree hit him, knocking him free of the tracks.

The next day, the train passed slowly. It was still really loud, but Amilcar concentrated on grabbing it and forgot the noise. The three friends boarded and climbed on top of a boxcar. Every car had more than 30 people riding on it. Amilcar did the math and estimated that 2,800 migrants were on this one train. 2,800 people with 2,800 reasons to be heading north.

After a few hours, the train began to slow to a stop. Everybody started to jump off, fearing that the Mexican immigration officers were doing a check. Amilcar didn't want to jump, so Oscar shoved him from the train. They ran into the 2 AM darkness, tripping and falling over one another. They became separated in the chaos, and Amilcar was alone and afraid for the next hour-and-a-half. He didn't know the way to the United States. What was he going to do?

As it turned out, the train had stopped only for repairs. When it started to roll forward again, he ran from his hiding place to catch it—and bumped into Oscar and Macaron.

"Why didn't you follow me?!" he asked.

"You don't know where you are going!" they said. Laughter turned to tears. Shoulder slaps turned to hugs. They thought they had lost each other. They were incredibly thankful that they hadn't.

They rode the train for three days. They were out of money, but the other migrants from Honduras, Belize, and Nicaragua shared food and water with them. The locals threw food and water to the migrants on the passing trains when they arrived at Veracruz. Both Oscar and Macaron had been to Veracruz before and knew a house that took in migrants. Such houses dotted the way to Mexico—a sort of Underground Railroad that covertly thumbed its nose at the injustice the migrants faced. They had nothing to give in return. Occasionally, they would stop to work a construction job or in a field to earn a little money, but mainly they relied on the kindness of strangers and money wired to them from friends and relatives already in the United States. Whatever money they had was shared. This was *their* journey.

Oscar knew what awaited them: 32 tunnels through Mexico's highest mountain range. He had heard about migrants freezing to death in the tunnels. He called his family, who sent him the $4,500 needed to pay a "coyote"—an individual who smuggles immigrants into the United States—to take him across the Arizona border. The more money you have, the farther out you can start your shot at the border and the safer it will be.

Now, they were two.

Amilcar and Macaron braved the tunnels together. Amilcar's backpack was empty. He wore one sweater, two pairs of socks, two shirts, two pairs of underwear, and one pair of pants—and it still wasn't enough. The two men huddled together for warmth. The train seemed to shake more in the tunnels. The sound and the zero-degree air pounded in their ears until they hurt.

When they arrived to Mexico City, the train workers ordered them off. They were so cold they could barely walk. They clambered off the train and started a fire next to the tracks. Amilcar boiled water for coffee in a plastic Coca-Cola bottle with a hole punched in it to release the steam. He thought it was a great idea until the bottle exploded, blasting scalding hot water on his right calf and scarring it forever. It was the first time he had felt his legs in hours.

It was decision time. They could shoot for Texas, Arizona, New Mexico, or California. Ultimately, Macaron was shooting for Atlanta, while Amilcar had his heart set on New York. They chose to cross at Juarez. They realized after six hours on the train that they were heading the wrong direction. Macaron climbed down and threw the lever that engaged the car's air brakes, forcing the train to stop.

They walked for a day to a village known for drug running to catch a train to San Luis Potosi. Police on horseback spotted them, along with four others waiting for the train. The two friends ran and hid, but the police had dogs that sniffed them out.

"Do you have any drugs?" the officers asked.

"No."

"Are you sure?"

"Yes."

"Take off all of your clothes," the officers demanded.

Amilcar was terrified. He thought for sure that he was going back to Honduras.

The dogs found drugs on the other guys, and the police let Amilcar and Macaron go.

The two friends agreed that no matter what, they would catch the next train. They walked ahead to a turn where the train would be moving slowly.

The train came around the bend, moving really fast, much faster than any of the other trains they had successfully caught. Amilcar ran as though he were chasing down a soccer ball in the open field toward a keeperless goal. He wanted to grab the train, but he held back. By this time, he had seen what "the beast" could do. He had witnessed other migrants lose hands, and he had heard gruesome stories about severed limbs and bodies cut in half.

Macaron hollered behind him. He was safely aboard the last car. Amilcar had to get on. He ran faster. Macaron hollered again. Amilcar looked over his shoulder. Macaron had a grip on the train's ladder with one hand and was reaching out with his other arm. It was a scene right out of an *Indiana Jones* movie. Macaron grabbed him under his arm and swung him onto the ladder.

Amilcar hugged the ladder and Macaron.

"I'm not going to leave you," Macaron said, his eyes filling with tears. "We're going to make it to the United States together."

In San Luis Potosi they stayed at a church that housed migrants and provided food and clothes. From here it would cost $1,500 to pay a coyote to take them across the border. Macaron had the money; Amilcar didn't.

"I'm not leaving without you," Macaron said.

An old woman who housed migrants took them in and helped them find jobs working construction during the day and working security at the site at night. They made $150 per week. After expenses, Amilcar had barely saved any money to put toward paying a coyote. Tired and depressed, the two friends spent what little extra money they had on alcohol and got falling down drunk.

They stumbled back to the woman's house, arm-in-arm, promising, "We will be together through the good and the bad."

After two weeks, Edwin showed up, and the three friends embraced, relieved. Amilcar asked him why he had gone on without them, and Edwin apologized for not jumping off; the train had been going too fast. Amilcar and Macaron told him about Oscar, the freezing train, and the police. Edwin was in Nuevo Laredo and had called Amilcar's mom in Villanueva to check on him. She told Edwin that he was in San Luis Potosi.

Now that Edwin was back, Macaron felt comfortable leaving Amilcar. The two friends said their good-byes and shared one last hug. They had faced a childhood in El Porvenir together, "the beast", the freezing cold, hunger, fear, and despair. Macaron left for Atlanta. It was the last time Amilcar would see him.

Edwin and Amilcar passed through Zacatecas and Torreón. With the help of a cab driver who motioned to a conductor to slow down, they caught a train and rode three days to Chihuahua where the locals threw rocks instead of bread, water, or burritos. They were sick of the migrants.

In her book *Enrique's Journey* (New York: Random House, 2006), Sonia Nazario recounts the journey of a teenager from Honduras to the United States, and reports on the negative attitude toward the migrants:

The Veracruz hospitality has vanished. One Mexico City woman wrinkles her nose when she talks about migrants. She is hesitant to slide the dead bolt on the metal door of their tall stucco fence. "I'm afraid of them. They talk funny. They're dirty."

The cousins ultimately arrived in Juarez. They sat with two Mexicans, and one Guatemalan, all staring across the Rio Grande at the American flag waving in the warm Mexican air. Or was it American air?

They discussed their options: They could jump the fence and make a run for it, or they could pay a coyote $4,000, jump the fence, walk a day through the desert, and then meet a car arranged by the coyote.

They could practically hear the American flag flapping.

They didn't have any money.

They looked east. They looked west. They ran north.

* * *

"Where did you come from?" the immigration officer asks.

"Mexico," the cousins say.

"Prove it. How many colors are on the Mexican flag?"

The cousins answer correctly.

"Who is the president of Mexico?"

Again the cousins answered correctly just as they do all of his questions. They had spent the past two months in Mexico; how could they not know the answers to such simple questions?

After narrowly escaping the machete-carrying bandits, Amilcar and Edwin are detained at 6 PM. By 3 AM, they are back in Mexico with a voucher courtesy of the US government for a bus ticket to Michoacán, Mexico, where they said they were from. Tickets at the bus station are two for the price of one. They get two tickets to Mexicali where they hope to cross into Arizona.

An old man in Mexicali named Artemio takes them in. They stay with him for 25 days, during which they call relatives to line up the $2,000 to pay a coyote to take them to Indio, California. Amilcar couldn't reach his friend in New York and decide to head to Indio where his uncle lives.

Under cover of darkness, they crawl across the border into the desert through a canal. They crawl for four hours, and then they wait in a grass field.

From October 2006 to May 2007, 31,993 migrants were apprehended by the US Border patrol, and six migrants were found dead. Migrants drown in ditches. They die of exposure to the heat and the cold, and of thirst. They are murdered by vigilante militiamen.

In April, President Bush gave a speech in nearby Yuma, praising the lockdown on the American border. No one is certain how many have crossed, but the number of apprehensions is down 68 percent in Yuma. Only 25,217 immigrants had been apprehended during the previous six months compared to 79,131 during the same period the year before.

"When you're apprehending fewer people, it means fewer are trying to come across," President Bush said. "And fewer are trying to come across because we're deterring people from attempting illegal border crossings in the first place."

US officials estimate that 12 million undocumented immigrants live in the United States; despite 13,000 border patrol agents patrolling the border, 400,000 more come each year. Amilcar was now among them.

Three months ago, he had hugged Betsabe good-bye. Since that time, he had been mugged, hugged, and deported.

A truck takes them to a hotel room with 13 other tired and dirty, nervous and ecstatic migrants. Two box trucks come to the hotel; Edwin is told to get into one and Amilcar the other.

Now, Amilcar is alone; his fate in the hands of smugglers.

The coyote directs 14 other migrants to cram into the back of the truck with Amilcar and shuts the door. Eight hours later, the door is thrown open and for the first time, Amilcar blinks this new country into focus.

He was in the United States.

I was in Cambodia.

An American Dream

December 2011

"Dinosaur, Dinosaur . . . ABC!" My daughter, Harper, almost three, is pretending to read from her library book. "Dinosaur, Dinosaur . . . stinky!" She looks at me and laughs. It's a deep, silly laugh that is as pure as joy.

Her bedtime routine is anything but routine. First, I give her a bath during which I end up half soaked, then I brush her teeth while she plays the drums on my head, and then I take her to her room. Annie comes up and reads to her for 15 minutes while I shower. When I return, Harper shuts off the light and turns on her Kenny Loggins *Return to Pooh Corner* CD. We rock in the rocking chair, and I tell her a story about the animal or muppet of her choosing with one caveat: She must always be a co-star. Then I put her to bed, get her a drink, rock her in her bed, lie down with her, start the CD over, and leave.

And that's if everything goes smoothly. Tonight it doesn't.

Harper is sitting in the rocking chair reading to me. Eventually, I demand that she get into bed.

"Now I'm going to be gone for the next couple of days. So you be a good girl for your mama, okay?"

"Dada, I have something to tell you." She pulls me close and whispers in my ear. "Dada, don't leave us. You're my best boy. I love you so much. I miss you when you are gone."

Her nighttime antics involve tummyaches, eyeaches, and toothaches. One time she, on purpose, pounded her head into the wall and then hollered, "Ouch! My head! Dada, I hurt my head!" But this was a good one. I was her best boy, and she didn't want me to leave. I rocked her on the bed longer than usual before putting her down. I was only going to be gone for three nights . . . that's it. When I traveled to Bangladesh, Cambodia, and China, I was gone for three months. But becoming a parent changes you in ways you never imagined. It makes you do things you never thought you'd do. You are missed when you are gone, and you are always needed.

"I have to go, sweetie."

"Why, Dada?"

"I have to find a friend."

*   *   *

"Kelsey!" Amilcar hollers through my phone. I know you aren't supposed to talk on the phone while you drive in California, but you also aren't supposed to walk here from Honduras and sneak across the border, either. "Are you driving an orange car?"

"Yes." I say, doing that head swivel thing when you are searching for someone who has already found you. "Where are you?"

"At the 76 station."

I turn around and head back to the station just off Interstate 10. A man standing next to a navy blue car begins to wave at me while I'm half a block away, sitting at a stoplight.

He's wearing cowboy boots, a cowboy shirt, and one of those belt buckles the size of Texas. He looks like he belongs on a horse in El Porvenir.

He comes at me with a big hug. No one driving by would have guessed that we had met only briefly six years ago.

He is older and wider and wiser, too. The tips of his hair are frosted with the slightest bit of gray, ever so slightly that you might not notice if you aren't within hugging distance. He's put on an extra 35 pounds since I last saw him.

We have a connection. I can't help but smile the same goofy grin that I had at the factory when I first met him. He does, too.

"The real reason I'm here is," I say, "where's my shirt?!? I want my shirt back!"

We slap each other's backs and just stare at each other. A T-shirt brought us together, how improbable is that?

"It's been six years," I say. "A lot has happened."

He recalls the story of Karla calling him and telling him about some American who claimed to have met him at the factory and wrote about him in a book.

Amilcar initially didn't remember me when Karla told him of my arrival in Honduras—which I couldn't believe. Meeting him changed my life. It wasn't so much what he said or what happened when I met him, but all of the unanswered questions I had about his life and the life of other such workers around the world that changed me. Yet he didn't remember my name, what I was doing in Honduras, or anything—except for one small thing. He remembered the shirt with Tattoo from *Fantasy Island* beckoning onlookers to "Come with me to my tropical paradise." He remembered me taking it off and giving it to him.

I've always been ashamed that I gave him the shirt I was wearing and posed shirtless beside him. It's something that I thought if I could go back I wouldn't do, because it aptly reflected the shallowness of my false start. That was until I discovered that if it weren't for the complete silliness of my giving him my T-shirt, he wouldn't have remembered me at all.

Other things he remembered about that day were that he thought I needed help and that he was drunk.

Meeting Amilcar feels like meeting a celebrity. He's someone I've thought about and someone I've talked about to the point he's almost become a legend. I still have so much to learn about him.

"Kesley, my wife gets off work at 3:30 PM and she will meet us here."

"Huh?"

"My wife . . . she's coming here."

He speaks a little English, and I speak a little Spanish. There's a lot that is lost in our language gap. A wife? What about his family and Jolanis in Honduras?

"My wife here," he says, "my wife in the United States . . . she's coming here and she can translate."

He mentions his kids and emotion creeps into his voice. He mentions Jolanis. He mentions immigration and opens his wallet and shows me his California working permit. He talks about fines and getting married.

Amilcar is married.

"Did you marry for love or for visa?" I ask.

"Sí, for love."

A maroon Honda pulls up and a 21-year-old woman gets out. Amilcar lights up and greets her with a hug and kiss while patting her belly.

"My baby," he says. She's three months pregnant.

"Nice to meet you, Kelsey. I'm Mayra."

Amilcar motions for me to get in the front seat of the car, and Mayra gets in the back. I grab the seat belt and pull it across me.

"It doesn't work," Amilcar says. "Just . . ." he motions me to tuck the seatbelt under my leg so it looks like I'm wearing my seatbelt. Sometimes appearing to obey the law is as important as obeying it.

We drive a few minutes, and Amilcar parks on the street.

"My first house," he says, pointing out my window. As with many things, from a distance the house looks okay. But as we walk to it, I realize that it isn't one house, but four small ones built really close together. Up close, you can see the chipped paint, the torn curtains. One of the houses has boarded windows. "Very ugly for Indio."

Amilcar lived here with three other guys.

"I thought I would work in the fields or in the factories."

When he first arrived, he got a job at a factory that shapes and delivers granite counter tops for the surrounding area. But then he hurt his ankle playing soccer, and his uncle helped him get a job at a shoe store where he worked the register and got experience in customer service.

He had experience selling; in fact, selling shoes was in his blood.

"Mom used to package bread, and I would sell it. Dad sold shoes. I never thought I would sell shoes, too."

His knack for selling shoes is a source of family pride. Back in Villanueva, his mom told me, "Even if you walked in and didn't want a pair of shoes, you'd walk out the door with a pair."

"One day," Karla had added, "a guy came to the store—a wetback [an illegal immigrant]—and he needed a pair of shoes. Because Amilcar had been there, he gave the guy a good deal."

We pull up to Zapateria Guardado, the store at which Amiclar eventually worked his way up to manager. GOING OUT OF BUSINESS SALE is painted on the windows. It was the job at the shoe store that paid for the construction of the $8,000 home where Jolanis and Genesis were living. Amilcar didn't make that much in a year at the garment factories in Honduras. The job also paid for his kids' education. He gave his brother $6,000 so he might be able to grow the family business of delivering bread. His mom's cough was more than a temporary cold; it was a chronic illness. He estimates he sent her more than $2,000 for her medicine.

"Ten-and-a-half?" Amilcar asks, pointing down to my shoes.

He's dead on.

"Wow, you were good at your job."

"I came over here for one thing: to make money."

A job like this was exactly why he had risked everything to come to the United States. And Amilcar was making it. His American dream was coming true . . . until it wasn't.

"I was so depressed," he says. "I was alone in this country. I started drinking and then drugs . . . cocaine." Amilcar felt guilty that he was drinking so much of the money he was supposed to be sending home to his family, but drink he did. He tried AA, and it didn't work. On December 31, 2007, he found a Hispanic support group of recovering addicts. His New Year's resolution was to never touch alcohol or drugs again; theirs was to help him. He's been clean ever since.

One day Amilcar was heading home after a shift at the shoe store when he was pulled over. After four years of looking over his shoulder and trying to act like he belonged, he stared his first immigration officer in the eye since that day when he jumped the fence between Juarez and El Paso.

"Immigration had me for 26 days," Amilcar says. "I had to meet with the judge. I was released, but had to pay fines."

His lawyer cost him $5,000, which he pieced together from money he had saved and a loan from his uncle. He paid a $10,000 fine, thanks to a loan from his boss at the shoe store. And he still would have been deported after all of that if Mayra hadn't proposed.

Their reluctant courtship started 10 months before the run-in with immigration. Mayra regularly visited the swap meet where Amilcar sold boots, and one of her friends pointed out a dancing Amilcar to her. He loves to dance. In the past he got drunk and danced at bars, but now he dances whenever he hears music. Mayra's friend egged her on to ask him to show her some moves. Shyly she slipped away.

There were more not-so-chance meetings at the swap meet and Amilcar asked for her number, but she wouldn't give it to him. Instead, she would call him from a private number.

After months of chatting, they went on a date to a park.

"I kissed him," Mayra says. "He was scared."

"Never in my life," Amilcar says, "has a girl kissed *me*."

They dated for three months before Amilcar told her about his other life in El Porvenir. She thought he had one child back in Honduras and was here legally. He also lied about one other thing.

"I can't take it anymore," Amilcar said. "I lied to you. I'm not 26. I'm 29. I don't have one daughter, I have three."

But she didn't care. She loved him.

Two days after he was released by Immigration, waiting for his day in court, Mayra proposed.

"I can help," she said. "Marry me."

"No," Amilcar said. "I don't want to marry you for the papers. I don't want people to think that about me."

Eventually he agreed, and, after he asked her parents, they got married. Her father was really nervous at first, but now he loves Amilcar. And though his new life was beginning, he hadn't forgotten about his old one.

"When [Immigration] let me go, I had to start all over. I worked in the granite factory again. I sold boots at the swap meet on Wednesday and Saturday evenings."

The plans for his home in El Porvenir shrank. His mom had to pay for her own medicine or go without. She told him that she understood.

Amilcar turns down a dead-end street and slows in front of a factory. Slabs of granite stand like counter-sized monoliths. This was his first job and his last one. Two months ago he hurt his back lifting an 800-lb granite slab with three other guys. To the employer, a Honduran with a seventh-grade education wasn't worth much without a back that could lift. They fired him.

Compared to the burdens that Amilcar carries each day, granite is weightless. But now his wallet is stuffed with appointment cards for a chiropractor. A month's worth of appointments is four times his monthly disability check.

Amilcar is suing the granite company. His American dream is a minimum wage job and a simple life that allows him to send a little money home to Honduras each month, and all this has been taken from him. We roll past without stopping. As we pull away I notice a message scrolling across his removable face stereo: "Failure . . . Failure . . . Failure. . . ." The car is in bad shape. My door can only be opened from the outside. I have to roll down my window and let myself out when we stop. The odometer reads just over 90,000 miles. Obviously, it's been tough mileage, aging the car much more than any gauge could measure. Still it pushes onward.

Next, he takes me by the apartment that he and Mayra share with his uncle. A sheet hangs down in front of the door. We have to push it to the side as we enter. It's a touch of life in Honduras. A 37-inch flatscreen TV sits on a small entertainment center. They don't have cable, and the TV is too thin for rabbit ears to sit on top, so the antenna is held up by a broom tied to a metal chair. There are three bedrooms. Amilcar and Mayra share one, Amilcar's uncle the other, and the third is crowded with leaning towers of boots. Snakeskin boots are atop armadillo boots atop traditional cow leather boots atop manta ray boots.

Manta ray boots—I have to try on a pair! Remembering my shoe size, Amilcar finds me a 10½. They're maroon, and I state how ridiculous I look in them. Amilcar agrees. He sells the boots for $150 to $250 and typically makes more than 100 percent profit on a sale. He also sells belts. Since he no longer works out of a store, he goes to his customers whether that be at their homes or at the grocery store during their smoke break.

Back at the 76 Station, we drop Mayra at her car. She's off to her second part-time job. She works 20 hours per week at a shoe store in a nearby mall and 20 hours per week fixing watches at the adjacent store.

We follow Mayra to the mall and Amilcar kisses her good-bye in the store before we head off for the food court. We talk about his mom's tortillas and how he would eat 15 in one sitting. And that's when he was skinny. Man, he misses his mom's cooking.

"American food. . . ." he says, patting his belly in a way that doesn't mean "delicious," but "fattening."

We're faced with the same old food court decisions: McDonald's, Panda Express, or Sbarro. He says that he wants Panda Express, but first he wants to get something for Mayra and approaches the McDonald's counter.

"Do you speak Spanish?" he says to the blue-eyed high-schooler behind the counter.

"Uh, no. I'll get someone," the boy says.

Amilcar has been here for six years and he can't even order a Big Mac.

"All you have to do," I say, giving him some grief, "is point to the menu and say, 'number one, please.' You can do that."

He tells me that I sound like Mayra. She's always after him to take English classes and at least try to speak English in instances like this. I know what it's like to be an outsider. I've spent months at a time in places where I had the communication capabilities of a toddler. It wears on you after a while, but Amilcar has been here for years. What must it feel like to be an outsider in your own home, living somewhere you don't belong but have to be?

Amilcar gets his Big Mac ordered and takes it to Mayra before we sit down to our Styrofoam boxes of Panda Express. I hesitantly ask a question that's been on my mind since I met Mayra.

"Does Jolanis know about Mayra?"

"No," Amilcar says. "I avoid telling her because I know she still loves me. Mayra always tells me, 'Why don't you have your daughters come here?' But I don't want to break Jolanis's heart. Kids should be with their mother."

"You know, she thinks you're coming back in a few years and you'll all be together living in El Porvenir. Do you love her?"

"Before I left we were fighting. We had a lot of problems. I want to see her happy."

"Is Jolanis a good mom?"

"Yes, 100 percent, yes."

Amilcar tells me that he talks to Genesis and Betsabe at least twice per week. He says that Genesis thinks she should have whatever she wants. She's having trouble in school. The teachers yell at her and beat her, and call Jolanis and yell at her. Betsabe was six months old when he left. She doesn't really know him, only through the phone and photos. He's impressed at how intelligent she is. As for Karen, he'd like to talk to her more, but her stepdad doesn't allow it. Amilcar calls them once per month to tell them that he sent money. When he talks about his kids, the color in his eyes rises and falls in pink crescendos. He unapologetically wipes his tears.

"Betsabe always asks me when I'm coming home. I always say, 'Soon.'"

"Are you a good dad?"

"I don't think I am because I'm not there to help the girls. I'm there mentally, but not physically. . . . When I go back, I'll tell them I'm failing them."

Amilcar can't hug his girls. We sit in silence as he feels and I imagine. I want to hug him. All along my journey, I've met mothers and fathers separated from their children, but that was before I was a father, before my little girl asked me not to leave and before my six-month-old baby boy won me over with his perfect little grin. I know I can't imagine what it must be like to leave everyone you love, including your kids; but at least now I know how all-encompassing a parent's love can be for a child. I think about all of the moments Amilcar has missed—the birthdays, the holidays, the milestones. The first time my daughter Harper pooped in the potty, I felt like I had won a Superbowl.

"It's a sacrifice for me to be here. I'm alone . . . except for Mayra. . . . Sometimes I feel like going back, but right now I'm still trying to become a citizen. Part of me wants to go back, and part of me doesn't. I want to work hard and save money, so they can have a better life. I don't want them to sell bread on the streets. I want to make their world a better place."

Amilcar wants his mom to meet Mayra. His mom, who he says is his role model, doesn't know about his pregnant American wife. Karla does. She and Mayra are already good friends, chatting on the phone and interacting on Facebook. He wants his family to meet his yet-to-be-born American son.

He wants his two worlds to converge.

We finish our Chinese food and walk back to Mayra's store so he can kiss her good-bye again. Christmas music is playing in the background, and it gives way to Rod Stewart singing a classic Motown song. He tells me that he likes this kind of music, not Mexican music. He likes Bryan Adams.

All the stores—Eddie Bauer, JCPenney, GAP—are advertising low prices for Christmas, but the prices are still too high for Amilcar.

*   *   *

We drive back to the 76 Station in the dark. When we arrive, I pull out my laptop.

"I want to show you the photos I took while I was in Honduras with your family."

I open the trunk and pop open my computer.

"Mi Abuelo . . . ahhh . . . mi babies." He gasps when he sees the photos.

His grandmother and grandfather stand in front of their home in El Porvenir. Genesis holding Betsabe (Figure 29.1). Genesis wearing her Miss El Porvenir crown and holding her scepter. He sees the house that he's built, the minds he helps educate, the kids he can't hold. His former life glows at him, lighting his face. It moves on without his presence, but with his help.

"Back . . . forward . . ." he commands. I'm not sure what he wants. It's like he wants every picture all at the same time. "Go back. Go back. Stop."

I stop on a picture of Jolanis. Her head is down, she's pulling the door of her house—of his house—shut. He smiles a sad smile.

"Do you want me to print some of these pictures for you?"

"Yes, print them all. I want them all."

*   *   *

Figure 29.1   Genesis holding Betsabe as Karla looks on.

I spend three days with Amilcar. We drive around. We drink mochas at Starbucks. And now we're eating grand slams at Denny's. We just hang, talking about our families and what the future holds.

The waitress greeted us in English and asked what we would like to drink. When it was evident that Amilcar didn't understand her, she tried to take our order in Spanish. When it was evident that I didn't fully understand her Spanish, she just scratched her head.

"You don't speak English," she said. "And you don't speak Spanish."

"That's right," I answered.

She paused for an explanation, but we didn't give her one. Admittedly, it's kind of a long story.

I had a lot of questions for Amilcar when we first met: What are you paid? Does this job provide a better life for you and your family? What are the working conditions like? I didn't ask any of them. I think that deep down I really didn't want to know the answers.

Now I know. I'm not happier for it. I'm not angrier for it. Ignorance isn't bliss; neither is reality.

I think about all of those economists that point to the garment industry as the first rung on the economic ladder. Let's not pretend that Amilcar, who's now shoveling a load of hash browns into his mouth, had a job in Honduras that was getting him anywhere. He risked his life running from his job, leaving his world and all his loved ones.

Last night I tried to express to Amilcar how meeting him changed my life, but Spanish and English failed me.

"How long did it take you to fly to Honduras from Indiana?" Amilcar asks.

"Let me see," I say, calculating when I left and factoring in the time change. "About eight hours."

Eight hours. That's it? I can nearly read his mind. Amilcar's journey here took him three months. To think that if he had the right job and the right papers, he could afford to see his family—and be there in eight hours.

We finish our meal and head to his chiropractor appointment. I have to be leaving. I have an overnight flight to catch. Tomorrow, I'll walk through the front door of my house, and my daughter Harper will yell, "Dada! You're home," as she runs to me and tackles my knees. My son Griffin will peek over Annie's shoulder and give me a tiny smile. I'll embrace all three of them in a giant group hug, and I'll say something sappy. I'll mean it more than ever.

Figure 29.2   The author and Amilcar reunited in California.

I ask a man filling out paperwork on the steps outside of the office to take a picture of Amilcar and me. We smile for the camera: two travelers, two dads, two amigos (Figure 29.2).

"Oh," I say, handing him the letter Jolanis asked me to give him, "this is for you."

I walk to my car, leaving him holding the letter, a message from his former life, just staring at it.

His journey is far from over.

CHAPTER
30

Touron Goes Glocal

On a sun-scorched hillside in Addis Ababa, Ethiopia, a woman in a bright yellow sunhat wearing pink jelly shoes swings a pickax. Jelly shoes are the last type of footwear you would select for this type of work. And the woman, old enough to be a great-grandmother in Ethiopia, is one of the last people you would select to dig out a tree stump. But that's what she—and dozens of women like her—are doing. The thuds of metal on earth and wood are followed by grunts of exertion. They sound like tennis players, putting everything they can muster behind a forehand, but faced with a much more daunting task.

The woman hands me her pickax, wipes her brow with a handkerchief, and chugs water from a plastic jug. All the ax swinging comes to a stop as all eyes turn to me. I swing the pickax and miss the stump. The women critique my technique and offer some pointers. The next swing makes contact and separates the slightest bit of root from the stump. Tomorrow I'll be sore.

This is the Ethiopian economy—earth and wood, arms and back, dirt and sweat—and it has been this way for generations. But up the hill, one young woman who combined her love for fashion and business is changing this community—one shoe at a time.

My adventures as an engaged consumer have brought me to soleRebels, a very different kind of shoe company.

I enter through a white gate off a dirt road where soleRebels founder and managing director Bethlehem Tilahun gives me a tour of the factory. It was Bethlehem who had invited me after stumbling upon my blog.

249

There's pretty much nothing "normal" about this shoe factory, which is not so much a factory as a home. A blue tarp shields hammering workers from the sun on the porch. Up a few steps and through the front door is the living room, which doesn't hold couches but sewing machines.

In one bedless bedroom, a man brushes glue onto a footbed. In another, a man punches eyelets in a leather upper.

soleRebels is a shoe company with a very small footprint. The leather, the cotton, and even the glue are all products from within 60 miles of the factory. The rubber soles are cut from flat tires discarded alongside the road.

"We're collecting the Ethiopian Army's uniforms and turning them into shoes," Bethlehem says as she points to the camouflage webbing on a pair of flip-flops. "We are green by heritage. From a long, long time ago, people were wearing these traditional kinds of recycled, rubber-soled shoes. We took that idea when we started this company. We didn't create anything; we modified it."

Bethlehem shows me into her office and takes a moment to discuss the day's business over a cup of tea with one of her partners, her brother Kirubel; soleRebels produces more than 80 styles—from brightly colored flip-flops to slip-ons and tie-ups that could be worn for an evening out on the town. The company just received a $40,000 order from Amazon in the UK.

soleRebels exports to 14 countries. They sold over $1 million of shoes in 2011 and project sales of $2 million in 2012, and $10 million in 2015. But in Bethlehem's mind, the most important math of all is this equation: sales equals jobs.

"soleRebels started as an idea," she says. "We thought that we could give an opportunity for the people to work because there was none."

She started the company with her own money and operates with a government-backed credit line from a local bank. soleRebels is on a social mission, but Bethlehem wants people to buy soleRebels because they like the shoes, not because they are feeling charitable. In fact, she questions charity's effectiveness.

"My community is a little bit isolated from the other communities, and there [are] a lot of aid organizations around our community . . . but there is no change in people's lives. So, we said, you know, 'Why don't we try to change this?' We are doing it from our heart."

soleRebels indirectly employs 300 people, from the weaving co-op where the company buys its fabric to the tire collectors that roam the streets looking for flats. Ninety people are direct soleRebel employees who reap benefits nearly unheard of in Ethiopia. They earn what the company calls a "proud" wage. They get health insurance, a school fund for their children, and six months of maternity leave.

"Before [working for] soleRebels, I cleaned houses and traded goods," says Wubuyau Legesse, a sewer and a mother who has worked at the company for nearly four years. "I have two kids. Before they didn't go to school and didn't study at all. Now they go to school. Life is really better now."

Bantegan Abebe, a man with a tightly groomed moustache, joins me in Bethlehem's office. After making some small talk, I learn that he's nearly a black belt in Taekwondo—a tough guy. I proudly share that I was the Kung Fu Club president of Miami University, but he seems unimpressed (as he should be).

"I work here for two years. We make shoes with our own hands, and when people wear them, we feel happy. It's really encouraging."

The job has allowed him to send his brother to school and help support his parents.

"What do Bethlehem and soleRebels mean to you?" I ask.

"I have no words. . . ." Bantegan says as emotion creeps into his voice, the tough guy façade cracking. "Bethlehem is really good for the community. I hope she is happy that we are really changing. She's with us in our hearts."

Bethlehem (Figure 30.1) was born, raised, and educated in Addis Ababa. Both of her parents worked at a leprosy treatment center—her father as an electrician and her mother as a cook. She studied accounting

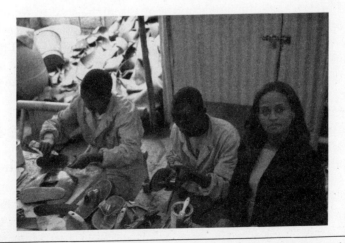

Figure 30.1   Bethlehem sitting next to two workers gluing soles.

and many of her classmates left Ethiopia soon after graduation. But she stayed.

"The other people are running from here," Bethlehem says, guiding me onto the porch. "It doesn't make sense for me. Every country has a problem. Ethiopia has a problem also. So we are trying to face our problems, solving them with our materials, our own way of thinking, and we can do it."

Bethelehem wants soleRebels to become the Nike of Africa. Both she and her company are constantly winning awards and recognition from organizations like the World Bank, the Clinton Global Initiative, and the International Monetary Fund. *Forbes* named her as one of the top 20 youngest power women in Africa.

soleRebels is changing lives.

When I leave the factory, I pass a blue shack housing a humming grinder. A man wearing a tan frock holds a rubber sole to it. Not long ago, the sole was part of a tire deemed useless and unwanted. The long-drawn-out bass note is broken by the scraping dissonance of rubber on metal. The sound follows me out the front gate and down past the women swinging pickaxes.

soleRebels is in the soul business. They also happen to make shoes.

* * *

The apparel industry has a lot of issues, including child labor and sweatshops, but these are all just symptoms of the real problem: poverty.

There's a reason a single mom of three children in Bangladesh will work for $24 per month. There's a reason a young woman in Cambodia will pay a month's wages as a bribe to land a job. There's a reason a worker in China will clock out and go back to work for free instead of telling his boss to shove it. They all have an extreme lack of options—because they all live in poverty.

New York Times columnist Nicholas Kristof agrees, and wrote in a January 14, 2009, column: ". . . sweatshops are only a symptom of poverty, not a cause, and banning them closes off one route out of poverty." But I'm not so sure about his assessment that working in a sweatshop is a route out of poverty. It might be for some, but working in a garment factory wasn't a route out of poverty for Nari or Ai or Arifa or any worker I've ever met. Their situations haven't improved. Amilcar looked at his family's needs, assessed his career as a garment worker, and decided to take his chances traveling north into an unknown future. A job at a "sweatshop" might be the best of a host of not-great opportunities, but it rarely does more than keep people just on the edge of extreme poverty.

Kristof claims that developing countries need more sweatshops. But I disagree. Developing countries need more jobs like those at soleRebels, jobs that allow parents to send their kids to school. The garment industry has huge—relatively untapped—potential to fight poverty.

Bethlehem projects that soleRebels will have 300 full-time employees by 2015. Let's say that every worker at soleRebels has six kids (based on Ethiopia's fertility rate). This means that over 1,800 kids will be supported by jobs at the company by 2015. The workers, with the help of the company, are able to send all six kids to school. And since these kids have an education, they don't grow up to be shoemakers. They do something that pays better, and they send *their* six kids to school. By the third generation, the 300 jobs at soleRebels will have impacted 64,800 people. Within six generations, the jobs will have impacted over two million.

I realize that this calculation might be a bit oversimplified, but my point is that a job, a *good* job, has an exponential impact.

Another brand that is changing lives is Alta Gracia, a brand manufactured in the Dominican Republic that makes T-shirts and sweatshirts for university bookstores across the country. They pay their workers a living wage, which happens to be three times the average wage at other such factories in the country. They are open to the workers unionizing, and allowing me to work alongside their employees on the factory floor. Actually, when I made my request, the brand's parent company, Knights Apparel, wasn't the only group that decided it would be okay. The workers liked the idea, too. I'm hoping to take them up on the job offer someday.

The fact that they are this open is simply amazing—as is the fact that I'm not the only one they've invited to their factory. Alta Gracia's union regularly receives visitors at the factory and has Skype calls with American students. The Worker Rights Consortium also regularly visits the factory and checks the pay-records at least once per week.

The *New York Times* reported on Alta Gracia from the Dominican Republic on July 17, 2010:

> *Sitting in her tiny living room here, Santa Castillo beams about the new house that she and her husband are building directly behind the wooden shack where they now live.*

The new home will be four times bigger, with two bedrooms and an indoor bathroom; the couple and their three children now share a windowless bedroom and rely on an outhouse two doors away.

Ms. Castillo had long dreamed of a bigger, sturdier house, but three months ago something happened that finally made it possible: she landed a job at one of the world's most unusual garment factories. Industry experts say it is a pioneer in the developing world because it pays a "living wage"—in this case, three times the average pay of the country's apparel workers—and allows workers to join a union without a fight.

"We never had the opportunity to make wages like this before," says Ms. Castillo, a soft-spoken woman who earns $500 a month. "I feel blessed."

"It's a noble effort, but it is an experiment," Andrew Jassin, co-founder of Jassin Consulting, an apparel industry consultant, quoted in the same story. "There are consumers who really care and will buy this apparel at a premium price, and then there are those who say they care, but then just want value."

You're a consumer. Do you care?

As I travel around the United States chatting with students, they usually respond to this question with a guilt-ridden "no."

And unfortunately, it's true; most of us don't care. We just shop mindlessly, basing our decisions on whatever fashion sensibilities we have and whatever we can afford. But I strongly believe that we *could* care, and that we would care—if we can bridge the divide between producer and consumer.

Allow me to introduce you to iPhone girl.

In August of 2008, a British man was eagerly waiting for his new iPhone to arrive. I'm sure he was doing that thing where you track it every 30 minutes online to see if it has left the warehouse in China or wherever. Finally, the day came. He opened the box, and it still had that new iPhone smell. He fired up his phone and discovered photos of a worker at the Chinese factory where his phone was made giving a peace sign and smiling for the camera. He posted the photos on Macrumors .com. In a matter of weeks the ensuing thread exploded with nearly 700 comments.

The iPhone girl became a sensation. Her smiling face was on cNET, on MSNBC, and in the *Washington Post*. Everyone wanted to know, "Who is iPhone girl?"

Reporters tracked iPhone girl to the Foxconn factory in Shenzhen. Foxconn, the largest private employer in all of China, employs more than one million people. Half of them work at the Shenzhen factory. Foxconn and Apple received a lot of negative press after a 2010 rash of worker suicides—17 total—at the Shenzhen plant. Suicides became such a problem that the company put up nets to catch workers who were so depressed that they opted to jump to their death rather than go back to work.

The Chinese newspaper *Southern Weekend* sent reporter Liu Zhiyi undercover for 28 days into the factory in 2010. He wrote, "[The workers] actually envied those who could take a leave due to work injury."

A company spokesperson called the iPhone girl incident a "beautiful mistake"—which it was for Apple and for Foxconn. They had been blasted in the press for the conditions in which iPhones were made, and here was photographic proof of a pretty, happy worker in a neat and clean factory, smiling.

And something beautiful did happen. When we see that iPhone girl has a slightly crooked smile and is wearing a slightly crooked cap and that she has a sparkle of personality in her eye, we can't help but care about her. The divide between producer and consumer disappears.

It used to be that when my grandfather bought a shirt, the life of the worker who made it wasn't much different from Grandpa's— although shirt-makers' jobs involved less manure (Grandpa was a farmer). Folks back then knew what life was like for the butcher, the baker, and the garment maker. They knew the story of their stuff.

I believe that we long for a deeper connection with our stuff. The proof is in the resurgence of farmers' markets and handmade crafts and the website Etsy.com, where you can buy handmade crafts directly from the producer. If you buy an ear of corn from farmer Dave out on State Route 32, or a necklace handmade by an artisan in a neighboring county, you can tell the story of where and who it came from when you serve that corn or give that necklace as a gift.

When we recognize that the people who make our stuff have hopes, dreams, and personalities, we can't help but care about whether their job pays them a living wage and allows them to reach those dreams.

But bridging the divide between producer and consumer isn't easy.

Back in 2008, I was working on a piece about where T-shirts come from for Condé Nast *Portfolio*. My research for the article required that I call all the biggest T-shirt brands and ask them where they got their shirts.

First I called Hanes, who were really helpful. They told me what percentage of T-shirts came from what country; Honduras led the way. They let me know that I could give them a call back if I had more questions.

Next up was Fruit of the Loom. They wouldn't confirm that the majority of their products are made outside the United States, or tell me anything, other than it was their official company policy to not talk about this.

It was the first time that I had written for the magazine. I could practically hear my editor's eyes roll on the phone when I told him that Fruit of the Loom wouldn't confirm anything. He would have the fact-checker call them. *Portfolio* was a business magazine, and they were used to getting companies to talk.

But the fact-checker was also stonewalled. He couldn't believe it. "Welcome to the wonderful world of underwear journalism," I thought.

Brands want us to think as little as possible about where our clothes come from. Think about the last catalog you picked up. The flowery description of the product likely ended with one of two things: MADE IN THE USA or IMPORTED. Or maybe if the product was leather and it added some value to it: MADE IN ITALY (even though sometimes that means that a product was made in Italy by imported Chinese workers). Brands are required by law to have the country of origin noted on their products, but other than that, they prefer not to talk about it or about the workers who made them. This is how they uphold the producer-consumer divide.

This isn't to say that the corporations themselves aren't thinking about them. Since Kathie Lee cried on TV in 1996, many corporations have worked hard to improve conditions in the factories from which they source. They've adopted codes of corporate social responsibility— and if you look hard enough on their websites, you might just find them. But for the most part, corporations have not made the effort to assure us that they are concerned with conditions in the factories and the well-being of the workers making their products.

They've either been burned themselves or have seen someone else burned by scathing reports of despicable conditions, and prefer to ignore the subject altogether. And really, I can't blame them.

There isn't a single worker who makes my clothes who lives a life that I would find acceptable. I'm not sure we can handle knowing how most of the world lives. Levi's recently ran a "Go Forth" ad campaign that featured all-American scenes of kids in blue jeans skipping through fields of grass holding sparklers and other shots that represented freedom. The scenes are set against Walt Whitman reading his poem *America*:

Centre of equal daughters, equal sons,
All, all alike endear'd, grown, ungrown, young or old,

Strong, ample, fair, enduring, capable, rich,
Perennial with the Earth, with Freedom, Law and Love,

It's hard to come to terms with this marketing image and the reality in which the workers who make their jeans in Cambodia and elsewhere live. The Cambodia Institute of Development Study conducted research to determine a living wage, and concluded that the minimum living wage in Cambodia was $90 in 2009. I'm okay with workers earning a living wage but think most consumers and the media would perceive this as, "Only $90! Those poor people." This is our problem, one that we should try and move beyond before corporations will level with us. If we continue to see garment workers' lack of opportunities through the lens of our own lives' relatively limitless opportunities, the conversation can't begin.

The Program on International Policy Attitudes at the University of Maryland conducted a poll in 2004 that found that 83 percent of those asked agree with the following statement:

> *Free trade is an important goal for the United States, but it should be*
> *balanced with other goals, such as protecting workers, the environment,*
> *and human rights—even if this may mean slowing the growth of trade*
> *and the economy.*

And when asked, "If you had to choose between buying a piece of clothing that costs $20 and you are not sure how it was made, and one that is certified as not made in a sweatshop, but costs $25, which one would you buy?" Sixty-one percent of those polled said they would pay $5 more for the piece of clothing certified as not made in a sweatshop.

To test the poll's findings, which were in line with other such polls, researchers at the University of Michigan and Northwestern University designed a study to observe the real-world spending habits of sock shoppers at a "well-known department store" in Michigan. They labeled one rack of socks with a sign that said, "Buy GWC . . . Good Working Conditions . . . no child labor . . . no sweatshops . . . safe workplace." An adjacent rack of similar socks was unlabeled. They gradually raised the price of the GWC socks and found that on average a third of customers were willing to pay more for them. The researchers believe that due to some of the customers' lack of understanding of the GWC label, the percentage of conscientious consumers is actually greater. However, even if a third of consumers are willing to pay more for GWC apparel, there is a major untapped market for such items.

While a labeling system would be an ideal way to inform conscientious consumers, there are many barriers to be crossed: How do
we define "Good Working Conditions"? Do they vary by location?
Who enforces them? Are the cotton farms that produce the cotton
held to these same conditions? How about the textile factories? Or
the oil refineries that produce the oil used to make synthetic fabrics?
Factories' conditions may change from year to year. Maybe a nation
devalues its currency, and a factory that was once compliant now is not
because it works its workers longer and harder to turn the same profit.

A labeling system might not be easy, but it's a goal toward which
we should aspire. It would require the efforts of activists, corporations,
and an informed public.

The Outdoor Industry Association and the Sustainable Apparel
Coalition are working on a labeling system "Apparel Tool"—that rates
products on their environmental impact. Target and Walmart are even
onboard. The tool isn't consumer-facing yet, meaning it's a tool for
companies and not consumers. Those involved want to get it right and
establish the label's integrity before we would see it on a rack anywhere.

This project was called the Eco-Index when I first heard about
it in 2010, and there was talk about factoring in social responsibility
into the scoring as well. But the focus today seems to be more on the
environment—and not on labor practices.

More and more brands are jumping on the bandwagon and offering environmentally friendly products. They're made from hemp and
organic cotton, glued with glue that does less harm to the environment, and packed in 100 percent post-consumer recycled boxes. And
while I'm happy to have these options, I still want more.

We care about our impact on the environment, but what about
our impact on one another? Saving the environment is in style, but
concern for the workers who make our shoes is not.

Don't believe me? Call up any brand and ask them how they
reduce their impact on the environment, and they'll likely have a long
list to recite to you. Then ask them about what they are doing to ensure
that the workers who make their shoes are being treated fairly. You'll
soon find yourself lost in the corporate phone chain.

The media gives corporations a reason not to advance the conversation. One radio program producer bluntly told me that her staff
thought I was naive because I said I didn't know when they asked if
the factories I visited were sweatshops. They wanted me to be up in
arms about the poor, poor workers toiling long and hard, being paid
little and respected even less. But it's easy to inspire pity and to cry

sweatshop. What's not easy is coming to terms with the context in which the factories and workers exist, and initiating dialogue based on this. Not doing so is naive.

When was the last time you heard a news report on a well-run garment factory or one that was working to improve their employees' lives? These don't make for good sound bites; so we hear only about the violations, and are left thinking that all clothes are made in sweatshops. Most corporations remain mute on the subject lest they draw attention. In the garment industry, there is only bad press.

Activists such as United Students Against Sweatshops have spurred brands along. They are largely responsible for improved conditions in apparel factories today, and have paved the way for brands like Alta Gracia and soleRebels. It's been over a decade since their movement exposed the industry to the general public, embedding the images of sweatshops in our minds. I've found that the leaders of the antisweatshop movement I've met have a very good grasp of the context in which the workers live; however, the leaders often overlook that context when delivering their message.

The most egregious violations and the most appalling statistics further their cause. Back in the Kathie Lee days, I think the shock may have been good for us. We needed it.

In 2010, I attended the annual SweatFree conference once again. This time it wasn't in Minneapolis but in Olympia, and I didn't meet anyone with fake blood on his shirt. The conference was two days long, and I was the last speaker on the last day. Again, I was amazed by the passion and knowledge present at the conference, but I'm pretty sure that I was the only one who said the p-word—poverty—during the entire conference.

I believe that we need to move beyond divisive discussions about sweatshops that make people feel as though they have to choose a side: you're either for or against them. Where is it getting us? How does it benefit the workers? We need to recognize two crucial facts: that the garment industry provides jobs that mean an awful lot to people in really poor places, and that these people could and should be treated and paid better.

It's been over a decade since the Kathie Lee incident, and most of us still assume our clothes were made in sweatshops; yet our shopping habits haven't really changed. This is the failure of corporations, media, activists, and our own apathy.

* * *

Since my trip, I've become even more obsessed with clothing tags. It's almost an irrepressible compulsion to such an extent that department stores freak me out; there are so many tags to be checked. Let me tell you, a fella obsessively moving at random from rack to rack checking out women's undergarments *is* weird. I know because I've seen the looks on my fellow shoppers' faces.

When I returned from my trip, my mom sent me to the Macy's at the Muncie Mall to pick up a cashmere sweater she wanted to give to one of her friends as a gift. It was a $100 sweater marked down to $12.50. While the sales clerk, Pam, was searching for the right size I asked her, "Do you ever get customers concerned about where the clothes were made?"

"I've worked here for seven years," she said. "And when I first started, we did. Now I think people are resigned to the fact that everything is made overseas, and they don't have any other choice."

"Well, the reason I ask is because I just returned from. . . ." I explained to her my journey from country to country, factory to factory, from worker's home to worker's home. I half expected Pam to let the conversation end, worrying that I might drop to the ground and pour fake blood on myself in own little die-in.

Instead, she hesitated and then reluctantly asked, "Were they sweatshops?" When she said "sweatshops," she lowered her voice and looked around for eavesdroppers. A few racks away, an employee was pulling off winter clothes to be added to the clearance items. She gave us a sidewise glance and then turned back to her work. I could tell she was listening.

"I hate to use the term *sweatshop*," I said. "It belittles the job that the workers do and the sacrifices they make to do it."

I told her about Arifa in Bangladesh who worked at a garment factory with the hopes of earning enough money so she isn't forced to send another one of her children to Saudi Arabia. I told her about Nari in Cambodia who had to pay a bribe to get her job making jeans that helps support her family back in her village and pays for her training as a beautician. I told her about Dewan and Zhu Chun and the long hours they work, the son they rarely see, and the debt they've acquired. I told her all of the reasons why we should care about the people who make our clothes.

I told her that I believe suffering human wrongs should not be a rite of passage. I don't think it's acceptable that Nari had to pay a bribe to get her job, that Ai doesn't have a contract with the factory, and that Dewan and Zhu Chun work over 100 hours in a week. And I could tell from the look on Pam's face that she agreed.

I told her that there was no way I could be sure that the sweater I was buying was made by workers who were treated fairly, but I could be sure of one thing: Whoever made it was someone's mother or father, sister, or brother.

When you go to the grocery store in Muncie, Indiana, you can shop with your ethics a bit. You can find organic fruits and vegetables and maybe some fair trade tea or coffee. But go to the Muncie Mall to buy a pair of pants, and you are on your own. Since I've returned, I've been doing a lot of thinking about what kind of consumer I am.

Am I a bargain hunter who doesn't care where or who made my clothes just as long as I get a good deal? Can I afford to worry about a garment worker in Bangladesh struggling to support her family?

Am I a red, white, and blue consumer who, after watching American jobs slip away, wants to support only American companies? Believe it or not, even though 97 percent of clothing is made outside the United States, it's possible.

If that's the case, then I can buy blue jeans and other garments from the All-American Clothing Company (www.allamericanclothing .com), which, incidentally, is located not far from where I grew up in Darke County, Ohio.

"Our mission is to support USA families and jobs by producing high-quality clothing in the USA at an affordable price," co-founder Lawson Nickols says on the All American Clothing Company's site. "By keeping our production in the USA we provide jobs and a tax base that supports our communities. We care about our country and the people in it; if we were only in it for money we would move our production overseas. We will NOT trade USA jobs for foreign profits. . . ."

Or, I could buy T-shirts from Cotton of the Carolinas (www .cottonofthecarolinas.com). From dirt to shirt, these items are 100 percent Carolina grown and sewn. Yet another great place I could shop for made in USA products, from billfolds to baby onesies, is ethixmerch.com.

Am I a full-on conscientious consumer who wants to be sure the products I buy are made under good working conditions by workers who are treated fairly? If so, I'll shop online at places like Maggie's Organics/Clean Clothes (www.organicclothes.com).

Or am I a low-impact consumer who wants to remove myself from the whole process as much as possible? If so, I can buy secondhand clothes or learn to sew (not likely). Did you know that at Goodwill you can buy an outfit and a book for under $10?

For most of my life, I have been none of the above. I was fortunate enough not to be restricted to bargains, yet I really didn't put much thought as to whom or where I was wearing. I was an apathetic consumer. I knew the people who made my clothes lived difficult lives, but I just didn't give the matter my time or attention.

Now I do.

Now I'm an engaged consumer. Until some type of GWC labeling system is available, I base my purchasing decisions on my own research. I visit the company websites of the products I buy or am considering to see how involved they are in monitoring the factories they source from. I consider shopping elsewhere if they only have a couple of paragraphs outlining their codes and how they self-police their factories. However, if they are affiliated with an independent third-party inspector like the Worker Rights Consortium, have a position or department that handles social responsibility issues, and acknowledge the challenges of ethical sourcing, I consider giving them my business.

Of course, this doesn't necessarily guarantee that their products are made under fair conditions, but such actions show signs that the company is engaged.

"Private monitoring, if done properly, can do a lot of good. But it's a tricky thing," T.A. Frank, a former corporate social responsibility monitor, wrote in *Washington Monthly*. ". . . we missed stuff. All inspections do. And sometimes it was embarrassing. At one follow-up inspection of a factory in Bangkok at which I'd noted some serious but common wage violations, the auditors who followed me found pregnant employees hiding on the roof and Burmese import workers earning criminally low wages. Whoops."

From Frank's story, "Confessions of a Sweatshop Inspector":

> Now, anyone in the business knows that when inspections uncover safety violations or wage underpayment more than once or twice—let alone five times—it's a sign that bigger problems are lurking beneath. Companies rarely get bamboozled about this sort of thing unless they want to.
>
> And many prefer to be bamboozled, because it's cheaper. . . .
>
> Now, I know about good and bad actors mostly because I saw them directly. But ordinary consumers searching on company Web sites—Walmart. com, Nike.com, etc.—can find out almost everything they need to know just sitting at their desks. For instance, just now I learned from Wal-Mart's latest report on sourcing that only 26 percent of its audits are unannounced. By contrast, of the inspections Target conducts, 100 percent are unannounced. That's a revealing difference. And companies that do what Nike does— prescreen, build long-term relationships, disclose producers—make a point of emphasizing that fact, and are relatively transparent. Companies that don't are more guarded. (When in doubt, doubt.) . . .

One of the largest brands to acknowledge their impact on the environment and on the workers who make their products is Patagonia Inc. In 2008, Patagonia launched an interactive feature on their website called The Footprint Chronicles (www.patagonia.com/usa/footprint), which traces the raw materials for their products from the source through design, manufacturing, and distribution. They recognize their business has both environmental and social impacts. The Footprint Chronicles takes concerned Patagonia customers inside the factories around the world that make our clothes. Social responsibility manager Nicole Bassett not only thinks about Patagonia's impact as a company, but also her own as a consumer. "I have trouble buying clothes," she told me during a phone interview. "The other day I saw these cute pajamas I wanted to buy, but I didn't recognize the brand. I couldn't buy them."

As an engaged consumer, I like to support Patagonia's efforts to be a better company.

Whether we realize it or not, we vote with our pocketbooks. The woman looking for boots that weren't made in China was casting her vote against China's deplorable human rights. Maybe I choose to support a product that is made in Cambodia, since the industry there is more regulated. Maybe I choose to buy from poor nations like Bangladesh to support their development. Maybe I choose to support a brand for its ethical stance or not support one because of its lack of a stance.

The truth is that it takes some effort to be an engaged consumer— but every bit of effort is worth it. Here are a few tips to help you become better at it:

- **Look at the tag of the shirt you are wearing right now.** Repeat every day. Most of us have no idea how global our wardrobe is. If everyone did this simple task daily, imagine how our collective global view would change!

- **Visit GoodGuide.com or download the GoodGuide app on your smartphone.** GoodGuide has a database of over 145,000 consumer goods and scores them based on three separate categories: health, environment, and social responsibility.

- **Encourage your city, county, church, school or university to source responsibly and support companies like Alta Gracia** (www.altagraciaapparel.com) **and Sustain U** (www.sustainuclothing.com), which produces 100 percent recycled apparel made in the United States. The resource page of sweatfree.org is also a great place to find other examples of these kinds of companies.

- **Wear a story and become a brand champion.** Share the tale of your favorite brands, the awesome products they make, and the lives of the producers they impact. I try not to leave the house without wearing at least one product I believe in.

- **Explore.** There are new ethical clothing companies springing up by the day. I recently was introduced to Forgotten Shirts, a company that uses cotton ethically sourced and T-shirts sewn in Uganda. The screen printing is done by Minneapolis teens as part of a tutoring program.

For more tips, visit: www.whereamiwearing.com/KelseysCloset.

I have three pairs of soleRebels that I wear with pride, because I know that the lives of the people who made them and their families are being impacted in a positive way. I share the story of the workers I met whenever I can.

What role do you want shopping to play in your life?

I answered what questions I could for Pam at Macy's, but she had more. She connected with the stories of the real people I told her about. I had wondered while I was in China if solidarity was possible between people who were located cultures and worlds apart. I learned in Macy's in Muncie, Indiana, that it was.

Pam's Muncie is changing every bit as much as the countries that made my clothes. The town was dubbed "Middletown" by social researchers for its inherent American averageness in the 1920s. Back then, Muncie was struggling while changing from farming to industry. Today, it's struggling while transforming from an industry of manufacturing to one of ideas and globalization. South of the White River, factories that once housed BorgWarner, Ball Corporation, Indiana Bridge, Broderick Co., Delco, Indiana Steel and Wire, and Westinghouse sit like empty skeletons. Every single company is gone. In 2006, General Motors left as well, taking 3,400 jobs with it. In 2008, they rigged the factory's smokestack with dynamite and pressed the button.

Although Pam's life was vastly different from the workers who make the clothes she folds, hangs, steams, and puts on clearance, there were countless reasons why she would connect with the lives I tell her about. Maybe she was a mother. Maybe her son left to find work somewhere that's more plugged into the global marketplace than Muncie. Maybe her husband was the fella who watched the demolition of the GM plant and bemoaned the new economy to a Reuters reporter, "How the hell am I supposed to live on $8 an hour?"

Globalization doesn't just happen to economies; it happens to people. Ways of life are changing in Union City, in Muncie, in Perry, in Dhaka, in Phnom Penh, in Guangzhou, in San Pedro Sula, and all across the globe. We might not share a religion, a language, or politics, but we share change and the burden it puts on our families and traditions. We long for simpler times and hope that the future and the change that it brings will be good.

But we don't know.

Still, we hope.

*　　*　　*

I began this edition with a quote from Martin Luther King Jr.:

> *We are tied together in a single garment of destiny, caught in an inescapable network of mutuality. And whatever affects one directly affects us all indirectly.*

Basically, Dr. King is saying that what happens in our community happens to the rest of the world. And what happens to the rest of the world happens to us. The global is local. The local is global.

Becoming an engaged consumer is one way that tracking my clothes around the world changed me. It also made me realize that we aren't simply going to shop or boycott our way to a better world. I began to examine not only my place and responsibilities as a consumer, but also as both a global and local citizen—or as I like to call it, as a *glocal*.

Not having an impact is all the rage right now. Lower your impact on the environment by lowering your carbon footprint. There's a guy called No Impact Man probably addressing an auditorium full of students right now somewhere. Don't buy this because of that. Don't do this. Don't go there.

This seems like such a passive way to live. I think about Bibi Russell giving up fame and fortune to return to Bangladesh. I think about how Bethlehem looked at her community in Ethiopia and didn't see poverty and desperation like so many before her, but instead saw skill, tradition, and hope.

The people and the organizations that have the biggest impact are those that have locals helping locals.

So I asked myself, "Where am I a local?" For better or worse I'm a local in Muncie, Indiana.

While so many of the people I met on this journey have a poverty of opportunities and resources, they often had a wealth of community. Yet I saw the opposite in Muncie. There are people who are dedicated to making our community the best it can be, but I sure wasn't one of them. How many of us know our neighbors? How many of us are facing poverty in and the problems of our own community?

I realized I needed to be a better local citizen.

And so I now volunteer with the local Circles initiative that matches community members living in poverty—called Circle captains—with three or four allies who aren't to brainstorm a path out of poverty. Circles matched me with a single mother of three children in Muncie. I sat down with her to do a monthly budget. By the end of our budget meeting we realized she was $600 in the hole. She had to reassure me, "Everything is going to be all right."

I became a big brother with Big Brothers and Big Sisters.

I'm filled with self-doubt: How much of a difference am I making? Do I have the ability to help? Then small victories come in the form of A's on my little brother's report card or a new job and a new attitude for my Circle captain. Maybe they would have won these small victories without me, but the one thought that keeps me pushing on is that maybe they wouldn't. Besides, trying to change others' lives has changed my life for the better. I'm trying to be okay with the fact that I *get* more from volunteering than I give. I feel more connected with my local community. I know better what it means to be a citizen of Muncie, Indiana.

I'm trying to be a better global citizen.

If you've graduated from college, you are more educated than 95 percent of the rest of the world. One-sixth of the world lives on less than $1.25 per day. Nobel Prize–winning economist and social scientist Herbert Simon estimated that "social capital" (a functioning government, access to technology, abundant natural resources) is responsible for at least 90 percent of what people earn in wealthy societies like the United States. Warren Buffett said, "If you stick me down in the middle of Bangladesh or Peru, you'll find out how much this talent is going to produce in the wrong kind of soil." We were born in the right kind of soil.

It was wise old Uncle Ben who told Peter Parker (aka Spiderman) that with great power comes great responsibility. Our relative wealth and our education are our superpowers, and we have a responsibility to use them for the less privileged.

We can't always control the impact that globalization has on our communities and on our lives, but we can control the impact our lives have on the world. I'm trying to be a better neighbor, consumer, donor, volunteer, and glocal. I'm trying to have the biggest and the best impact I can.

Annie and I now give more. A young family supported on a writer's/speaker's income isn't exactly a jackpot of philanthropy, but we're trying to do our part, dividing our giving between local and global causes. We try to give with intention, searching for the best ways to share what we have.

I'm not just trying to be an engaged consumer. I'm trying to be more engaged, period.

We need to look outside of ourselves and recognize how connected we all are. We are surrounded by invisible people who make the trash disappear, make our clothes, mine the coal that keeps our lights on, and put food on our tables, and all of the others who support our lives. And we are the invisible ones to some. We need to open our eyes, and to see one another.

"Where am I wearing?" is such a specific question and one that sent me on a global journey to see where I fit in the world as a consumer. I have many more questions: Where am I eating? What are my responsibilities? What is my impact? The more I know, the bigger my questions grow. And they always seem to come down to this one root question . . .

Where am I? In a world of American Dreams and Fantasy Kingdoms, where am I?

The search continues.

*　*　*

It's been seven years since I stood shirtless with Amilcar, a sea of garment workers breaking around us, outside of his factory near San Pedro Sula. I was 26 at the time, on a silly quest pursuing the tag of a clever T-shirt. At the time, I had no idea what the experience would eventually lead to.

Now, I'm 33. I'm married. I'm a homeowner. I'm the consumer, father, husband, glocal, giver, and donor that I never would have been if not for Amilcar.

I still think about him every time I put on a T-shirt. Just as I think about Arifa (Figure 30.2) and her children each time I pull on a pair of boxers, about Nari and Ai and the families they support every time I slip into a pair of jeans, and about Dewan and Zhu Chun whenever I slide into my flip-flops.

Figure 30.2   Arifa in Bangladesh, one of millions around the world who make our clothes.

When I walk into my closet, I think about the hundreds—if not thousands—of people around the world who had a hand in making my clothes. Jeans are no longer just jeans, shirts no longer just shirts, shoes no longer just shoes, clothes are no longer just clothes.

Each is an untold story.

APPENDIX

A

Discussion Questions

Here are a few questions to get your discussion rolling. You can find a 116-question discussion guide complete with eight activities at www.whereamiwearing.com/waiw-teaching-tool/.

The Mission

1. Kelsey states that "globalization was a foreign problem" and that everybody was against it. In a source other than this book, find out what globalization is and explain it briefly.

2. What was the original reason Kelsey decided to travel to the countries where his clothes were made?

3. What is the difference between what activists believe about the garment industry and what some economists believe?

4. How did the United States' trading relationship first begin in Asia?

5. What did the Decent Working Conditions and Fair Compensation Act intend to do?

6. Why don't companies want their customers to think about where their products are made?

7. Why did Kelsey find being "a college-educated, white male living in the United States" a problem?

Activity

Where were your jeans made? Look at the tag. Now consider the components of your jeans: thread, cotton, zipper, rivets, dye. Research companies and countries that could have possibly made each of the components of your jeans. How many countries might have had a hand in making your jeans? Discuss your findings as a group.

Made in Bangladesh

8. When did many of the department stores in Kelsey's hometown start to go out of business? What was the reason?

9. Why did Kelsey have to lie in order to see the factories?

10. Fantasy Kingdom is Bangladesh's equivalent to Disneyland. How many Bangladeshis can be admitted to Fantasy Kingdom for the price of one Disneyland ticket?

11. Five of the children Kelsey took to Fantasy Kingdom had never attended even one day of school. What did they do for a living?

12. Why do you think Kelsey spent $67.00 taking children to an amusement park when the money might have been better spent on something more practical for them?

13. What percentage of Bangladesh's exports involve the garment industry?

14. After a *Dateline* program showing child laborers inside a garment factory in Bangladesh, American consumers started boycotting clothing made in Bangladesh out of concern for the children. Look up what a boycott is and explain it. Why didn't they want our help?

15. What kinds of injuries occur in the textile factory?

16. Where does Arifa, a garment worker in Dhaka, Bangladesh, keep the family food?

Activity

Nobel Peace Prize–winner Mohammad Yunnus formed Grameen Bank, which gives microcredit loans to people who couldn't get loans from traditional banks. Visit www.kiva.org, a site that allows you to lend money to individuals around the world. Write a paragraph explaining who you would lend to and why.

Made in Cambodia

18. In Cambodia, where beggars line the streets, a woman spends money to purchase a bird that she doesn't keep. What's her reason for paying for the bird and letting it go free?

19. What did the violent events in Chicago in 1886 eventually lead to in the United States?

20. Why are certain areas of Cambodia dangerous to walk in? Why do families continue to live there?

21. What countries are *consumers* of Levi's?

22. What percentage of Cambodia's exports are based on apparel?

23. How many girls live in the apartment together in Cambodia, and what is their sleeping arrangement?

24. What is the difference in the amount of living space between Kelsey's home in the United States and the garment workers in Cambodia?

25. What do some children do to get around child labor laws?

26. What was one of the last US garment manufacturers to give in to globalization and move their factories overseas?

27. If most garment workers are women, what do the young men do?

28. How many Cambodian farmers now make a living as scavengers at the Stung Meanchey Municipal Waste Dump? How much do they earn on average? How much do children earn? Why the difference?

Activity

Ever dream of running your own sweatshop? Probably not. Even so, try your hand at running a virtual sweatshop at www.whereamiwearing .com/your-sweatshop. Discuss with the group some of the decisions you faced. Who made it to the highest stage and how did they succeed? Write a review of the game.

Made in China

29. Why are flip-flops the shoe of choice in developing countries?

30. What qualities does China have that entice factories to locate there?

31. Why do Dewan and Zhu Chun work many more hours than they are legally allowed to, even when they don't get paid for the extra time?

32. When Kelsey goes to visit Dewan's and Zhu Chun's village, what does he mean that "the room is missing a generation"?

33. Why does Kelsey say "there aren't too many places in the world . . . like Guangzhou." Why? What is unique about it?

34. When the United States was industrializing, we cared more about the workers' lives. Why is it easier to ignore the people who now make our clothes and other products?

35. In an American Walmart, fish tanks would be found in the pet section. What section are they in the Walmart in China? Why there?

Activity

What did your grandparents do for a living? How about your great-grandparents? How does your lifestyle and desired profession compare to theirs? Trace the professions of your great grandparents through to your parents' and ultimately to your desired profession. Write a few paragraphs about what these jobs say about the times we live in and about the changing national/global economy?

Made in America

36. In visiting the factory that made his shorts in Perry, New York, Kelsey finds out the reason American Classic Outfitters (ACO) had been successful in competing against foreign factories. What's the reason? What has changed since Kelsey's visit?

37. What did the *Washington Post* call Honduras?

38. Why did Amilcar's family move from their village to the city?

39. What caused Russell Athletics to reopen their factory in Choloma?

40. Karla told Kelsey she was happy unions existed, but she would never join one. Why wouldn't she?

41. How much did Jolanis's house cost to build? How long would it take to earn that much working as a garment worker in Villanueva?

42. What was the reason Edwin gave for not carrying any photos or phone numbers of family members?

43. What's a "coyote," and what part did they play in Amilcar's journey north?

44. What jobs has Amilcar held since arriving in the United States?

45. What did Amilcar lie to Mayra about? Why do you think he lied?

46. Have you ever been in a situation where no one spoke your language? How did that make you feel?

47. Why hasn't Amilcar told Jolanis or his kids about Mayra? Do you think he should?

48. Amilcar said he doesn't think he's a good father. Why?

49. soleRebels isn't a "normal" shoe factory. What's different about it?

50. Think about recent graduates from your hometown. Where are they finding jobs?

51. Kelsey writes that child labor and sweatshops are just symptoms of the real problem. What is the real problem?

52. What does Nicholas Kristof say about sweatshops, and how does Kelsey disagree with him?

53. What does Kelsey mean when he writes that "a good job has an exponential impact"?

54. Kelsey states he is now an "engaged consumer." What does he now do before purchasing clothing?

55. Beyond becoming an engaged consumer, how did this journey influence Kelsey's life?

Activity

Talk to the person at your school, city, or church who buys clothing (T-shirts, uniforms, licensed apparel). How do they decide what to buy? Where are the products made? What kind of consumer would you label your organization as? Share your findings with the group.

Note to Freshman Me

Dear Kelsey,

Hey man, it's me, or I mean you, 15 years in the future. How's 1997 treating you? I know that you're getting ready to head off to college, so I wanted to weigh in with a few words of encouragement and some advice.

Get a PhD in Undecided

Right now, you have no idea what you want to be when you grow up. I've got some bad news: It's 2012, and I still don't know what I want to be when I grow up.

But this is actually a good thing. Your curiosity is going to take you places that you wouldn't believe. Let's just say that at one point you'll go to Bangladesh because your underwear were made there. It's kind of a long story, long enough to fill a book (hint, hint).

You don't have a major. You're undecided. That's okay. A lot of your classmates think they know what they want to do, but really they're undecided, too. In fact, the average college student changes majors 3 times, and the average person will change jobs 10 times between the ages of 18 and 42. Get your PhD in undecided. Let your curiosity choose your way.

Not Being Able to Speak Another Language Will Be One of Your Biggest Regrets

Your freshman year of college won't be the brightest spot in your academic career. You will, however, master the spread offense of Madden NFL on PlayStation. Let's just say that your yards per carry with the Detroit Lions Hall-of-Fame running back Barry Sanders will be somewhat higher than your GPA.

Actually, on the very first day of college in your very first class, you get booted. Remember that Spanish test you were supposed to take to test into Spanish 102? Well, you really should have taken it. I know you were the Spanish Club president of Mississinawa Valley High School, but, let's be honest here, you didn't have to be able to speak Spanish to be the Spanish Club president. All you had to do was eat copious amounts of Mexican food. In Spanish 102, you actually have to speak Spanish. You should have dropped down to 101 instead of dropping Spanish for Latin, which you don't have to speak.

You'll never regret learning something.

You Never Know What Class Will Change Your Life

Next year you'll stumble into an intro to anthropology class. All you'll know at the time is that archaeology is a subfield of anthropology, that Indiana Jones is a pretty cool archaeologist, and that someday, deep down, you long to stand in some unmapped jungle and holler, "It belongs in a museum!" at a Nazi. Yes, that's a pretty silly reason to choose to take a class, but this class will lead you to declare anthropology as a major, which will inspire your curiosity about how other people live around the world, and teach you empathy. Curiosity and empathy are your most important tools.

You'll take a sociology class about globalization. You'll learn about genocides, child labor, and sweatshops. You'll process these lessons with your head and not your heart. You'll get a B+ in the course, but this course will plant a seed that grows into a big idea.

Become Part of Your Community

For the next four years you have the opportunity to become part of the Miami University and the Oxford, Ohio, communities. Embrace your new home. You'll never have more time to volunteer, to give back, and to plug into where you live than right now. In 2012 you'll have two kids, a wife (can you believe that Annie actually sticks it out and marries you?!), and a demanding career, but you'll find the time to be a part of your community. If I can do this, you can do this. Play two hours less of Madden NFL a week and volunteer. I promise that you'll get more than you give.

Travel

Find a way to study abroad. Work two summer jobs. Sell your baseball cards. Visit the study abroad office and ask about scholarships. There's only so much you can learn from a textbook or from a professor. Get out there and experience the world.

You'll learn more from people who live in mud huts and tin shacks than you'll ever learn from a college professor. But before you go and drop out, know that college will uniquely prepare you to receive these lessons.

Your Worthless College Education

You'll graduate with a degree in anthropology, and your parents will buy you a nice shiny frame to hang it on the wall. I hate to tell you this, but the degree is worthless. You'll never get a job because of your anthropology degree. But, here's the thing, your degree is priceless.

Your college education is way more than a piece of paper to leverage to a better job and a brighter future. You will actually learn stuff in college. Don't forget to do that.

The Path

A few years after you graduate, you'll have worked as a SCUBA instructor and have traveled extensively. To the outsider you'll seem rudderless, a twenty-something with no direction. You won't know where you're heading, and then one day you'll show up at a garment factory in Honduras and suddenly everything will fall into place. All of those anthropology courses, that sociology course that you didn't think you got much out of, that degree that you never used to get a job, and your love for travel, will lead you to that moment. It will give you direction. That moment will change your life. It turns out that all of your passions, interests, and curiosities put you on the path you were supposed to be on the entire time.

If you or anyone else who reads this needs some encouragement along the way, e-mail me Kelsey@kelseytimmerman.com or you can find my Freshman's guide to going glocal at www.kelseytimmerman .com/GoGlocal.

—**Kelsey**

P.S.: If you ever enter a bathroom in Cambodia that has an attendant who is wearing a red bow tie, turn and run.

Where Are You Teaching?

A Guide to Taking *Where Am I Wearing?* to a Glocal Context

J.R. Jamison, M.A.

Associate Director, Indiana Campus Compact
Educator, Advocate, Author—And, Frankly, One Who
Gives a Damn

Just like you, I finished reading *Where Am I Wearing?* and my mind began racing. It was early in the fall of 2011, and I couldn't stop thinking about the lives of Amilcar, Arifa, Nari, Ai, Dewan, and Zhu Chun—and the countless others whose names did not make it into the book—and wonder where they must be now. Did Nari reach her dream of opening her own salon? Or is she still ironing the Levi's I wear before they are shipped off to the United States? Perhaps she's moved on to craftsmanship and is, with the quick dash of her foot and easy slide of her hand, sewing the well-known Levi's logo onto the back of my jeans. I do hope she's reached her dream; if not, I hope she's at least making a fair wage, has fair hours, and gets to visit her family more often than she did in 2007.

As an educator, my mind began to think about the applicability of *Where Am I Wearing?* to the everyday lives of college students in the United States. As fate may have it, I live in the same town as Kelsey

Timmerman—Muncie, Indiana. Before I read *Where Am I Wearing?*,
I had no idea who Kelsey was; though I imagine we must have passed
each other a time or two in the grocery store without a simple nod
or smile, as we Americans so often do these days. And that's when
it hit me—this book has taken me around the world and infused my
brain with geography, politics, culture, people, and where I'm wearing. What is it about this book that will not only make me a more
engaged consumer, but a broader consumer of my own geography,
politics, culture, people, and the city that I *wear* every day? Perhaps
it begins with acknowledging the *other* that we pass each day; perhaps this broad lesson is one way of applying what I've read and
learned into action.

I now know Kelsey, and, because of geography, I have the unique
opportunity to pick his brain on a regular basis. And, though, by training,
I'm the educator, I learn much from his adventures. One *aha* that I've
had from all of this is what Kelsey calls the glocal, or, in other words,
taking a global experience and applying those passions not just in a global
context but in a local context. If I, other educators, and students couldn't
put on another article of clothing after reading *Where Am I Wearing?*
without thinking about the multiple fabrics that make up the lives of
those who make our clothes—how can we, too, never again drive to
another part of town without thinking about the kid we tutor, his
family, cyclical poverty?—And how we could change our local communities, and global communities, through education, time, virtues, and,
frankly, just giving a damn.

For me, the answer is service engagement and, broken down
more, service-learning. In the sea of languages, those words could
mean a variety of things for you. As you think about your discipline and
how *Where Am I Wearing?* connects to the content and to the glocal,
use the following definitions as a framework:

Service Engagement—*is any endeavor that brings the community
into the campus and the campus into the community, reciprocally, often
addressing a social concern. Forms of service engagement include: service-
learning, co-curricular community service, and volunteerism; and some
internships and field experiences. The sum of these activities leads to a
campus that is fully engaged with the community.*

—Jamison & McCracken (2007)

Service-Learning—*is a credit-bearing, educational experience in which
students participate in an organized service activity that meets identified*

community needs and reflect on the service activity in such a way as to
gain further understanding of course content, a broader appreciation of
the discipline, and an enhanced sense of civic responsibility.

—Bringle & Hatcher (1996)

To be a campus that cares about service engagement and wants
to develop future citizens who think deeply about what they're reading and their actions in a glocal context, often the first step is to begin
service-learning courses. The inherent hyphen between service and
learning is not always grammatically correct yet intentional. Service
and learning cannot stand alone; a marriage must exist between the two
for service-learning to be at its best, and the hyphen is where the true
transformations exist.

Allow me to take the time to give you a few brief examples of
what this might look like:

Discipline: Fashion Design & Merchandising Level: 200+

The content in the classroom is focusing on the history of the
industry, understanding textiles, and developing business models,
but how much of the content is on understanding the people and
lives of those who make our clothes? What impact could future
fashion design and merchandisers have on the global economy and
lives of people if they understood these complexities from the start?
How does one create and sell sustainable lines that are good for the
environment and fair for the people? Perhaps the learning starts in
their own backyard. An example of this would be to have students
read *Where Am I Wearing?* and have them spend time working
with a local community agency focused on poverty while learning
the stories of those they serve. The students could work with the
agency to put on a fashion show that educates the participants and
audience of how to dress for success while shopping in bargain
or secondhand stores. In the classroom, what are the connections
between the local stories and those within the factories? How do
both stories impact how one designs and/or sells? What could the
future of fashion design and merchandising look like if we learn
about, and at times with, the maker and the consumer?

Discipline: Sociology Level: 100+

The content in the classroom is getting students to think about
self, society, race, gender, and class. What better way to learn that

than to get them involved in their local communities while thinking about the global context of what they're learning in and out of the classroom? While students are reading *Where Am I Wearing?*, they could be volunteering their time at a homeless shelter or serving at a battered women's shelter to learn first-hand about the complex nature of life all while breaking stereotypes about class and gender. During class time, students could reflect and connect course content with what they're learning in *Where Am I Wearing?*, what they're experiencing at their community site, and compare and contrasts the lives of those in the book with those in their local community. How are their lives different? How are their lives the same? As a sociologist, how will this change how I better understand self, society, race, gender, and class?

Discipline: Business/Economics Level: 300+

Business/Economics students are our future industry leaders. If we engage these students in service-learning, we are creating future leaders who are also civic-minded. As students are preparing for field experiences, they could be reading *Where Am I Wearing?* while applying their skills with a local community agency. They could work with local community center sites throughout the semester teaching local teenagers about the culture, history, and economies of our global world; in particular those places where the US conducts most of its business. In the higher education classroom, the connection of course content with that of *Where Am I Wearing?* tied with the service-learning experiences should, ideally, heighten the actions of how a future business leader acts in a global economy.

These examples are brief and thus would take more thought regarding the people and learning involved, but the examples should give you an idea of how you could transform your classroom into one that helps students understand the course content and the glocal world in which we live. The most important piece of information I can leave you with regarding service-learning is that it is a two-way street. You cannot develop a project or program and then approach a community agency. Rather, you must approach the community agency with your idea and have them, as your co-educator, expand upon and make the project complete. You know the content; they know the real-world complexities of the local community.

For deeper examples of what this might look like for you, regardless of discipline, I encourage you to visit the website of Campus Compact (www.compact.org). Campus Compact is the premier resource for the intersection of service engagement and higher education, and the organization currently has a network of 35 formalized state offices and over 1,100 institutions of higher education located in all 50 states, the District of Columbia, US territories, and four countries. Through Campus Compact, you can search the service-learning syllabi database that has service-learning course examples for every discipline from all over the United States and a few international institutions. Additionally, through the website, you can connect with local state Campus Compacts that often have grant opportunities and networks to assist you with your service-learning endeavors.

And ask yourself: Where am I wearing?—as a broader consumer of my own geography, politics, culture, people, and the city that I *wear* every day.

For more service-learning resources and to learn how others are incorporating Where Am I Wearing? *into their classes, visit* www.whereamiwearing .com/service-learning.

References to Appendix C

Bringle, R.G., and J. A. Hatcher. 1996. "Implementing Service-Learning in Higher Education." *Journal of Higher Education* 67: 221–239.

Jamison, J., and J. McCracken. 2007. "Enhancing Student Learning and Retention through Service-Learning." Funded grant No. 2007 0320-000 from the Lilly Endowment Inc., 2007–2010.

Jamison, J., D. Nickolson, and J. Bryant. 2011. "Setting Sail into Service-Learning and Navigating the Workbook." In *Charting the Course for Service-Learning: From Curriculum Considerations to Advocacy—A Faculty Development Workbook*, ed. M. Eisenhauer, N. Marthakis, J. Jamison, and M. Mattson, 1–4. Indianapolis, IN: Indiana Campus Compact.

Acknowledgments

Following my clothes around the world might seem like a solitary quest, but from the first glimmer of the idea, through the writing of this book, I was anything but alone.

My *Where Am I Wearing?* journey pales in comparison to the 16-year one I've been on with Annie, to whom this book is dedicated. Before Honduras, she was my longtime girlfriend. Between Honduras and Bangladesh, she became my fiancée. And after China, she became my wife and the mother to our two beautiful children, Harper and Griffin. Her patience is legendary. Her laugh is everything. I still owe her a honeymoon sans garment factories.

I suckered Kyle, my brother, into accompanying me to Honduras. He saved me from a deadly poisonous snake in the jungle, but couldn't save himself from the parasite-carrying mosquito that bit him. He eventually came down with malaria. After the spinal tap, a few short stints in hospitals in Indiana and France, and a year of recovery, he's okay. (Sorry, Kyle.) When he's healthy, there's no one I would rather share a dugout canoe with.

You'll never meet a more practical guy than my dad. At the age of 28, he owned a construction business and had two kids. So having a son who, at 28, goes to Bangladesh because his underwear was made there isn't the kind of thing one would think he'd support, but he did. If I have an ounce of his hard work, determination, and integrity, I have enough.

Before I set foot out of the United States, it was my mom who taught me there was a much larger world. Every mom and child I come across on my travels, I look at through her eyes. Her family has also been very supportive. Aunt Cathy has always kept me supplied with journals, Uncle Randy has been a loyal member of the "Travelin' Light" readers from day one, and my Grandma and Grandpa Wilt have always encouraged my getting out and seeing the world.

Annie's parents, Jim and Gloria, have always been there for us to pick up the slack when I'm God-knows-where doing God-knows-what. Annie got her patience honest.

My cousin Brice bought me the Tattoo T-shirt that started all of this. If anyone is to blame, it's him.

Captain Ralph Chiaro will never get a chance to read this book, but, without his friendship, my life and this book would have likely steered in a much different direction. I owe him so much, and it tears at my insides to think that I'll never get the chance to sit, just the two of us, the rolling Atlantic beneath us, and thank him.

If everyone had an English teacher like mine, the world would be a better and much more grammatical place. Kyle and I once bumped into my English teacher, Dixie Marshall, at a play. She introduced us to her sister: "This is Kyle Timmerman, one of my best students ever," and turning to me, ". . . this is his brother Kelsey." Even so, she never gave up on me and continued to teach me about gerunds and split infinitives a decade after I last sat in her class. She pored over the manuscript countless times with her red pen.

The good folks at Bootsnall.com jumped behind my idea early on and hosted my blog, www.whereamiwearing.com. Without their support, many of the cool people who stumbled onto my blog likely wouldn't have found it. The readers of my blog have been great, and I owe them all a round of drinks. No matter where I was, I was never alone.

Without my agent, Caren Johnson Estesen, this book wouldn't have landed in the inbox of Richard Narramore, my editor at John Wiley & Sons. If you go to Bangladesh because your underwear was made there and come back and write a book about it, you are an author. If you go and come back and don't write a book about it, you are just some weird dude. More than anyone, Caren and Richard are responsible for making me the former.

I really couldn't ask for a better publisher. The team at Wiley, including Lydia Dimitriadis, Kim Dayman, Amy Sell, and Christine Moore, has been so supportive. And I'm continually amazed by the energy, passion, and running ability of Larry Olson.

J.R. Jamison at Indiana Campus Compact did a phenomenal job with his piece on Service-Learning. I look forward to many more conversations with J.R. about going *glocal* in the future.

Dr. Nancy Bush at Wingate University was kind enough to share her fabulous discussion questions with me. She also stumbled upon the first edition of this book and championed it as a common reader at Wingate, the first university to adopt it as such. I owe hugs and high-fives to Nancy and all of the professors and university administrators who have shared this story with their students.

Ashley Ford, a fantastic young writer and engaged citizen, worked wonders with the discussion guide.

I wouldn't have been able to bridge the divide between producer and consumer if it weren't for the hard work and patience of my translators: Eduardo and Gabriel in Honduras; Dalton and Ruma in Bangladesh; Chuuon, Phalline, and Sima in Cambodia; Angel, Pink, Luther, and Huang in China.

Most of all I'm indebted to Amilcar, Arifa, Nari, Ai, Dewan, and Zhu Chun, who let me into their lives and put up with my questions. This book is as much theirs as it is mine.